Dream Chasers
of the West

Dream Chasers of the West

A Homestead Family of Glacier Park

B.L. Wettstein

RIVERBEND
PUBLISHING

Dream Chasers of the West: A Homestead Family of Glacier Park
© 2006 B. L. Wettstein
Published 2010 by Riverbend Publishing, Helena, Montana
Previously published by Log Cabin Publishing, 2006

Printed in the United States of America

ISBN 978-1-60639-021-4

5 6 7 8 9 SB

Permission to use the poem "Homesteader's Wife" by Beth M. Volbrecht courtesy of John C. Barsness, Executive Director, Montana Arts, Bozeman

Cover design by DD Dowden
Text design by Barbara Fifer

Cover photograph: The G.C. Smiley homestead on Lake Lubec in 1919 with Clara, GC, and her father, Charles Miller, standing in front of the log cabin with Glenn on horseback. The surviving bunkhouse is on the back cover.

Riverbend Publishing
P.O. Box 5833
Helena, MT 59604
1-866-787-2363
riverbendpublishing.com

To Clara,
whose adventurous spirit helped settle
the West (1883-1965),
and
Melina,
whose memory made the past come alive (1919-2005)

Publisher's Note

This is the story of a homestead family in Montana in the early 1900s. The names, activities, and opinions of people in the book are derived from family letters, taped interviews, and personal memories that are impossible to verify. The author disclaims responsibility for information published herein. The personal letters have been reproduced exactly as written, without corrections. The author attempted to credit those who contributed poetry and photographs, and apologizes to any who were inadvertently overlooked.

CONTENTS

Reynolds Township, Minnesota, 1914

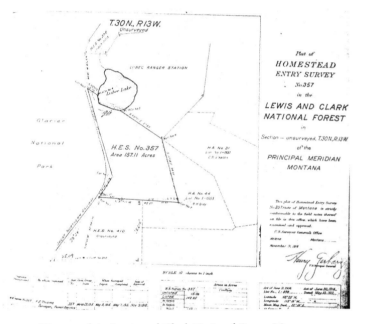

Homesteads in Lewis and Clark National Forest, Montana

PREFACE

In 1913, Clara Augusta Miller, an unmarried woman from Long Prairie, Minnesota, set out alone to homestead on the plains of Montana. With a penchant for adventure, she fought against drought, prairie fire, and poverty before she met another homesteader chasing his own dreams in the West.

Dream Chasers of the West tells the poignant story of their struggle for survival on the southern fringe of Glacier National Park before most Americans knew of its existence. This is the saga of intermingling lives of settlers destined to leave their impact on the development of the West, people who experienced despair and anguish, and whose graves lie largely unmarked and unvisited. It was a time when men were tough, and their women were tougher.

B.L. Wettstein

Clara Augusta Miller Smiley in 1915

Introduction

During the mid-nineteenth century, European emigrants flocked to America searching for a better life. To accommodate the flood of newcomers and to expand the frontier of the vast new land, a group of men in the East, elected officials who believed that a farmer could live well on 160 acres of rich American soil, wrote the Homestead Act. They established guidelines allowing adults to secure 160 acres of native land by paying a minimal filing fee, erecting a 12' x 12' residence, and living on the property for a period of five years. It encouraged people to move farther west to develop new farmlands from virgin soil, and when Abraham Lincoln signed the Homestead Act in 1862,[1] land-starved families surged forward by the thousands to settle areas of Minnesota, Wisconsin, Iowa, the Dakotas, Nebraska, Oklahoma, and points farther west.

In spite of the honorable intentions of the Homestead Act, the high plains country of Montana continued to be sparsely populated; only vast cattle ranches and open range prevailed. The uninhabited land supported short prairie grass for grazing, but transient farmers in search of a permanent place to settle declined free homestead acreage on the arid plains and continued west to the fertile valleys of Oregon and California. Early settlers traveled in covered wagons; latecomers used the rapidly expanding railway system.

In the 1880's, unlike other railroad barons of the time, James J. Hill, builder of the Great Northern Railroad, received no land grants nor government aid to build his railroads. He raised his own capital and expanded his rail system across the wastelands of northern Montana and the northern Rockies.[2] If he could get a family settled onto every 160 acres of land, and there were millions of acres available, his railroad would be their only means of transporting grain out of northern Montana to markets in the East enabling him to recoup his investment.

Enlightened to the fact that a farm of 160 acres in Montana could not support a family, and after further deliberation about the lack of settlement, the government passed the Enlarged Homestead Act of 1909.[3] It increased the amount of land to 320 acres per family and encouraged farmers to practice dry land farming, a technique developed by Prof. Thomas Shaw of the University of Minnesota. He proposed that half the acreage be tilled and planted, while the other half should be plowed and lie fallow to conserve moisture until the following year.[4]

Although his advisers considered it a brash idea, James J. Hill embraced the concept of dry land farming and became the nation's greatest promoter of Montana settlement. He helped colonize the state with inexpensive loans to perspective home-steaders, his railway provided cheap one-way transportation for people and their household goods, and he flooded the country with thousands of posters, advertisements, and brochures ex-uding the richness of Montana land.

The early years of the new century conspired with him. Plenty of rainfall and optimum growing conditions resulted in record-breaking wheat production. With the potential for be-coming rich, successful settlers encouraged friends and relatives to share in the bounty, and the dream of James J. Hill ceased to be a mirage and became reality.

He traveled extensively throughout the East to promote dry land farming. Exhibits of record wheat yields and experimen-tal farming techniques accompanied him. Newspaper coverage dignified his dream of having every available tract of land under cultivation. Descriptions of endless expanses of rich farmland stretching to the farthest horizons tantalized landless folk who put their faith in the truth of the press.

His representatives traveled abroad to encourage immigrant settlement on the munificent land. They promised rich soil and good water supplies; they described mild winters and adequate precipitation where farmers could grow crops year around,[5] but his representatives neglected to mention grasshoppers that could reduce bounteous crops to bare dirt in a matter of minutes or prairie fires that rolled across drought-stricken flatland fueled by horrendous winds. They avoided questions about bone-chilling blizzards that blew out of the Canadian wastelands, loneliness that drove isolated farmers mad, and droughts that plagued the plains and sucked the life from every living thing.

Precipitation sometimes exceeded fifteen or sixteen inches a year, an adequate amount to grow grain, but in some years it mostly fell in the form of snow while summer crops withered in high temperatures and low humidity. A year of good precipitation during the growing season might be followed by several years of inadequate rainfall when creeks dried up and lakes disappeared. But the potential homesteaders didn't question the enthusiasm of the frontier prophets who propounded the riches available to those adventurous enough to accept the challenge. They went on faith.

Realizing that vast tracts of Montana continued to be uninhabited, the Three Year Homestead Law of 1912 was passed. It reduced the time needed to "prove up" a homestead from five years to three years; in addition, it permitted the settlers to be absent from their land for five months of the year.[6] The land-hungry people didn't read between the lines. They didn't question why the law had changed. They didn't stop to think that perhaps they'd need five months to find other employment to meet their basic needs. It didn't discourage them, it encouraged them, and the homestead hopefuls came in waves across the grassy plains aboard the Great Northern Railroad, otherwise known as the "High Line" because of its close proximity to the Canadian border.

During the great onslaught of homesteaders into Montana in the twentieth century, frustrated cattlemen watched the settlers plow lush grassland into furrows as far as the eye could see. Barbed wire fences obstructed their cattle drives. The stockmen scorned the settlers and their grubby way of life in their isolated shanties on the plains, but the latest momentum of western expansion was at hand, and Clara's undeterred ambition to own a piece of that land determined her destiny.

On a Government Claim[7]

O.S. Grant, Perkins County, South Dakota

I'll write a few lines if only I can,
And tell you about my excellent plan.
You'll find me out here on a western plain,
Starving to death on a government claim.
Hurrah for this country, the land of the free!
Home of the grasshopper, chinchbug and the flea.
Oh, I'll tell you of it's joys and sing of it's fame,
While starving to death on my government claim.
My Mansion is built of the natural soil,
The walls not erected according to Hoyle.
The roof has no pitch, but is level and plain.
I'll sure get wet on my government claim.
Oh, I have a good time, I live at my ease,
On canned goods, crackers, old bacon and cheese.
Then come to this country, there's room for you all,
Where the winds never cease and the rains never fall,
Where the sun never sets, but sweetly remains,
'till it burns up the crop on our government claims.
Oh, how happy I feel on my government claim!
There's nothing that will make a man hard and profane.
I've nothing to eat and nothing to wear;
The mosquitoes possess both our water and air.
It's here I am settled and here I must stay;
My money's all gone and I can't get away.
There's nothing to lose and there's nothing to gain,
While starving to death on a government claim.
Hurrah for this country where blizzards arise.
Where the sun never sets and the flea never dies.
Come join in the chorus and sing of the fame,
Of the "Honyock" who's stuck on a government claim.

Rudyard in 1914. Photo courtesy of Rudyard Depot Museum, Rudyard, Montana, Jan DeLaney, Co-curator.

Anticipating the yield at Wilbert's homestead in Rudyard.

PART I

A Woman Homesteader

*Clara was older than most women heading to Montana, and
she was unmarried, another quality that set her apart.*

In late March of 1913, Clara Augusta Miller boarded the
Great Northern Railroad for her first venture out of central
Minnesota away from family and friends. Filled to capacity,
the passenger cars reverberated with the clamor of foreign lan-
guages and reeked with pungent odors of ethnic foods. Small
stoves with ill-fitting stovepipes leaked greasy smoke.[1] Dirty
diapers, smelly youngsters, human waste, and stale sweat permeated the interior where passengers were held prisoner without hope of parole between stops on their way to the promised
land of Montana.

She pushed her way down the crowded aisle to a vacant
seat, removed her coat and hat and stashed them on the over-

head rack along with a basket lunch and small suitcase. Her three brothers had supervised the loading of her household goods and now stood on the station platform waiting for the train to pull out. Each of them worried about her foolhardy plan to file on a homestead alone, but with no visible display of emotion, they watched the train pull away except for her youngest brother, Charley, who at the last minute, ran alongside her window and waved farewell.

Charley Miller

As the steel wheels clattered along the High Line on its way toward free Montana land, lengthening shadows concealed familiar landmarks as Clara studied her reflection in the window, a determined woman searching for independence. Tendrils of reddish blond hair framed her face, excitement heightened the color in her high cheekbones while fine lines around clear, blue eyes gave testimony to years of exposure to the sun. The weeks of preparation for her departure had been exhausting, but now she settled back to experience her first taste of freedom as the train lurched its way into the mystique of the West.

Most of the passengers were like Clara, children of earlier settlers now seeking their own fortunes. Others were filled with greed or had fraudulent enterprises in mind, but for the most part, her traveling companions were courageous, ambitious people who desired independence and a better life for their children as they left loved ones behind in their quest to claim free land in Montana.

For less than $50, a family could reserve a boxcar for their possessions, while others preferred to rent "Zulu" cars that also provided sleeping facilities. They took farm animals and machinery along with furniture, household goods, fence posts, barbed wire, buggies and wagons. Some brought trees, shrubs, flowers, and seeds as well as enough lumber and tarpaper to build a house.[2]

Clara kept to herself. She cared for her needs, observed the families around her, and occasionally offered a helping hand. As she was subjected to the din and stench of her assigned car twenty-four hours a day for days on end, melancholy foreboding began to infiltrate the shadows of her mind as she watched the monotonous plains pass by. Gone were the pasture lands and wooded, wilderness tracts of Todd County. Gone were the rich, rolling fields of dark loam along the river bottom, the earthy perfume of freshly plowed furrows.

Patches of snow, dirty remnants of a bruising winter, littered the flatlands; occasional herds of antelope searched for green, telltale signs of spring. Unkempt shanties of homesteaders lay scattered across the horizon. She wondered whether her future might be spent in such disarray, but quickly dismissed such misgivings. In her mind, the wealth of the land was more important than the buildings. Cousin Wilbert Ruck had located a half-section with a house for her, a barn would materialize after a year or two of good crops. Meanwhile, she would work the land and let its strength take care of her needs. All I want in life is a piece of land, she thought. The rest will fall into place.

Interminable hours passed as the Great Northern made its way across the prairie. Clara reminisced about her early childhood in Wisconsin and the final move of her family from southern Minnesota to Todd County in 1897. Her father, Charles Miller[3], located 160 acres of affordable rich, black land along the banks of the Long Prairie River a few miles west of the Ruck relatives. He delivered his family to a log house, a two-story affair on a hillside nestled beneath a canopy of oak, maple, and box

August Ruck and Charles Miller. Photo courtesy of Sandra Bareister, great-granddaughter of Ernestina Ruck

elder trees on the dusty river road. The immigrant family arrived with five children, a wagon load of household items, a team of horses, and eight dollars.

The land provided sustenance during their first season, and the five children attended the one-room country school, District 77, adjacent to their property, for three months in the spring and three months in the fall. Emma, the eldest child, finished eighth grade and continued her education to become a teacher, but academics held no interest for Clara. She preferred to work in the fields where she listened to the slurred whistle of the meadowlarks, imitated the rollicking songs of the bobolinks as they hovered and darted across the fields. Sometimes she caught a glimpse of a badger shuffling along the riverbank; she watched the muskrats building winter houses in the

The old log house on the Miller farm in Todd County.

reeds, red-winged blackbirds whistling to each other from the tops of cattails where they bobbled in the breeze. The gentle aroma of freshly mowed meadow grass intoxicated her with an unexplainable love of the land. Whimsical fantasies frolicked inside her head as she labored in the fields; her lively imagination produced capricious tales that she eagerly shared with the family, for she was a born storyteller but, except for brother Charley, her humorless audience listened with bored indifference, considered her a dreamer, a profligate squanderer of time.

No longer interested in teaching school, Emma moved to Minneapolis while Clara remained behind and worked the land with her brothers. But, as Clara approached her late twenties, she sensed a void in her life; she had nothing to show for her lost youth. The Ladies Aid Society of the Whiteville Methodist Church held no interest for her. Her passion for playing the organ was dying a slow death; she was too exhausted to play. Even the purchase of a new piano couldn't sustain her interest in music. No ardent suitors knocked at the door, and since her aging parents had retired from the field work, Lou's overbearing tyranny became unbearable.

Louis Miller

Lou, the oldest of her three younger brothers, a morose bachelor, viewed his world through cold, blue eyes obscured by eyelids that hovered at half-mast. An ominous figure, a man of few words who allowed no room for human error. A lank and sinewy farmer with large, callused hands. A stillborn sense of humor. Each morning he handed out work assignments for the day. He expected Fred, Charley, and Clara to complete their tasks by an assigned time, and he expected Clara to do the work of a man.

Strong and tall with muscular arms, sturdy legs and ankles, she worked from dawn until dark. She swung the scythe through timo-thy-covered meadow, gathered it into piles with a wood rake nearly four feet wide, and pitched it onto the hayrack when one of the broth-ers came with the team. During the harvest she followed the binder and gathered sheaves of grain, stacked them into shocks like golden teepees.

Fred Miller

She hoed acres of potatoes, mucked out the barns, pitched manure on the fields. She helped with the garden and cared for the chickens. And in the evening before barn chores, Lou inspected the day's work to make sure that his standards were met. Perfectly straight rows of corn graced his fields. Symmetri-cally stacked shocks of grain stood amongst the stubble. He frequently pointed out one neighbor's careless handiwork with disgust and commented under his breath, "Just look at those crooked rows!"

Clara's spirits faltered under his domination. She longed to escape, but she'd never known a life away from the farm. After much soul-searching, she followed Emma's lead and moved to Minneapolis, where she sought a different lifestyle—one that offered more freedom, perhaps even marriage. Within days of her arrival she accepted a cooking position, but it was hard work without amenities. Dissatisfied that she had no time to work in a garden, to plant flowers and vegetables, she opened the Min-neapolis newspaper in search of a new position and perused a provoking article about free homestead land in Montana.

The Great Northern Railroad now stretched to the Pacific Ocean, and along the way bountiful acres of rich, grassy plains waited to be claimed. A colorful poster at the market displayed the sketch of a house and barn along a country road, a peaceful, pastoral setting where rolling wheat fields and heavily laden fruit trees completed the lure of a typical homestead as depicted by artistic promoters.

Clara's dreams of independence flashed before her. She envisioned herself on such a farm. She might not raise cattle, but she'd keep a Jersey cow for her dairy needs, and she'd raise flocks of poultry. Clara quickly realized that James J. Hill and his Great Northern Railroad were offering her a ticket to freedom. "Gee whiz, with just a few dollars," she reasoned, "I could own a piece of land, a lot of land that would be all mine."

Exhilarated, already anticipating the joys of emancipation, she pondered the move and its estimated cost. By living frugally, she reasoned, she could pay the train fare, the filing fee, and buy supplies for the first year. After that, the money from her crops would sustain her. She could be master of her own fate.

With the rekindling of her adventurous spirit, Clara collected her wages and gathered her savings; she returned to the family farm determined to present the bold plan to her parents and brothers, but her unexpected arrival made them wary.

Pa and Momma stared aghast at the brashness of her decision to homestead alone in Montana. Lou and Fred leaned back on their chairs, crossed their arms, studied her from beneath half-closed lids. Charley grinned, but sat silent. The brothers knew about the high wheat yields on the Montana plains; they had read cousin Wilbert Ruck's glowing reports of his homestead at Rudyard. Aware of Clara's ambition and her talent with farming, and knowing that she would go whether they gave permission or not, the brothers proposed that if she'd agree to file on a homestead at Rudyard where she could be near family, they would give her a share of the family farm

Wilbert Ruck playing guitar at his homestead.

as a grubstake. Clara listened to their proposition with an open mind. She and Wilbert had been close childhood friends. She needed the money; it would assure her independence.

She helped the brothers with chores and busied herself buying household goods, garden seeds, and hand tools while waiting for Cousin Wilbert's response. Visions of vast wheat fields lulled her to sleep at night, and the contemplation of raising a munificent garden enhanced by a fleeting glimpse of a tranquil house and farm buildings rounded out the tableau of domestic bliss. A chicken coop…yes! She'd raise leghorns, maybe Plymouth Rocks, and sell eggs to the neighbors. She wrote notes to herself and made lists; she packed and organized with unrestrained excitement. Within the week, Wilbert's letter arrived. He knew of an available homestead with a house a few miles out of Rudyard, and he had the horses and machinery to plant her crops.

Impervious to the dangers that awaited her, a woman with few material possessions but an infinity of dreams, Clara watched the empty miles of the Montana plains unfold as the Great Northern rumbled westward. Being a strong woman who loved the smell of fresh earth and the feel of dirt on her hands, she prepared herself to accept the challenge of a lifetime.

What actually transpired when Clara announced her intention to go to Montana to file on a homestead? Did she first discuss it with Emma? Was there a confrontation with her family or had their patience been exhausted with this daughter, this sister who once abandoned the family farm and now intended to leave a position in the city to run off to the wilderness?

Visualize six adults sitting around the dining room table in the evening, the tall kerosene lamp, its burning wick emitting a gentle glow. Pa and Momma huddled together, the three brothers presenting a solidified front, Clara alone, steadfast in her decision. A somber audience meticulous in envisioning the worst scenarios, offering caution, discouraging risks as they listened to another of her capricious dreams. Perhaps they offered her a share of the family farm in hope that she'd make a commitment in life, settle down. Clara's stories to her children didn't reveal detailed circumstances of her departure except for the fact that the family paid her off and helped her depart.

With frequent stops along the High Line, the Great Northern left the bleakness of North Dakota behind and rolled onto the wastelands of northeastern Montana. The crowd of passengers began to thin as families and their boxcars were off-loaded at scheduled stops. The north-central towns of Malta and Havre caused the longest delays, with Havre recording dozens of homestead entries every day. And the settlers kept coming. There was land for all, and there was someone eager to help them find it.

Land locators, specialized entrepreneurs, loitered around the Montana train depots in anticipation of making a fast buck when weary families, ignorant about the frontier, stepped onto the depot platform. With all of their worldly goods gathered around them, the exhausted newcomers saw a dingy, one-horse town with wide streets, a general store, a saloon or two, a bank, a church, a few houses and a school all huddled in the shadows of towering grain elevators. And beyond that, the wasted emptiness stretched as far as the eye could see. Nothing but windswept prairie lay before them.

Not a tree, not a hill offered relief from the vastness of northern Montana. A sudden hopelessness enveloped their tired bodies and fatigued minds. They had arrived. Land was free, but how were they going to find a suitable tract?

At the depots of Malta, Dodson, Zurich, Chinook, new towns along the High Line, Clara observed the hectic pandemonium from her window seat as families tried to organize themselves. Well-dressed men approached each family and led the husband aside for a private conference. They pointed off toward the north or the west, they made elaborate gestures, they laughed, and shook hands, then moved off to greet another bewildered family.

Unbeknownst to her, Clara was witness to the feeding frenzy of the local barracudas, men well-informed about available land. For a fee of $20 to $50, they loaded the new arrivals, five to ten at a time, into an open wagon with rough board seats and drove them from site to site until each newcomer found suitable acreage for his family. When they returned to town, the land locator helped the husband register his filing fee and pointed the family entourage in the direction of their new property.[4]

Nearly every man who lived in Montana for a period of time considered himself to be a "land man." Most of them were honest men who provided a valuable service, while others worked the system to their advantage then moved farther west. They bought relinquished homesteads, added a few improvements, and resold them for unbelievable profit. Others showed a desirable piece of property to several parties, then registered them on different tracts, a bait-and-switch scam of the lowest kind. Some of the locators specialized in spinsters, sweet-talking them out of their savings. It was a lucrative business that paid far better returns than farming.[5]

On Thursday afternoon as the Great Northern dispersed a few families at Rudyard, Clara slipped into her heavy wool coat, secured her hat, then stepped down from the train onto the depot platform to claim her menagerie of goods. She surveyed the treeless, dusty street of a desolate community, an inhospitable island in a sea of prairie grass. A grain elevator hovered over the rails at the edge of town; a general store and the feed store claimed their territory on the main street making it easy for the men when the womenfolk shopped. The few nondescript houses at the end of the block looked on with bored tenacity. Small businesses with dusty windows peered into the deepening twilight as the wind whipped across the platform and dust devils twirled like dervishes, howling and whining, disappearing into the distance as replacements chased behind in an endless game of tag through the streets before churning out over the prairie.

Exhausted and dirty, Clara admitted to herself that Rudyard wasn't the way she'd envisioned it. She had expected a thriving community of new businesses, expansive streets, lovely new homes. Wisps of trepidation clouded her optimism as she met the ugliness of Montana face to face.

A middle-aged man approached, called out. "Hey, Cousin Clara! Over here!"

She turned with relief. "Oh, Wilbert, I'm so glad to see you!"

Wilbert, a man of slight stature, huddled inside his sheepskin jacket, pulled his hat further down over his forehead against the wind, and approached with a smile. He enthusiastically pumped her hand. "Welcome to Montana, Clara. It's sure gonna be swell to have more family around. It gets pretty lonesome out here for me and brother Elmer."

Accustomed to being self-sufficient, Clara helped lift trunks, boxes, and tools into the back of the wagon. Cautioned about the price of goods on the frontier, she had expediently followed Wilbert's advice and brought flour, sugar, spices, soap, washtubs, and housekeeping goods. The prairie wind teased like an impudent child as it pirouetted before her, tangled the long coat around her ankles and tugged at the stout buttons. It coaxed tendrils of fine hair from the security of her hat thrashing them across her face until she secured the strands with a hairpin. After four years of this incessant companion on the plains, Wilbert continued to load her freight as he shouted against its mournful whine, "The train always seems to be late these days with so many new settlers coming to the West, but there's land for all!"

Clara pulled herself into the wagon and settled next to Wilbert on the springboard seat as he urged the horses forward and continued to tell her his plan. "It's getting pretty dark out now, so we'll stay at my house this evening, and then tomorrow I'll take you out to a nice half-section of land I've located. It's several miles farther out than my place, but there's a soddy already on it. A soddy on the prairie makes a nice little house. They're cooler in summer and warmer in winter than a house made of lumber." He continued, "Before long it'll feel just like home."

I wonder if that's true, she thought as she tucked wisps of hair under her hat. Wilbert headed the team across the railroad tracks and out of town on a trail across the prairie, a level, treeless expanse of nothing. She gathered the collar of her coat to her throat as the chill of an early spring evening nipped at her cheeks.

Located one mile from town, Wilbert's house, similar to the shacks of homesteaders she'd observed from the train, offered modest accommodations for his bachelor lifestyle. The black silhouette of a barn could be seen against the skyline, assorted farm machinery lay off to the west. Relieved to be with family again after the melee on the train, Clara accepted his humble hospitality and settled in for the night.

At dawn, Wilbert hitched the horses to the wagon and the two of them jolted away from civilization toward the desolate area of available land. The rising sun shone brilliantly from horizon to horizon, and the warmth of a spring morning after a good night's sleep erased discouraging memories of her arrival at Rudyard. Clara contemplated the flat terrain of her surroundings and the wide expanse of blue sky. Farther off toward the southeast, the gentle slope of the Bears Paw Mountains offered a pleasant diversion from the prairie.

After a seven mile journey with the wagon bouncing and hiccupping across the open land on a rutted trail, Wilbert reined in the team at the edge of a ten-acre field that had once felt the scratch of a plow. The remaining 310 acres of the half-section presented an ocean of virgin prairie grass. Clara stood up in the wagon, shaded her eyes, and studied the barren, infinite wilderness where the curvature of the earth fell off on either side. The openness of the plains suddenly appealed to her. The vastness of the wasteland challenged her intrinsic desire to vanquish it into billowing, golden fields of wheat as she climbed down from the wagon to pursue her dream.

A lonely sod house blended into the tawny prairie background where tangles of lifeless grass protruded above islands of snow. A few sprigs of green pushed toward sunlight, a half-hearted promise of spring. "Welcome to your new home, Clara. Me and Elmer are sure glad you're here. We know you're gonna like it."

They walked together into the field where broken earth from past crops was soft and free of rocks. She picked up a clump of fine-grained soil. With her hands cupped to protect it from the wind, she held it to her face anticipating an earthy aroma, but it crumbled between her fingers. "This soil is odorless," she said with a frown. "It doesn't smell at all like our Minnesota land. And it's fine and powdery."

"Don't let it fool you, Clara. It's a fertile loam that's been deposited over the years. All you need is a little rain, and you'll be able to grow anything," Wilbert declared as he, too, crumbled clods of soil between his fingers, watched it trickle to the ground. Clara accepted that there was much to learn about the land in this wild Montana country, allowed her dreams to soar.

Wilbert unloaded her provisions then departed with good intentions to return in a few days. As his wagon disappeared from view, Clara paused, considered the expansive grasslands and her unencumbered freedom to wander at will. The bright sunshine and gentle breeze that ruffled the dead prairie grass proffered its own kind of beauty, but no other signs of human habitation appeared on the horizon.

I'm alone, I have no neighbors, she realized as her eyes swept the treeless landscape. Who will buy my eggs, she wondered. If Wilbert's busy, who will help me with the field work, but his assurance of the fertility of the soil lingered foremost in her mind, and she ignored the truth that lay before her.

Once again Clara brushed fine wisps of hair back from her face and sighed with resignation. She saw that the door and window of the soddy faced south, the gable ends faced east and west. It looked snug enough to withstand the wind, but the squares of turf in the low walls pitched haphazardly from one corner to the next. Staggered like brickwork, each level of sod lay face down; straggly roots protruded from the outside walls and fluttered in the breeze. The end near the door sagged a few inches lower than the rest of the shelter, and cotton rags filled the void between the one four-paned window and the sod above. A red hand pump near the door offered the only relief from the drab surroundings as she worked the handle in anticipation of fresh water. She rinsed her hands, dampened her handkerchief in the trickle, freshened her face with its coolness.

She walked around the back side of the soddy. Edges of rough boards projected from the roof. She examined the layers of roofing above the boards, a woven mat of willow poles, an upper layer of brush, and a layer of grass topped off with a final layer of sod, grass side up to catch the rain. A rusty stove pipe tottered above the greening roof at the west end where arctic winds had buckled it toward the south.[6] Farther west away from the house, a hovel of sod enclosed the one-hole toilet while a nearby shelter resembled a barn. The outside looks all right, she thought as she turned to examine the inside of her soddy.

Heavy hinges held the solid wood door to a frame on the outer edge of the wall where several layers of sod lay side by side. Clara stepped onto the dirt floor. No scrubbing here, she observed with satisfaction. A low, Acme range claimed its territory at the far end of the room, the nickel trim concealed beneath layers of dust. A roughly-built table and two oak chairs absorbed beams of daylight beneath the only window; a cast iron bed, its springs in contorted disarray, lay adjacent to the north wall. Rows of shelves covered the space behind the stove; drops of candle wax on wooden crates bore testimony of earlier inhabitants who had unsuccessfully pursued their dreams. She absently scratched at the wax with her thumbnail and contemplated the former residents. I wonder why they left, she mused.

Shredded debris dropped from above. Strips of muslin that once stretched tightly below the rough boards of the ceiling now hung like shrouds capturing bits of dried sod. The bouncing movement of a mouse making his way across the suspended walkway brought a frown to her face. "I'll soon take care of you," she murmured as she prepared to settle in.

The early days of April passed quickly as Clara rose at daybreak and began setting her house in order. She scrubbed the rough table and chairs until the patina of the wood grain glowed in the sunlight. She secured the sagging bed springs together with heavy twine and stuffed an old comforter with dry grass to use as a mattress. She removed the muslin from the ceiling and subjected it to the rigors of her washboard, then stretched it over the prairie grass to bleach in the sun. She swept the ceiling boards, swept the walls, replaced the muslin. Her heavy broom polished the earthen floor until it shone like slate; she then moved her meager belongings into place. Smugly satisfied with her accomplishments, she plumped up the bed pillows and tied back the new kitchen curtains, smiled at its cozy ambience.

Each afternoon before dusk, Clara ambled across the flat land relishing the arrival of spring. She watched for kits around fox dens and studied abandoned rodent holes for signs of burrowing owls. The distant cry of killdeers accompanied her as they searched for nesting sites on the prairie. She returned to the soddy laden with armloads of dry, dead grass that she had twisted into fuel knots, and in the twilight, she wrote lengthy letters to her family describing the happiness she felt.

Playful breezes of spring, the couriers of hope, cavorted and tumbled across the prairie scattering fragrances of awakening life. Clara's ambition to prepare the land was overpowering. While waiting for Wilbert to come with his plow, she spaded the corner of the field nearest the house for a garden. Turning the soil brought contentment, energized her as she pushed the spade into the ground with her foot, wriggled it loose, lifted the root-bound clod into the air, and plopped it over back into the hole. A few quick chops with the sharp blade cut and loosened the tangled mass as she repeated the process and worked her way across the garden plot.

With a heavy four-tined digging fork she sifted and broke the clods into finer soil, buckets of which she carried and distributed along the west end of her soddy to become a raised hotbed for tomato and cabbage seeds. The softened soil captured the afternoon rays of the sun as it swept toward the north; the walls of the soddy absorbed and reflected the heat onto the nursery.

When Wilbert returned with his horses and plow, Clara's face glowed with excitement as she proudly led him to admire the delicate leaves of tomato seedlings spreading their arms to embrace the warmth of spring. She gave a quick tour of her new home and offered a cup of tea; he was her first guest.

They sat at the polished table. Wilbert removed his broad-brimmed hat matted with sweat, caked with dust, and tossed it across to the bed. He emptied the teacup into his saucer, blew across it several times to cool the searing liquid, then lifted it to his lips with both hands, slurped it with satisfaction. He admired the neatness of the interior of the soddy with pots and pans hanging from pegs, a new set of dishes displayed on the shelves. The freshly blackened Acme range enhanced the brilliance of its nickel oven door and side brackets; light reflected and bounced from its handles to the crystal globe of a kerosene lamp on the shelf where candles once flickered. The heavily carved frame of the Miller family portrait perched at one end of an embroidered dresser scarf atop a trunk; a curling wand with ivory handles, a matching comb and brush, a mirror, and an array of articles for her toilette lay on display. On the earthen floor near the bed, the circular pattern of a braided rug complemented the decor. "You've got this place cleaned up. It's looking real fine," Wilbert said appreciatively as he took another slurp from the saucer.

Enthusiastic about his approval she said, "It's a swell place, Wilbert, but now I want to get my filing fee paid so no one else can claim it."

Wilbert settled back in the chair with outstretched legs, crossed his arms and confided, "Well now, Clara, there's no hurry about that. Lots of folks live on the land for a year or more before they get the papers signed. Besides, I know the couple who built this place, and I'm about the only one who knows they left. The young wife just couldn't tolerate the wind and loneliness no more, so the husband never bothered to file. He just took her back east to her family. They won't be back. Let's just wait awhile."

He stood and stretched his arms over his head in preparation for the task at hand. He reached for his hat. "Now let's get out and start to plow that field for you. Since it's already been broke once, we should be able to do three or four acres a day."

For thousands of years the prairie grass laid claim to the land, its tangled roots reaching six to eight feet into the earth searching for moisture; now it stubbornly fought the sharpened shares of the plow even though it had been turned once before. Clara held the reins and walked off to the side of the team while Wilbert steadied the plow, forced his weight upon each handle, forced the steel shares deep into the soil. The team pulled and jerked against the resistance, slashed contours that scarred the natural beauty of the prairie, ripped open furrows that flopped over, rode piggyback on each other toward the horizon and back until the ten acres once again lay conquered.

Wilbert advised her to plant flax the first year, but she had never considered planting anything but wheat. Her brothers had never planted flax; she was apprehensive about it herself, but Wilbert assured her that it was the fastest way for a newcomer to make money, so she shrugged off her preconceived ideas and went with the advice of experience. Next year I'll plant these ten acres in wheat and have Wilbert turn over another ten acres for flax, she decided as she sent her letters with him to be mailed in Rudyard, then planted peas and early garden vegetables as she hoed and caressed the soil, faithfully tended her hotbed of tomatoes and cabbages until his return.

After a late spring rain when touches of emerald graced the wasteland and budding larkspur promised to paint the prairie, Wilbert returned. Clara stood at the edge of the field watching the mating ritual of a male sage grouse. His mottled brown body blended with the prairie grass except for a deep white V at the base of his throat and a touch of yellow above his eye. With a ruff of white feathers jutting upward from his breast like a feather boa, he spread an erect tail of sharply spiked feathers. Booming sounds erupted from his chest as he pranced, pivoted, and postured before a drab, uninterested female.

Unimpressed with prairie romance, Wilbert swung down

from the wagon. "It's time to plant your flax. I'll take you into town to buy seed and household supplies, and I'll bring you home again. But you know, Clara, it's eight miles into town from here. I can't always take time away from my work to help you. You'd better think about getting yourself a team of horses and a wagon."

Clara watched the frustrated cock scuttle into the grass, then turned and looked at Wilbert in disbelief. Horses frightened her. She'd always refused to ride a horse. Her brothers had wondered how she'd survive on a homestead without horses, but hoped that nearby neighbors might help her out. But she had no neighbors. Now she found herself in a dilemma with Wilbert suggesting that she buy a team of her own.

All the way to Rudyard she mulled the situation over in her mind, first from one perspective, then another. Money was not the problem. She had enough money for a team and wagon, but she feared their awesome power. She was not an aggressive master, and horses needed to be ruled with a stern hand.

They bought flax seed and supplies, and collected their mail before heading over to Wilbert's place to meet Elmer. Clara prepared an afternoon lunch while Elmer stroked the fiddle and Wilbert accompanied him on the guitar, but the time passed too quickly as she wrestled with the notion of owning a team of horses. She didn't know how to harness a horse. Pa and the boys had always done that job.

Jolting across the prairie back to the soddy Clara gazed toward the empty horizons and murmured, "Maybe you're right. I do need a team of horses and a way to get around. You can't always come a-chasing after me, but what would I do with them in the winter?"

"Well," he said slowly, "it would sure make your life a lot more pleasant to be able to come and go on your own. Eight miles out is a long ways." He paused. "That little enclosure out behind your house would be shelter enough for horses during the summer, but you shouldn't try to spend a winter alone on this Montana prairie. Go on back and visit Emma and the family for the winter. My barn has a couple of extra stalls. I'll take care of your team."

"But Wilbert, I don't know how to buy a horse. I don't know anything about them." She shuddered at memories of the farm horses snorting and tossing their heads. Realizing that the situation was beyond her control, she finally relinquished her fears to his common sense. "Wilbert, maybe you can find a good team and a wagon for me. You know a lot of people around here. If you find a well-behaved, calm team, send them out to me, and I'll pay on delivery. Will you do that?" she queried, hoping all the time that he'd refuse, but her hopes were dashed as he agreed to see what he could do.

The month of May wore on as Clara scattered flax seed across the furrows and scratched it in with her rake. She wore a broad-brimmed hat for protection from the sun, tied it under her chin to prevent the wind from carrying it away. The skirt of her dress brushed her ankles and sturdy oxfords supported her weight as she worked her way up and down the field across the ten acres while bountiful crops spilled out of her cornucopia of dreams.

She finished planting her garden, precise rows of potatoes, onions, beans, and greens, then busied herself manicuring the land around her soddy. Unseen, nocturnal sounds of the prairie lulled her to sleep at night, a reveille of bird songs welcomed her at dawn, but one morning soon after her discussion with Wilbert, the sound of jingling harnesses awakened her. She cautiously opened the door.

Near the pump, a team of horses hitched to a grain wagon, a heavy, high-sided vehicle with wood spoke wheels and a springboard seat, awaited her appearance. A saddle horse trailed along behind. "You must be Clara," said the stranger who jumped down from the wagon seat. "Wilbert told me you was looking for a team of horses!"

From the doorway Clara surveyed the shaggy animals. They still sported their winter coats, and they looked calm enough, but one could never tell. She stepped forward. She walked around the team and studied them from all sides. She tentatively patted the black on the rump, stroked the nose of the roan. She asked questions about the temperament of the beasts but nothing about their age or condition. The cumbersome wagon looked clumsy and uncomfortable for the long ride into town. "I was really hoping for a buggy," she said.

"Won't work," the man confided. "If you wanna be a farmer, you gotta have heavy equipment to haul your grain and supplies."

She remembered that Wilbert had stated specifically that she needed a team and a wagon, so without haggling, she agreed to the price.

Realizing that he'd made a good deal and that this woman knew nothing about horses, the horse trader replaced his hat and stepped forward to give her a few instructions. Flashing an impish grin, he darted quickly around the team from side to side, under their bellies, around their chests, releasing harnesses, removing bridles and bits, lifting away the horse collars, slipping on the halters. Within minutes he'd finished unharnessing the team and stood back.

She shrugged her shoulders in bewilderment, so he reharnessed them once more as she paid close attention. He started with the collar and finished with the team once again hitched to the wagon all the while offering words of reassurance that these horses were as gentle as lambs. Under his guidance Clara unhitched the team by herself, removed the leather traces, and slipped their halters into place. Together they led them to the enclosure behind the house where the horse trader deposited a few sacks of grain and accepted Clara's money. As he rode off on his saddle horse, she pondered what to do with her new purchase.

Over the next few days Clara staked them out for fresh grass and cleaned their stalls. She buoyed her courage for a confrontation as she brushed away their shaggy coats, patted them on the rear, stroked their long faces, and whispered words of reassurance, more for her benefit than theirs. "I have to do it," she told herself after another restless night fraught with worry. "I can't put it off any longer." With grim determination she prepared to hitch the team to the wagon for a leisurely trip into town.

Remembering the horse trader's instructions and trying to recall how her brothers had hitched up a team, she scratched, patted, and cooed at them as she slipped each horse collar into place and attached the hames. So far, so good. Taking one horse at a time she untangled the harness and threw it over the back. She drew the front straps around the chest, down between the front legs, reached under the belly and connected them to the side straps. The horses stood quietly while she fastened each breech harness around the hind end. Growing confident, she stood on tiptoe and replaced their halters with the bridles and bits. She attached the reins, reached up for the bridles and led both horses outside the enclosure.

She backed the black horse into place and fastened him to the wagon with ease, but when she led the roan toward his partner, he rolled his eyes, laid back his ears, and jerked the bridle out of her hand. Clara cried out, covered her head with her arms, and backed against the soddy for safety. Spooked by her cry, the terrified black bolted forward dragging the half-hitched vehicle in his wake. He galloped across the prairie while Clara cowered against the wall, watched the wagon fade into the horizon.

But her determination to master the beasts was greater than her fear, and once again she approached the roan without success. Time and again he watched her with haughty eyes, backed away in spite of her coaxing and sweet talk while the renegade black eventually tired of dragging his encumbrance and circled back where he settled down to munch the prairie grass a safe distance away. With her energy expended, Clara disappeared into the soddy for a cup of tea and deliberated about her next course of action.

She calmed down, and they calmed down. A few hours later she approached each horse with false words of endearment, released them from their traces, and returned them to their enclosure. It was a fiasco not to be repeated.

At dawn, Clara opened her parasol for protection from the sun, and walked seven miles over the grasslands to Wilbert's. "Get rid of them, Wilbert," she pleaded. "I don't know how to handle horses, and I'm too scared to learn."

"But how will you get around?" he asked. "You live so far out of town."

"Gee whiz," she answered. "How do you think I got over here today? There's nothing wrong with my legs!"

Wilbert sold the team. Although the brothers continued to check on her from time to time, Clara remained stubborn and determined to survive on her own. They understood. That's the way the Miller cousins were.

Cloudless skies filled her days, coyote harmony lulled her to sleep at night while the flax grew tall, then turned the ten acres into a rippling ocean of blue. With her garden flourishing and her flax showing promise, Clara felt free to pay Wilbert a visit from time to time. Carrying her parasol at a jaunty angle, she enjoyed the refreshing walk across the prairie in the dewy hours of dawn. A frustrated killdeer performed its conspicuous distraction, a forward hobble, a broken wing dragging on the ground. Flittering butterflies accompanied her while a multitude of wildflowers, nodding daisies, asters, prairie sunflowers, black-eyed Susans beckoned her onward as she composed fanciful stories in her mind then shared them with Wilbert.

In return, Wilbert frequently gathered her mail and delivered eggs from his chickens, baskets of strawberries from his garden, and arrived in time to share her supper. She amused him with new stories and embellished familiar ones. He strummed his guitar, and together their voices wafted over the prairie. Clara thrived with independence, her enthusiasm was irrepressible.

Clouds appeared on the horizon from time to time, lightning flickered false promises across the evening sky, but rain didn't fall on her field. She despaired at the unrelenting heat. Only two weeks before, Wilbert had shown her the plump kernels at the base of each bloom on the flax, indicators of a bumper crop, but now the soil dried to dust as July approached August, and she watched her crop of flax turn yellow then brown with no moisture to ease the torment of the earth.

The leaves of the beets, rutabagas, and turnips became thin, papery sheets, then broke from the stem and tumbled along the ground. The crisp brown leaves of tomato plants fell to the earth; the fruit, yellowed with sunburn, dried on the vine. Her precious cabbages petrified on the stem.

By early August the flax withered and died where it had eagerly sprung out of the earth two months before; a hazy pall hung over the parched flatlands where wildflowers had once billowed above the shortgrass prairie. Sleepless nights plagued her with doubt about the homestead. She'd reaped nothing from her attempt to tame the land. Her savings had been depleted on train fare, seeds, and supplies. All she had left was the money from her share of the family farm. She had no food to survive the winter; she'd have to return to Minnesota until next spring, and she dreaded facing brother Lou's inability to understand her plight.

A mid-August sunrise. Vulnerable and alone, Clara prepared herself for another blistering day. She arose early, dressed with care. Wore heavy oxfords, selected a filmy, cotton dress with flared skirt, one that allowed the air to cool her thighs, donned her broad-brimmed straw hat, and began the dusty trek to Rudyard to post an anguished letter to her family, a worried letter of disappointments, unfulfilled dreams. She hadn't seen Wilbert for some time, and she needed to buy food since the demise of her garden. White cumulus clouds gathered on the western horizon. Breathless air suffocated the land. The morning rays of old Sol beat down on her parasol, waves of oppressive heat ricocheted off the great nothingness as she blotted rivulets of sweat from her face, her throat, and pressed on.

Clara craved human contact; she was vulnerable and fragile when The Land Man came into her life. Perhaps she succumbed to his charms because of her loneliness and dire circumstances. No one knows, but between the imminent crop failure and her return to Minnesota for the winter, she entrusted him with her savings to buy a half-section of land adjacent to his homestead near town.

In late September of 1913, after spending nearly seven months on her homestead, Clara boarded the Great Northern and returned to Minnesota for a reunion with her family. En route, she distributed The Land Man's business cards to perspective female homesteaders. She mailed him a postcard filled with family news. She sent a second postcard asking how the land deal was progressing. In frustration, she wrote a detailed letter disclosing the news that her family refused to advance her more money.

Every morning Clara walked down to the mailbox in hope of finding a letter from The Land Man. It finally arrived. Her hands shook with excitement as she examined the neatly typed address on the envelope. Did he get that land for me? Does he miss me? Will this letter contain a proposal of marriage, she wondered.

With a hammering heart she slipped the long-awaited letter inside an apron pocket away from the prying eyes of the family, then stole away upstairs to the privacy of her bedroom where she could absorb each treasured word in private.

Rudyard, Mont.
October 6th 1913
Miss Clara A Miller
Long Prairie Minnesota.

My Dear Clara—Your two cards and one letter at hand just now and I am so glad to hear from you. I got home and found no mail from you and I thought you had forgotton me…

Well maby you will make a land man yet. Ha' Ha' as you say you handed my cards to ladies on the train that talked Montana, maybe we can go into pardner-ship yet. Yes Clara I am trying to enjoy my self the best I can but you must remember I am all alone out here and am so anxous you come out but if we ever land any thing in this country we sure ought to make up for lost time…*I am not going to see you loose this claim here by the side of me* if it is possible for me to get it for you. *It does not make any difference if Papa dont help us,* I am one of these kind that can help my self and dont you forget it, and I am not going to expect him to help you a cent now but *I am sure if you get the land and every thing goes off all right he will be perfectly willing to lend a helping hand sooner or later. however now is the time we need it most,* but I am no beggar. and I never beg people against their own opinions. as the other children have cut up so about him helping you then I would not have it if he offered it to me, I will get you this Claim now if it is possible if it costs me $1500.00. cash, I am not broke yet and I still have a little credit. so dont get discouraged. you have been to true a fried to me for me to turn you down even if your own folks have, in a finantial way speaking, *It is right they should help you and if they feel it right to loosen up a little send what amount you can to the Havre National*

Bank Havre Montana, if it is $50, $100, or $500. and instruct
them to turn the money over to me when I have the Land for you.
I will send you inclosed a letter to the Bank if you wish to send
them the money. and instruct them to hold the money untill the
place is yours I will leave the amount blank and you can fill it
in when you get ready to send the money. send any amount you
can and if you cant then I will do my best single handed for you,
I am not going to give up now I can tell you that, I was not born
in the give up season, so I am going to do the best I can for you
under any and all circumstances.

as I have told you Dear I want to settle down and I feel you
would just suit me and I am willing to get things shaped up so
we can have something some day, I have a deal or so now pend-
ing kist like yours have another one to try to pull of next Saturday, so I am getting in the harness again, and suppose I will be
busy form now on.

But done let the Boys discourage you by telling you that
you will not get the land here so near town…Oh' well look over
them and just say as little as possible and dont do any thing to
make them sor at you, keep quiet and I will try to do the rest. I
am your friend and a true friend, and you I hope will find it out
sooner or later, and then maybe you will be sorry for being so
mean to me when you were out here. But I think I have about
as much patiens as any man living, how many men do you think
would go throught what I did, (enough said you know the rest.)
Ha' Ha'

My that sweet little…right arm of yours is sure a haven of
rest to my weary poor self, and I do love to cuddle up in it and
have you love me there is some class to that. Now about the land
No you are not a contester you get the land after all you get it
outgih and would not have to contest as you have only signed
filing papers, and in whos name is the land now well Dear it is
in Claude B. Reinharts name, Nora Windle has no thing to do
with it whatever now, she is intirely out of it, *if those tow fellows*

*are paid off the land goes to you as soon as you get your filing on it
and that I will attend to at the proper time,*

*that is if I can get them out of the way in any way reasonable
and that is what we need the money for, you know, no trouble at-
tatched to it whatever if these parties are gotton out of the way,* you
wo get a clean streight filing on it without any trouble whatever,
and the land would be allowed to you and you would get the
allowance papers sent you there from the Government Land Office here.

Now do you believe me when I have written you before that
I was *very effectionate,* it is my nate *dear Darling* and I cant help
it and is not a bad failing if I had a wife to be effectionate with as
you say Dear I should marry that is right,

Well I will clse for this time,

am yours Most Sincerely,

....

[unsigned]

Clara carried the letter with her for several days; she
read and reread its sweet message. She washed windows and
scrubbed floors with wild abandon in an attempt to eradicate
immodest fantasies. Her hands fairly flew over the keys of her
parlor organ as refrains of romantic ballads hung in the air; her
mind lingered over intimate moments when the two dreamers
had shared visions about that Montana land next to his; she
could almost hear his voice murmuring tender endearments
and feel his lips at her throat. His disarming smile hovered in
the recesses of her fancy; she longed for the spicy scent of his
cologne, but deeply hidden within the confines of her soul, she
felt that her true destiny lay with the land, and foremost in her
mind was the need to possess that special half-section close to
town. The thought of losing it to someone else haunted her.

In a final attempt to coerce the men in her family to loan
her the money, Clara approached them once more. She de-

scribed the fertility of the soil, the quality of the buildings, its nearness to town, the willingness of The Land Man to help her procure it and file the paperwork, but the men were hopelessly unyielding. For nearly twenty years the sweat of the siblings had mingled with the dark earth of the river valley to enlarge the family estate to 240 acres. If Clara wanted a better homestead, she could do it the Miller way. She could work for it.

Discouraged by her brothers' adamant parsimony, Clara eagerly awaited Emma's arrival from Minneapolis—Emma, whom she hadn't seen since March. Her sister's savings were substantial; perhaps she would grant her a loan.

Emma arrived for noontime dinner and entertained them with descriptions of her daily life as companion to a judge's wife. After the departure of the brothers to muck out the barn, Momma and Pa withdrew to the poultry yard to tend the turkeys, allowing the girls to

Emma Miller

be alone with the problem at hand. The aging parents had discussed Clara's need for money between themselves; it was their hope that Emma could talk some sense into Clara, but Clara had always been their ethereal dreamer, and they didn't have much hope of any change.

Emma, forewarned by her family and anxious about Clara's need for money, helped wash the dinner dishes and assumed an anxious camaraderie as they moved into the parlor together. Feigning gaiety, Emma lightly strummed her mandolin and Clara accompanied her on the organ as they reviewed their repertoire of favorite melodies from younger, carefree years when they'd saved their egg money and ordered the musical instruments from the Sears, Roebuck catalog. After a few minutes, Emma set her mandolin aside and lowered herself into Pa's oak rocking chair with the high, spindled back and wide arms. She settled onto the quilted pad that protected his bony hips and smoothed the creases from the long skirt across her lap; she quietly rocked with folded hands and crossed ankles. The Miller family's reputation for being self-sufficient would exact a grueling toll from Clara's self-esteem as she entered her final plea for money, so Emma waited in silence allowing Clara ample time to gather her dignity.

Clara adjusted the stops above the keyboard of the organ, slipped the sheets of music into the side cabinet and placed the round stool close to the pedals. With nothing more to do, she removed a handkerchief from her pocket and pressed it lightly to each temple as she walked to the leather sofa. Not allowing herself to relax against the back cushion, she rigidly perched on the edge while her sister continued to rock.

Clara studied the handkerchief in her lap as she wadded it into a ball tight like the nerves of her body, then unfolded it and smoothed it with her fingertips as if erasing the misfortunes of her frontier life. She cleared her throat several times before attempting to speak; her temples pulsated, the knotted muscles at the nape of her neck throbbed. Her voice quivered like the high, reedy sounds of her organ when she reluctantly revealed the contents of the letter, her need for additional money from the family, and their refusal to grant it.

Emma gently rocked back and forth, the quiet cadence calming her own unease as Clara revealed the perils of life on the frontier. She listened with grave misgivings while her sister elaborated about the hardships she'd endured alone at her soddy, the infestation of mice and vermin, the occasional rattlesnake seeking respite from the broiling Montana sun, the rationing of well water, the drought, and the continual threat of grasshoppers chewing their way across the land. She nodded in agreement when Clara shared the burdensome worry about her increasing reliance on Wilbert. Emma fully understood Clara's dilemma, the great distance from town without neighbors and transportation, but she was skeptical about the business venture with The Land Man.

"You went there to homestead on free land, Clara. Why do you suddenly need money to buy a piece of property?" she asked. "Surely there is another homestead site near Rudyard that you could file on. I just don't like the sound of this deal."

The steady rocking of the chair ticked away the minutes as a silent Emma contemplated her sister's need for money. Clara rose from the sofa and walked to the parlor window where she brushed aside lace curtains and gazed out over the dry stubble field of oats and the mottled browns of disheveled cornstalks waiting to be cut, but visions of Montana danced in the recesses of her mind obliterating the late October vista across the river valley. In exasperation, she turned back. "You've always been a suspicious person, Emma. How many times have I heard you say that everybody is a crook until they're proven innocent, but The Land Man is different. He owns the property next to this piece of land. He really wants me for a neighbor, and he'll do anything to help me."

She returned to the edge of the sofa. Leaning closer to Emma, she confided, "He even talks about getting married!"

Emma stopped rocking and searched the face of her sister, the face of a strong woman, proud of her heritage and honest of heart. She saw the gnarled hands of a woman accustomed to hard work and sacrifice, but she also saw a slender, middle-aged woman whose wispy hair curled around her face, a face weathered after years of exposure to the elements. She could see vulnerability in those clear blue eyes; Emma unwillingly comprehended the situation.

"Will you share his letter with me?" she asked quietly.

Slowly Clara withdrew the envelope from her apron pocket and handed it to her sister. She watched Emma's face as she painstakingly unfolded and perused the contents of the precious letter. She hoped that Emma would see The Land Man's concern for her welfare and loan her the money.

Emma looked up. "How long have you known him?" she asked.

"A few months," Clara replied hurriedly as she removed herself from the sofa and retreated to the window while Emma continued to examine the letter. She busied herself around the room fluffing pillows, straightening curtains, and rearranging family portraits displayed on the organ.

Emma watched her sister pace the floor, a sister innocent and inexperienced in worldly ways in spite of her age. Emma returned to the letter. She read it again. She reread some paragraphs several times. She loved her sister, but Clara's stubborn belief in the honesty of other people had always resulted in disappointment. There was no way to be diplomatic about The Land Man and his letter.

Clara returned to the sofa. The rocking chair sat silent as Emma stared into the distance at a menacing Montana apparition of a greater magnitude than she'd ever imagined. Once more she glanced at the pages before her, then turned to confront her sister with unrefrained honesty. "I can't accept that this letter was written by a man in love. I believe it was written by a con man trying to bilk you out of your savings and as much money as he can squeeze from your family." She remained cool, calm, unemotional. She prided herself on her ability to be rational under duress. "Clara, let's be reasonable. He didn't write the letter in his own hand, he typed it. That doesn't sound like a man in love."

She rose from the rocker. "Look at this, Clara," she said as she pointed to the first page. "He says that he will get the claim for you himself even if it costs $1500 because he can get a little credit, but then he tells you to get whatever amount of money you can and deposit it into his bank account. Further on, he states that he has a deal or so pending just like yours and another one he hopes to pull off on Saturday. What are these deals just like yours? Didn't he ask you to pass out his business cards to women who want to settle in the West?" She waited for a response, but Clara turned away.

"Look," Emma said patiently as she passed the letter into Clara's hands and pointed to the last page. "He didn't even sign his name at the bottom. He typed a dotted line. I cannot lend you any money under these suspicious circumstances." Clara took the letter and glanced at the dotted line where her lover's name should have been. The battle was over, and she'd lost.

Emma returned to Minneapolis on Monday morning after repeating her suspicions about The Land Man, and the family continued to deny Clara's request for a loan. Apprehensive about the future, Clara contacted Wilbert, who came to the rescue when his friend at the Browning Mercantile in Browning, Montana, offered her employment for the winter months. It offered a way out of a difficult situation, and she accepted immediately.

Only Charley accompanied her to the train depot. "Don't worry about me, Charley," she said tentatively. "Everything will turn out swell." She turned away and boarded the Great Northern for points farther west than she'd ever been.

Built in 1907, the Browning Mercantile catered to the needs of local homesteaders, ranchers, and Blackfeet Indians.[7] Shelves laden with preserved foods and grocery items reached to the ceiling and covered the length of the walls on either side as one entered the front door. Showcases of clothing, millinery items, and dry goods displayed additional merchandise on the countertops. A tall, potbelly stove in the middle of the room kept the store comfortably warm as shoppers checked their lists and stockpiled their needs until the next trip into town. Clara enjoyed the responsibility of waiting on customers and meeting other homesteaders, adventurers like herself. She had a pleasant disposition, and displayed indefatigable energy; her height and strength were beneficial in lifting heavy items from the topmost shelves.

Life in the frontier town of Browning offered a variety of activities. In addition to the church socials, it had the Orpheum Theater where she could take in a silent movie for a quarter; sometimes traveling musicians or a local orchestra provided live entertainment in the evenings, but aspirations of owning that special property closer to town demanded a frugal lifestyle as Clara hoarded her nickels and dimes.

In mid-March, one year after she had first ventured west from Long Prairie, she boarded the Great Northern in Browning with seeds and supplies for the next seven months, and departed east toward her homestead while harboring secret dreams of a better life. Wilbert met her at the depot and shared winter gossip while she posted a letter to her family requesting that they ship her organ and music books out on the Great Northern. Music had always been an important part of her life, and the organ would help her pass the long, lonely nights. She related Minnesota news about friends and relatives, revealed her dream to Wilbert of purchasing that half-section of land closer to town as he headed the team across the prairie.

The impoverished soddy looked much as it had when she'd arrived the previous year. Clara busied herself cleaning out the remains of rodent activity and tidied up the place in anticipation of The Land Man's arrival. The warm days of late March with plenty of moisture promised a good growing season and encouraged her to dream of a bountiful harvest

Days passed as she waited in vain for news of her new property. Finally, Wilbert delivered her organ in the back of his wagon and shared the latest gossip: The Land Man was engaged to be married. A wave of desperation swept over her as she learned the awful truth. The bride-to-be was a young woman of twenty-two who had recently purchased the 320 acres adjoining his.

Clara was struck dumb. That was supposed to be her land, but she had no receipts for the money she'd left with The Land Man nor the monthly deposits into his account. She didn't have his signature on the one and only love letter of her life. She had no proof of any relationship between them. This can't be happening, she thought. Why was I so stubborn when Emma tried to warn me?

Devastated by The Land Man's dishonesty, she backed away. A great gust of wind whipped the hem of her dress, lifted her dusty hair, whispered mournfully in her ear to turn away, to escape this evil disclosure. She raised a hand to her brow and struggled to maintain a lady's decorum in spite of her desire to cry out.

Bitter nausea burned at the back of her throat as though the purging of her gut could provide relief from his venomous betrayal. She swallowed convulsively against the bile as she turned, retreated inside the soddy, retched and vomited soured dreams into the slop bucket. Physically spent, emotionally broken, she stumbled across the room and collapsed onto the bed. She felt old and ugly, but worst of all, she was destitute.

Who was The Land Man? Although his letter was typed and unsigned, it had been written on letterhead stationery belonging to a man who had been charged, several months before Clara's arrival, with violating the Mann Act, a law passed by the U.S. Congress on June 25, 1910, prohibiting the interstate transportation of women for immoral purposes. The law was better known as the White Slavery Traffic Act. The Land Man initially proclaimed his innocence when charged with bringing a woman from Kansas City to the Havre area for immoral purposes, but he later admitted guilt. He was sentenced to serve six months in the Lewis and Clark County jail, and to pay a $250 fine.[8]

When the author mentioned his name to a woman in her mid-90's who'd grown up in Rudyard, she smiled and said, "He was a ladies' man, a rounder. When his name was mentioned, people just kind of smiled. There was not a lot of stock in him. If his name was mentioned, you knew something was in the woods. With The Land Man, you knew there was a little trick in there someplace."[9]

Was he also the perpetrator of this scam? Perhaps. No public records could be found of the landowners mentioned in his letter to Clara. However, there are no public records of Clara's two years at Rudyard because of her failure to file on the land, not an uncommon practice during the homestead era as families migrated from site to site seeking the rewards promised by the posters of James J. Hill and his Great Northern Railroad.

In later years, Clara told her children about her relationship with The Land Man, and how she'd firmly believed that he was interested in her welfare. Emma's terse comment to them was, "Your ma lost all her money on that homestead," reinforcing her own belief that all men were crooks until proven innocent.

Once again Wilbert planted her ten acres in flax, a repeat performance of the previous year. The warm weeks of spring eased toward summer. Gentle rains continued to fall, her garden prospered, and vast expanses of feathery silky-headed pasqueflowers, daisies, and goldenrod created a collage of brilliance across the horizon. An occasional antelope lingered at the edge of the field while the raspy, evening call of ring-necked pheasants created music for her dining pleasure, but she heard and saw nothing.

Scathing memories. Foolish, romantic notions of marriage with The Land Man. Shattered dreams splintered like a mirror, each glittering shard reflecting self-incrimination and disgust. She fantasized the beauty of his flawless young bride, an apparition that flailed her self-esteem with brutal abandon.

By rising at sunup and pushing herself to exhaustion, she tried to subdue the shame inflicted by the loss of her money. She attacked the soil with a vengeance hacking the lifeblood from weeds, innocent recipients of her anger, in her attempt to reap something from the land.

But loneliness sapped the life from her spirit as she toiled alone. When darkness fell, she played the organ with wild abandon in the dim light of a kerosene lamp. Throughout the late summer evenings crescendos of frenzied arpeggios flowed from the humble doorway as she pumped melancholy misery across the prairie beneath the stars.

The heat of mid-August descended upon the land as the vicissitudes of homesteading became apparent to those settlers willing to see, but Clara's indomitable desire to subdue the hostile terrain into the proverbial land of milk and honey consumed every waking hour in the struggle to regain some of her lost wealth. Once again, however, her flax began to wither as the infernal wind swept across the dry grasslands from the southwest. Wilbert's visits were less frequent as he, too, tried to impose his will upon the land. She missed his lively retellings of Minnesota gossip, and she longed to hear the gentle strumming of the guitar, but she hadn't ventured a walk across the prairie for fear of encountering The Land Man, the cause of her degradation.

In late August while sitting down to another supper alone, a wave of homesickness wracked her body as she thought of her family back home along the bank of the Long Prairie River. In the sultry dusk of dog days after the evening milk chores, they used to sit out on the front porch together. Emma would fetch a chilled, home-grown watermelon from the depths of the cellar, a watermelon that Lou had protected with shotgun blasts from his upstairs bedroom window toward local hooligans who tried to raid his watermelon patch at night. Lou would slice the dark green melon into long pieces and pass it around. They'd grasp the ends and bite out hunks of sweet, red pulp while juicy trickles escaped from their lips and dripped from their chins. Spitting contests between Charley and her provided nightly entertainment as they stood at the edge of the porch and exploded their missiles into the ensuing darkness.

The solitude of her liberated life weighed heavily on her mind as she picked at her food and wished herself elsewhere. Painful self-incriminations about The Land Man's ease in duping her out of her savings had healed somewhat during the passing weeks, but scars of suspicion now flawed her once resplendent faith in the honesty of her fellow man.

A sudden skitter of movement caught her attention. The ears and beady eyes of a mouse appeared above the edge of the table. He was timid and she was apprehensive, but in her loneliness, she appreciated his presence for dinner.

The little rodent sat in the corner above the leg he'd used as a ladder and watched her with unblinking concentration. She studied him in return, gathered a few crumbs from her plate and slid them toward the uninvited guest in a slow, deliberate move. The withdrawal of her hand offered an invitation to dine as her male caller crept forward and nibbled at the bounty. As quickly as he'd appeared, he disappeared into the night, and she sat alone once more.

However, she'd made a friend, a friendship based on trust. Thereafter, he joined her at each meal and sat in his corner until she presented the daily special. At first he was cautious and demure, but after a few days he scampered up the table leg to be on time. He never came close nor approached her plate, but sat patiently in his corner like a high-born gentleman and waited to be served. They fulfilled a need in each other.

And the hot, dry wind continued to blow. It pummeled the northern plains undeterred by trees or canyons or cities. It drained the earth of moisture and bled the will to live from helpless creatures unfortunate enough to be confined to that desiccated wasteland.

Clara continued to watch the sky for signs of rain. Thunderheads—heavy, cumulus clouds—appeared on the horizon. A particularly dark storm appeared in the southwest as she stood in the doorway and watched the blazing thunderbolts of an angered Zeus split the air and smite the fields. The winds increased and a barrage of thunder separated the heavens then moved off into the distance leaving behind broken promises of salvation from the drought.

Clara stepped outside. Heavy, tumultuous smoke appeared in the distance as she recognized the punishment Zeus had bestowed upon the land. A prairie fire leap-frogged across the plains toward the soddy. The wind increased as she feverishly pumped a bucket of water. Fox families, coyotes, jackrabbits, and mule deer raced ahead of the crackling conflagration as churning winds and billowing plumes of smoke gave way to a low wall of swirling flames rolling across the broad expanse of rain-starved grasslands, rolling over the virgin acres of the homestead toward her field.

Clara knew her only hope of survival lay locked within the soddy. Working with haste, she stuffed the cracks around the door and window with wet rags. She soaked towels and blankets in the bucket of water until smoke invaded the thickness of the walls and choked off her breath. Cries of stampeding wildlife became mute as the insatiable appetite of the inferno swept forward devouring everything in its path. In final desperation, Clara lay on her belly and hugged the earthen floor facing away from the flames. She pulled the soggy blankets over her body, draped her head with towels to screen the smoke from her lungs.

The roar of exploding grasslands and towering flames obliterated all hope of escape as it raced up the sides and over the top of the soddy. Convulsed with fear in her final entombment on the prairie, Clara let painful, smoke-filled gasps emanate from beneath the soggy heap. Minutes of terror seemed like hours as she cowered, pressed her face more tightly against the wall to escape caustic smoke curling through each crevice, every crack behind her. She waited to die, wondered about the pain of burning flesh while treasured memories of home briefly flashed across her dimming consciousness.

Deadly silence surrounded her. The beastly roar of the prairie fire had faded into the distance when she finally raised her upper body and listened to the hushed stillness. Keeping her head covered, she bellied along the floor to stay below the acrid smoke, itself held prisoner inside the soddy. She reached for the door latch, pulled herself up, cautiously cracked open the smoldering door. She brushed aside the wet towels that draped her face and peered toward the blackened furrows of flax, the remaining stumps of the garden, and the smoking, charred nothingness of the prairie. Although tendrils of ash continued to swirl along the ground and reeking clumps of grass exuded smoky residue, the flames had dispersed. Still clutching the wet towels, she staggered outside and drew great gulps of tainted air into her lungs, raised her arms to that ravaged hell and whooped in triumph, "I'm alive! By golly, I'm really alive!"

She tried to work the pump handle, its red paint now blistered and blackened, but the heat from the steel burned her hands. The charred door and soot-streaked windows drove home the near-calamity of the last few minutes; shudders engulfed her body. Persistent wisps of smoke eddied along the ground, but the tinder-dry fuel had been exhausted. Off in the distance toward the northeast horizon, she could see the final death throes of the prairie fire as an isolated cloudburst alleviated the misery of the land.

She stumbled along the perimeter of her homestead acres retracing the steps of earlier days when she'd been filled with exuberance for owning this piece of the earth. Kicking up clouds of ash and surveying scattered carcasses of animals and birds unable to stay ahead of the wall of flames, witnessing the unrelenting cruelties of the Montana frontier, she wondered what other plagues this land might bestow upon her.

Hungry and bone weary, Clara returned to the soddy and prepared a cup of tea using the last of her fuel; she sat down to a cold supper. The sound of pattering feet up the table leg brought a smile to her weary face. "Hello, my friend," she said to her guest as she slid his portion across the table. "I see you survived, too." She studied him thoughtfully and added, "We make quite a pair, don't we?"

Wilbert arrived the next morning assaulted by the devastation of the land and the stench of decay. Clara met him at the door. Her haggard face and snarled hair stunned him to silence. Heavy residue of ash caulked the deepened creases of her face; dark circles framed sunken eyes, the aftereffects of a sleepless night, its black depths haunted with recurring nightmares of the all-consuming flames.

Wilbert glanced around and evaluated the burned-out homestead, the ash-covered soddy with its blackened door. "These past two summers have been tough, Clara. Elmer is talking about pulling up stakes and moving to Missoula to try his hand at raising sugar beets." He looked pensive. "Maybe you ought to consider moving back to the family where life isn't so hard on a woman alone."

She stood silently beside him. They studied the decimated prairie together considering her future. Because he'd encouraged her to come to Montana, Wilbert felt somewhat responsible for her two years of hardship. Clara, however, was disappointed rather than defeated. Surviving the fire had strengthened her faith.

"I won't let this country get the best of me, Wilbert," she said. "You know that the ash will fertilize the land. Next spring the fields will grow greener and taller than ever. I've had two difficult years out here. Next summer will be better." She patted him gently on the shoulder. "You know I'm a born farmer. Gee whiz, it's in my blood, Wilbert, and this is my home. I'm a-gonna go to Browning for the winter, but I'll be back."

Clara returned to Browning a little older, perhaps wiser. Going home to Minnesota to live with her brothers was not a viable option. In the first place, she didn't know whether she would be welcome, and secondly, there was no way she could make money. And she wanted to make it on her own.

On October 3, she turned thirty-two; all she had to show for her life was a burned-out homestead and no prospects of a husband. She had no money for machinery, no money for supplies, and no money for seeds. Thus, she faced another winter of frugal living with the scraping together of nickels and dimes, but she didn't mind because she had tasted a bit of independence, and it was sweet.

In Pike, Montana, a little community west of Glacier Park, a homesteader frequently hopped aboard the Great Northern bound for the bustling east-side town of Browning, a diversion from the isolation of his log cabin during the winter months of short daylight hours and inclement weather. Tall and personable, an attractive man in his early forties with a pleasant sense of humor, Glenn Smiley bought supplies at the Browning Mercantile. No one knew much about him except that he'd been in the area since 1910.

Clara filled his weekly grocery order in her no-nonsense way. She was wary of the attention he paid her, the jokes he told, the stories he shared, but the more he talked about himself, the more she appreciated their similar backgrounds. Both sets of parents had been settlers in a new land; his mother had been named after the territory in which she'd been born, Iowa. His angular body, his clear blue eyes, and hearty laugh set her at ease. He listened with compassion when she shared the trauma of her isolated life in the soddy and her hardships with drought and fire. He was considerate and undemanding. He set no expectations, and from time to time she joined him after work for a silent movie or local concert whenever he stayed in town.

Even though the hardships of life on the frontier outnumbered the rewards, thousands of people pursued free land in Montana. Each of them had a reason for leaving the past behind,

Glenn Cecil Smiley

and Glenn Cecil Smiley was no exception. Born and raised in Center Point, Iowa, he married the love of his life, but after the birth of their fourth child, she died of complications. Her death left him devastated. He longed to escape the environment where everything he touched reminded him of his loss, so his mother-in-law agreed to raise the children, and Glenn departed for the Montana wilderness where he hoped to make a new start, perhaps someday bring his children to the West to live with him.

Accompanied by his long-time friend Jack Hyde, he arrived in 1910 in Midvale, a freight car depot servicing a valley community on the southern edge of the newly formed Glacier National Park, a pristine wonderland of chiseled peaks and ridges. Canyons and glacial cirques lay whittled and gouged, contorted by vast rivers of ice during the Pleistocene epoch, smoothed by the last ice age eleven thousand years ago. The climate warmed, the mighty glaciers receded leaving behind hundreds of alpine

The G.C. Smiley homestead at Lake Lubec.

lakes tucked away in hidden valleys like carelessly scattered jewels, jade and blue sapphires faceted by reflected sunbeams from riffling waters.

First came the game trails meandering through the wilderness, migration paths that followed the seasons, then the Indians in search of provisions, then mountain men, explorers and fur trappers. Now settlers had recently moved into the Lewis and Clark National Forest farther west, and the precipitous country lured the two men into the wilds. They hired horses and rode the narrow trail toward Marias Pass until they approached the ranger station at Lubec, a scattered, forested community in the heart of a mountain valley where Lake Lubec lay nestled at the base of Squaw Mountain.[10] At 5000 feet above sea level, the lake reflected the grandeur of the valley, the towering spires of the pines, the distant forests in the pristine mountain air. The spectacular wilderness welcomed him, offered a paradise in which to work out his sorrow, and thus, Glenn settled on the shore of the lake where he could watch the sun rise over the towering pines and see reflections of craggy cliffs at sundown.

Relatively flat land surrounded the lake shore. Tall pine and tamarack grew in profusion, and the Great Northern Railroad passed on the north side of Lake Lubec. Neither of the men were experienced carpenters, but they cut the timber and fashioned a log house near the lake. Glenn insisted that his oversized door open onto the flanks of Squaw Mountain to take advantage of the view.

Most people believed that homesteading meant farming, but the elevation was too high and the land was too poor to support crops, so he raised a few cattle and started a logging company. During the summers he abandoned Lake Lubec and went into the wilderness to cut posts, poles, and firewood. He neglected his cattle, and his log home was not a home at all, but a mere shelter from the wrath of nature. Glenn soon realized that he couldn't raise his children on the frontier alone nor would they be able to adjust to the isolation of Lake Lubec after their city life in Iowa. When his father died, he inherited an Iowa farm that he deeded to his mother-in-law, who continued to raise the children.

After four years of living in the wilderness and several visits from his mother, Iowa, and sister, Edna, his mourning eased. At the age of forty-three, he wanted the companionship of a woman again.

Winter passed quickly for Clara as she pursued the simple social activities of Browning, but she realized that her meager winter savings could not cover the cost of provisions to see her through another summer at the homestead. Her inability to manage money was a fact of life. Embarrassed at her predicament and fervently seeking advice, she confessed to her new friend. "Golly, I don't know what to do, Mr. Smiley. I haven't saved enough money to buy supplies for my homestead, and I can't move back to my family. Do you think they'd hire me to work at the Browning Mercantile permanently?"

Glenn respected her independence. He covered her hand with his own and remained silent as he gazed away and considered the future. He had plenty of money; he could offer to cover the cost of her supplies for the upcoming growing season until she harvested her crop, but he suspected that another year of prairie hardships might break her spirit.

Clara searched his face for clues. She fidgeted with her tea cup, studied the cornflower design on the side, traced the gold rim with her finger, waited.

He considered daily life in Browning, with its booming businesses, its ranches, and irrigation workers trying to subdue the wild prairie land, and the Blackfeet Indian community that reluctantly tolerated homesteaders who settled on the fringes of their allocated land. "There's no future for you in this town," he finally answered. "You'd soon detest the confines of reservation society such as it is. You need open spaces and freedom, Clara."

He allowed time for her to ponder his concerns, then continued. "Why don't you marry me and move out to my homestead? I have a log house near a lake." He recalled her descriptions of the soddy and added with a grin, "It even has a floor!"

She was dumbfounded. He'd never shown any romantic interest in her; he'd been her friend. "Gee whiz, why would you want to do that?" she asked in amazement.

He laughed at the surprised look on her face. "You're a hard worker and fun to be with. I need someone to watch over my cattle and care for my house when I'm logging in the summer, and you need a place to live. We could help each other."

Memories of The Land Man refused to stay buried. She occasionally re-read his cherished letter, dreamed about his flashing dark eyes and devilish grin in spite of his nefarious behavior, but this man before her was a true friend, one concerned about her welfare. Unwilling to hurt him, she confessed, "But I don't love you, Mr. Smiley."

He appreciated her honesty, tried to put her at ease. "My first wife loved me enough for many lifetimes," he answered, "and when I die, I want to be buried beside her, but for now, Clara, we could have a good life together. You wouldn't be burdened with me all the time because I'm away logging most of the summer. I know that you'd miss your homestead, but you'd have my place. You could sew and write stories. Several neighbors live close by. What do think?"

She considered him a good man, a sincere, caring man, and they shared a mutual respect for each other. He was offering her a secure future. There was just one impediment of his homestead that she had to confront. "Mr. Smiley, could I have a garden? Could I raise a big garden with tomatoes and potatoes and rhubarb and cabbage?" She worried about being a burden to him. "I could grow all of our vegetables for winter and save you lots of money. Is there a place for a garden?" Visions of an expansive garden near the lake encouraged her to consider his offer. If I can have a garden, life will be just swell, she thought.

He hesitated a moment before answering, "Yah, you can have a garden. Take as much land as you need."

Marriage offered her a chance to start over. During her formative years Clara had worked beside her mother in the fields with her brothers, and more than anyone, she knew the importance of having a man and woman work together to survive on the frontier.

"Can I bring my organ, Mr. Smiley? I have a nice organ. We could sing together and invite the neighbors over. Should

I ask Wilbert to fetch my organ and send it on the train? You know how much you love music."

"Clara, there's no way to get your organ to my homestead."

"Why not? Wilbert hauled it in the back of his wagon eight miles out to my soddy. Why can't we get it to your place?" she persisted.

"Clara, it just won't work. It can't be done. Your organ will have to stay behind," he answered.

Not easily discouraged, she smiled to herself. Once I see his place, she thought, I'll figure out a way to get my organ delivered.

She wrote to Wilbert about her upcoming marriage and explained the intended abandonment of her homestead. He collected her personal articles from the soddy then met her at the Rudyard depot, where he studied his impetuous cousin from beneath the battered brim of his dusty field hat. His brow furrowed in consternation. He understood Clara's free-spirited way; he tried to warn her. He removed a match stick from his mouth, held it between his thumb and forefinger and stabbed the air with it as he spoke trying to explain a simple fact of life. "Once you're married, you won't be able to do whatever you want. You'll have to answer to your husband."

Clara straightened up from sorting her possessions and laughed. "Oh, Wilbert, he'll be gone logging most of the summer, so I'll have all the freedom I want. I'm going to plant a huge garden and raise a few chickens. Maybe I'll get a couple of cows. It's only a few hours from here by train. You can come and visit us from time to time. Mr. Smiley says it's real pretty up there!"

Wilbert wasn't so sure about the freedom aspect of marriage, but he accepted that it might provide a better life for her than living alone in the soddy. Clara believed that the troubled memories of her Rudyard misfortunes would be left behind once she boarded the Great Northern to meet her soon-to-be husband. He was a dear friend; she knew she could grow to love him.

Glenn met her at the Shelby depot and offered assistance with her collection of household goods and gardening equipment. In a comic gesture, he flashed the marriage license and assured her that all was set, then escorted her to the Sullivan Hotel where he'd booked separate rooms. Clara felt safe, almost loved, as she passed the evening alone washing and styling her hair in preparation for her wedding.

She joined him in the hotel dining room for breakfast. Slim-waisted and tall, wearing a long, beige dress with an eyelet lace collar and a simple string of pearls, the bride looked lovely. He rose and helped her with her chair.

She had never seen him in a suit before. He's a fine looking man, she thought as she admired his new haircut and close shave.

He returned to his seat. He reached for her hand across the table, held it lightly and smiled into her eyes. I wonder if she can cook, he mused silently.

She reassured him with gentle pressure from her fingers and returned his smile. How many seeds should I buy, she pondered.

Hand in hand they walked to the Toole County Courthouse in Shelby, where the Rev. Homer F. Cox waited to receive the middle-aged couple. There were no attendants; no friends joined the bridal party. Local employees at the courthouse witnessed the ceremony that was nearly over before it began. And so it came to be that on the fourth day of April in 1915, Glenn C. Smiley and Clara A. Miller were united in Holy Matrimony. He gave her a gold band, she gave him a smile.

*Glenn and his logging crew prepare to go into the mountains for several
months cutting posts and poles. Clara is left behind
to survive as well as she can.*

*A small building near Jack Hyde's homestead offered shelter to the train crew.
There was an extra set of tracks in the flat area where homesteaders could flag
down the train, but it was not a scheduled stop.*

PART II

Entering Grizzly Country

"Entering Grizzly Country" now warns a poster from the U.S. Department of the Interior to trekkers who hike the back country of Glacier National Park, but there were no warning signs when Clara Miller Smiley, a new bride, arrived on April 4, 1915. And so, Clara, a woman who trusted everyone and whose generosity became legend, began her married life on a homestead at the southern fringe of Glacier National Park.

With formalities out of the way, the newlyweds were eager to board the train to Lubec and begin a new life, but they had different interests, separate agendas. Glenn wanted to get back to his cattle, but Clara insisted on buying seeds for her garden. He watched in silence as his bride bought peas, beans, tomatoes, cabbage, corn, potatoes, and rhubarb. Her face glowed with excitement; she could smell the richness of the soil and feel the life within each tenderly selected packet of seeds.

The groom purchased flour, sugar, yeast, and lard; he looked forward to good home-cooked meals after the slim pickings of the last four years. Finally, at the station platform, he secured the trunk with two leather straps, transferred their supplies and all of Clara's possessions from Rudyard into brown burlap bags and tied them securely. "Why are you doing that?" she asked as they waited for the Great Northern to arrive.

He continued to fill the bags. "Oh, it just makes it a lot easier when we get off the train," he answered.

Her smiling eyes snapped with excitement as she helped load the heavy bags into the passenger car. Her new life was beginning with the security of a good husband, a snug log house, and an expansive garden on the shores of Lake Lubec.

The Great Northern labored its way to higher elevations as it followed the contours of the foothills toward Glacier Park where a few tourists departed to experience spring in the mountains, and local folk returned home from their shopping trip to Browning. In 1915, no highway yet traversed the wilds of the northern Rockies. Motorists who had driven their autos as far west as Glacier Park now secured them onto flatbed cars of the Great Northern and joined the passengers inside. They continued their journey farther west to Kalispell where they would disembark and drive their cars to more distant destinations such as Spokane or Seattle.

Clara had admired the towering peaks of Glacier Park from a distance of several miles, but never in her wildest dreams had she perceived them to be so spectacular. Off in the distance, rugged crags and endless forests welcomed her with open arms; melting glaciers created a waterfalls symphony over sheer rock walls as moss and spring flowers pushed up toward the spring sunshine. The dramatic diversity of the wilderness unfolded before her as the train snaked its way toward Lake Lubec.

Glenn stood up. "Okay, now, Clara. We'll soon be there. We have to move everything out the back door and be ready to jump."

She looked into his eyes with alarm. "Jump? Jump off the train? Why didn't you tell me? I've never jumped off a train before in my life! I'm a-gonna end up with a broken leg on my wedding night!"

Fellow passengers observed the couple with interest as Glenn tenderly stroked her cheek with the back of his hand and smiled with reassurance. "It's not so bad, Clara. The train doesn't stop for us local folks, but it slows way down, you know, so it's real easy to get off. Just kind of look for an easy place to land, bend your knees a bit, and hop right off. There's nothing to it!"

I doubt that, she thought to herself as the train lurched ever upward following the twisting grade toward the top of the pass.

They slid their goods to the back of the car where Glenn opened the door and moved them out onto the platform over the coupling. Clara stood behind him, braced herself, watched the dizzying kaleidoscope of trees flash past, clutched at a narrow railing as the jerk and pitch of the train threatened to topple her off the back. Her stomach churned, and the hypnotic rhythm of steel wheels pounded in her temples; she squeezed her eyes shut and swallowed the fear burning the back of her throat.

Glenn balanced the trunk on the bottom step, saw the landing site up ahead. He shouted at her over his shoulder, "Now we're gonna be there pretty quick, so you be prepared to jump."

She grasped the railing with both hands, practiced bending her knees, rehearsed the ultimate jump as she looked over his shoulder and saw the nearness of a mountain lake before them. A distance of four feet separated the bottom step from the steep incline of the railroad bed. Her eyes widened with apprehension as Glenn grasped the handle of the trunk and eased it off the step toward the ground; he reached back for the burlap bags and tossed them off the train. She could hear the rattle and clatter of precious pots and pans as they tumbled and bounced down the slope. Without further ado, her new husband leaped from the train and disappeared from sight as the train continued up the grade. Clara heard him shouting at her in the distance, "Come on, Clara, jump! Jump!" But she couldn't see him! Where was he?

Just a few hours before, she'd promised to love, honor, and obey. Easing her way to the bottom step, instinctively bending her knees to absorb the shock of hitting the ground and holding her long skirt above her ankles, she obeyed. No longer thinking of the consequences, no longer worrying about what might happen, she followed his lead and jumped from the train. Clumps of dead grass, matted and tangled by the weight of winter snow, lay spread before her, softened the shock of a brutal landing, and welcomed the new bride to her mountain home.

She balanced briefly on her feet then plopped backward. Vibrations of the train thundered beneath her body, she could hear the creaking of boxcars, steel wheels chattering over cracks between the rails, the screeching of steel against steel as the massive engine towed its burden around the corner and out of sight. Her smiling eyes were not smiling. She felt battered and bruised. She shouted at her husband as she brushed the dirt off the back of her coat and the hem of her wedding dress, "Mr. Smiley, you said the train would slow way down. Well, it slowed a little bit, but not way down!" He waved and grinned at her as he began to gather the bags; he knew she could do it.

She looked around. The brute strength of the mountains terrified her. At Rudyard it was flat—she could walk for hours and never see a change in scenery—but Mr. Smiley's homestead was in the heart of the Rockies. She tipped her head back, pondered the height of Squaw Mountain. "Oh, my," she said to herself.

Although it was mid-afternoon, the April sunshine at 5000 feet didn't produce warmth. Pillows of snow lay frozen beneath the trees. Her bones felt the sharp bite of the frolicking wind as it coursed through the tamaracks and rattled the branches. She looked around again. The darkening mountains appeared foreboding and ominous. She instinctively felt wild animal eyes staring at her from the deep forest; she was apprehensive about life at Lake Lubec.

She studied the ground with its projecting slabs of shale and scattered tufts of bunch grass. She surmised that the soil wasn't conducive to growing anything, but her new husband stood there grinning with pleasure at the way she'd jumped off the train without breaking her neck, so with a heavy sigh she joined him at the trail, picked up two bags, and strolled by his side toward the cabin.

She'd caught a quick glimpse of it across the lake as the train rounded the final corner along the side of the mountain. It didn't look to be too far away, but because of the quicksand along some of the shoreline, the path detoured inland through the forest. Glenn pointed out a little shelter bordering the woods where they might take cover during inclement weather, but April 4 was a pleasant day, and they continued on toward home. The surprise of having to jump off the train made Clara a bit anxious about the quality of the log house that awaited her arrival.

The softness of forest duff beneath their shoes, the overhead canopy, a dizzying movement of shadowed greens, reluctantly relinquished the newlyweds from its silence to an alpine meadow where greening spears forced their way from beneath humped tussocks. They followed a muddy path to a bridge, three logs lying lengthwise, their cracks filled with gravel, over a swollen stream gurgling with the melt-off waters of snow fields hidden in the clefts of Squaw Mountain. Across the lake leafless shrubs cluttered the hillside; blackened trees, their limbs gnarled and twisted, the skeletons of fire, mutilated the horizon.

"When did that happen?" Clara asked as she stopped for a brief rest and pointed toward the charred timber.

"In the summer of 1910, hundreds of lightning fires decimated this country. The cabin was about half built, and Jack and I'd been watching the smoke sweep our direction for days, but when the fire came over the rise, we hardly had time to lash logs together and ride it out in the middle of the lake. Luckily the wind switched."[1]

Clara tried to imagine a sweeping wall of flame coming through the trees, the two men floating on the raft, the heavy smoke. She was glad that the cabin now sat in the middle of a wide clearing. The thought of fire made her shudder as she recalled her own near tragedy, but she picked up her bags and followed Glenn across the meadow.

A low bunkhouse hugged the edge of the lake where gentle waves lapped at the shore. A pole corral contained a few horses that whinnied at their approach. She quickly dismissed them and looked around for the neighbors that Mr. Smiley had promised, but nary a plume of wood smoke could be seen.

His log cabin, a low shelter twenty feet long and sixteen feet wide, awaited their arrival. Chinks of white plaster contrasted against the dark logs. The ridge pole was off-center. One side of the roof was wider than the other side; the whole thing looked lopsided, but it was the door that riveted her attention. Immense. Cut into the log wall at an angle as though the walls had leaned away before the door could be put into place. She'd never seen such a door; it nearly reached the roof under the gable.

Glenn propped the bags against the side of the cabin and swung the door open. Its sturdy casement gaped before them, but she stepped to the side and examined the heavy vertical planks of the door itself, its crossbars, heavy bolts, massive hinges. She lightly fingered it inside and out, examined the lock. The strength of the door reassured her. That ought to keep wild animals out, she thought. She stepped over the threshold. The inside walls were peeled logs chinked with plaster, but wide cracks between the floorboards puzzled her. She knelt down and studied the nearness of the rocky soil below, gazed up at her husband. Glenn shrugged helplessly, "Jack and I built this house ourselves. We didn't know the boards would shrink."

"Well, I won't need a dustpan," she commented as she straightened up and continued her inspection.

"This is the first house I ever built," he admitted. "The door and big window are on this end of the house so I can enjoy the view, but it's the wrong end of the house because of the high winds and storms." He paused and looked toward Squaw Mountain, then added as an afterthought, "You'll have to be real careful of that door when we get those 100 mile-an-hour winds whistling through here. It could be lethal if it gets to swinging!" Disillusioned with the penurious quality of the soil and the homestead's remoteness from civilization, Clara didn't respond to his latest warning. It simply presented another challenge to take in stride.[2]

To the right of the entrance a square table and chairs caught the light from the window; off in the distance she could see the railroad tracks winding toward the summit. Her eyes swept along shelves to the far end of the room where two double beds nestled opposite walls. A kerosene lantern hung from a hook in the middle of the room; stacks of newspapers tumbled from the bottom shelf of a narrow table between two rocking chairs. A cook stove, the only source of heat, lay adjacent to the east wall, its stovepipe exiting through a hole in the logs. It had a warming bin at the top and a porcelain hot water reservoir at the far end. She walked over and checked the oven, slid the shelves in and out. That part looked pretty good. She continued her inspection. A small table at the far end of the stove held a white, enameled wash basin; a bucket of drinking water claimed the rest of the space. An oak mirror tilted at an angle above a shelf where Glenn stashed his shaving mug, razor, and toiletries. A towel draped from a nail. The toe of her shoe brushed against an empty slop bucket; a mousetrap snapped. Empty shelves gaped above the beds; leather harnesses hung from spikes along one wall, a pair of snowshoes decorated the other, a saddle sprawled in the middle of the spare double bed.

Wary of his new wife's fastidious inspection, Glenn silently followed her around the room straightening chairs, watching her face for a reaction. When the neatness of the cabin's interior seduced a cautious smile from her lips, he bolstered her uneasy thoughts with lame enthusiasm, "Oh, this will be just fine, Clara. Don't be discouraged. With a little of your feminine touch, you could get this place looking pretty nice!"

The sun dropped behind the horizon, its dying rays gilding the snowcapped ridge of Squaw Mountain; violet shadows dappled the rippling water of the lake while Glenn split kindling and started a fire in the cook stove so Clara could prepare a tasty meal. He retrieved her trunk, she distributed the treasures of the burlap bags onto the empty shelves and prepared supper in her wedding dress.

Darkness had enveloped the alpine valley when they ventured outside. Crossing the meadow to the edge of the lake, they stood hand in hand beneath the glittering pavilion of stars and studied the heavens searching for Orion, the North Star, the Big Dipper. Across the breathless stillness, the haunting question of a great horned owl drifted from the forest and lingered on the air, meadow mice scuttled beneath the grass, the mournful howl of a wolf echoed from the hills. They stood for several minutes in silence, then turned and walked back to the lonely cabin. As the massive door swung shut, the tremolo laughter of a loon, the ultimate sound of the wilderness, chortled across the water as if he alone knew the perils that lay ahead on the shores of Lake Lubec.

Homesteader's Wife

She longed to write a masterpiece
To win the world's acclaim,
Her mind was full of plots and plans and literary style;
But her good man worked from dawn to dark
And it would be a shame
To neglect to keep his house and home
The while.

She'd have liked to paint a picture
That would win the critics' praise,
To spend her heart in color that would riot like her
dreams,
To express her tortured longing
For beauty in her days,
But she spent such endless hours
Sewing seams.

She longed to sing great arias,
Her voice was good they said;
She could feel the power to quicken hearts with notes that
thrilled the skies,
She had little time for singing
She'd a family to be fed,
And she spent such endless hours
Making pies.

Clara Augusta Miller Smiley

PART III

Homesteader's Bride

"She longed to write a masterpiece, To win the world's acclaim/But her good man worked from dawn to dark, and it would be a shame/To neglect to keep his house and home, the while."—Beth M. Volbrecht, in "The Homesteader's Wife"

While his cattle roamed the valley searching for spring grasses, Glenn prepared for the arrival of loggers and informed Clara of his impending departure for the summer. She faced the next few weeks with apprehension; she needed something to occupy her time. She wanted a flock of chickens, perhaps some ducks and geese, and she wanted a Jersey cow. She could keep the cow in the corral while he was gone.

"Oh, Mr. Smiley, please get me a Jersey cow," she pleaded. "A Jersey will give me cream for baking, and the milk makes wonderful cheese. It won't take much to feed her. I'll do all the chores, and it'll give me something to do."

Desperation loomed in her eyes as lonely months of isolation in the mountain wilderness approached, but he had to deny her request. "We don't have a barn, Clara. You can't have a cow without a barn in this country with the cougars and grizzlies. They won't bother the horses, but a small cow alone in a corral wouldn't last two weeks," he explained. Disillusioned with this isolated homestead, the near hopelessness of having a garden, and now her inability to own a cow reduced her to tears.

There must be something I can do for her, Glenn thought as he glanced around the clearing searching for ideas. He finally said, "I can build you a little chicken house with left-over lumber from the cabin. That won't take me long, and then you'll have eggs for baking and chores to do." He wanted to make her happy. "I'll get started right now. You go inside, and I'll call you when it's done."

Clara brushed away the tears. With determination, Glenn spent the afternoon with poles, boards, and nails as he hammered together a rustic chicken house, a shelter of his own design.

She could hear him whistling to himself as he sawed and hammered behind the cabin; her spirits lifted as she envisioned a snug little coop with a flock of contented hens scratching nearby, perhaps fluffing themselves in a dust bath. She prepared a shopping list of chick mash, ground oats, middling and bran, a narrow chicken feeder so the hens couldn't scratch out the grain, and a watering trough. Perhaps she should have one of those inverted glass fruit jar dispensers for the baby chicks as well. Answering an enthusiastic call from her husband several hours later, Clara hurried out back for the unveiling. He stood a few feet off to the side of his masterpiece and awaited her inspection.

A precarious arrangement of spindly logs and boards stood before her. The steep roof slanted to one side; the small hinged door gaped open at an angle. She stood back and surveyed the shabby shelter created by a man who knew little about carpentry and nothing about chickens. The random collection of building materials and haphazard construction amused her. It doesn't look like much of a chicken house to me, she chuckled inwardly, but it'll do the trick. "Mr. Smiley," she said turning toward him with a grin, "you really are trying to make me happy."

Seeing her smile of appreciation at the helter-skelter array before them, Glenn breathed a sigh of relief as he walked to her side, stepped back and admired his own handiwork. "It really does look pretty good!" he admitted. The next day he caught the train into Browning and returned with the requested items from the list and twenty yellow chicks for his bride.

In late April, logging hopefuls, mostly returns from the year before, began to arrive on horseback and moved into the bunkhouse. They brought bedrolls, canteens, a variety of revolvers and shotguns to shoot small game, the mainstay of their diet, and rifles to protect themselves from wolves, black bears, and grizzlies that might be attracted to the tantalizing aroma of sizzling bacon.

The plan was to leave at daybreak. Glenn owned a wagon and team of horses to haul their supplies to camp, horses they could later harness for skidding logs. Clara observed the commotion with interest; she knew nothing about logging. She watched the men load the flat, heavy wagon with chains, hooks, pulleys, buck saws, cross-cut saws, saws with handles on both ends, single-bit and double-bit axes, adzes, sawhorses, steel cables, peaveys, cant hooks, come-alongs, and winches. The leathery camp cook inventoried bags of flour, sugar, dried beans, sides of bacon, and coffee, staples for a crew of hungry men who would work fifteen hours a day. He checked the pots and pans, the three-legged Dutch oven used for baking biscuits over the coals, the lidded cast iron kettle for the bean hole, the coffee pot, and the cook tent.

On the day of departure, Clara heard the men in the bunkhouse stirring before first light as they roused each other, hawked globs of phlegm, slammed the toilet door. She rose quickly, pulled on warm clothes and lit the lantern. She combed her hair, washed in tepid water dipped from the reservoir at the end of the stove, then built a fire and began to prepare her husband's breakfast. She worked in silence as she set the table, sliced bread, peeled potatoes, cut thick slices from a slab of bacon.

While her husband had fitfully slept in anticipation of another summer in the woods, Clara had restlessly tossed in tangled sheets as her imagination churned up tragedies that might occur in his absence. Now she sat at the table, stoic and resolved, but tasted nothing. Glenn buttered thick slabs of bread, repeatedly filled his fork from the plateful of sliced potatoes fried brown and crisp, glistening with grease, used his knife to cut the bacon. He choked down his coffee, refused to meet her eyes as he ate in silence.

She couldn't swallow. Her tea cooled; an oily brown film floated on the surface then congealed on the inside of the cup. Her skin lay taut and stretched across her cheekbones; lips set in stubborn determination tried to restrain her fears, the pallor of her face matched the chinking in the walls. The silence continued. Only the sound of Glenn's knife and fork, his chewing and swallowing, and the men saddling their horses, calling to each other, broke the hush. She refused to share her fears; they had a pact. She would take care of his cabin, raise her chickens, and try to keep an eye on the cattle in return for a secure place to live.

He cleared his throat, pushed back from the table, stood and reached for his low-crowned hat with its braided band, secured it on his head. He grabbed a heavy, wool jacket and headed outdoors to the crew.

Clara cleared the table, then wrapped a shawl around her shoulders and stepped into the brisk dawn. The meadow lay beneath a blanket of feathery hoarfrost; ice-covered spears of awakening beargrass caught glints from the brightening eastern sky. Her warm breath hovered in mid-air as she stood near the cabin door, the stolid wife, the homemaker left alone to protect the family's worldly goods, a bride whose misery lurked behind a tentative smile.

Glenn joshed with his men and welcomed late arrivals coming out from town; he never turned a man away who wanted work. The men checked the cinches on their saddles, their horses impatiently stamping, snorting great plumes of steam as they tossed their heads and champed at their bits. Great furrowed globs fell from beneath raised tails; the pungent stench of horse manure cloyed the calm mountain air.

Clara pulled the shawl tighter around her body, held one corner to her nose. The cook climbed onto the wagon seat, whistled at the team of horses, and guided the heavy load toward the trail. With bedrolls tucked behind their saddles amidst the jangling camaraderie of spurs and scabbards, the hired men mounted their horses and fell in behind the supply wagon. Riding tall in his saddle, Glenn turned his horse to face the cabin, raised his hand in a quick salute and called out, "Take care, Clara! We'll be back in a few weeks."

She smiled bravely, "Goodbye, Mr. Smiley," but he'd already turned and cantered away to catch his crew as he rode toward the timbered mountainsides without a backward glance, leaving her alone at Lake Lubec with no neighbors, no friends, no relatives, no means of escape.

Throughout the month of May, unpredictable weather brought plunging temperatures and spring snowstorms interspersed with warming chinook winds. Clara created a brooder house behind the stove in the cabin where she nurtured her twenty chicks. She spaded a plot of land near the lake for a garden in spite of black flies and blood-thirsty mosquitoes that moved in for the kill whenever the wind died down. She used horse manure to fertilize the poor soil in her determination to coax vegetables from the reluctant land.

The temperature warmed, but the wind continued to blow. The cabin shuddered as gusts whipped down the draw. Sheets of ripples coursed across the lake, limbs of subalpine firs tossed in frustration, and through all of this, Clara worked her garden until the soil was ready for planting. She moved her chicks, now lightly feathered, from the cabin to the chicken house and admired all that she'd accomplished.

Claud and Sadie Dowen lived two miles farther west into the wilderness near the summit of Marias Pass on a plateau where they raised a few head of cattle. Claud, a carefree, robust man, appeared from time to time on his rounds to help the neighbors, while Sadie's jolly, weathered face searched for adventure. She cut a sharp figure in her tightly-cut riding pants as she galloped astride her horse. She befriended Clara and invited her up to her homestead to spend a night during Glenn's absence, but Clara's fear of riding a horse was greater than her need for friendship. In addition, Glenn had described in great detail the treacherous road up the side of the cliff to get to the Dowen cabin, so she politely declined the invitation.

She waited. Lived alone. A timelessness pervaded the valley, a place where clocks had no meaning, where time was measured by seasons, years, eons, by the upheaval of the land, the melting of glaciers. Minutes and hours meant nothing. Serviceberry shrubs exploded with white blossoms along the perimeter of the meadow, a striking contrast against the deepening summer greenness of the forest. A doe and her twins grazed in the meadow, eagles perched in dead snags while ospreys rode the air currents in their search for fish that carelessly cruised below the surface of the water. Lupine and Indian paintbrush created a natural flower garden, but Clara was oblivious to the beauty. She felt no sense of belonging, no sense of ownership.

She concentrated on projects of her own. Tiny containers

of tomato plants adorned the table where she'd buried the seeds in fine soil and nurtured them until they were ready to set out. In June she planted her garden with meticulous rows of vegetables and rhubarb. She hoed the soil until the weeds sulked away to a new location, and finally, she set out the baby tomato plants and staked them against the wind. The lengthening daylight hours of mid-June warmed the soil, and green rows of seedlings thrived. Once again she could feel the strength of the earth beneath her hoe.

The feathered chickens roamed the compound by day as they pecked at gravel and terrorized bugs; she locked them in their custom-built shelter at night. She lathered and rinsed the laundry in the lake, but the powerful wind snapped the clothes pins in half, so she knotted the clothes to the line that stretched between the house and the toilet. She kept busy to forget her loneliness, to avoid melancholy queries about her decision to marry.

On an evening in late June, the temperature dropped several degrees. An ominous chill settled into the valley as Clara secured the lock on the chicken house and went inside the log cabin. She built a fire to discourage the ensuing dampness that crept out of the night, sat at the table and hand-stitched kitchen curtains by the glow of the kerosene lamp. Worried alone.

The morning light revealed her worst fears. Heavy frost blanketed the meadow grass. Yesterday's vibrant tomato plants lay limp and black; the garden graveyard gave testimony to the killing spree of a summer freeze. Only the rhubarb survived. Disheartened by the latest turn of events, she pulled up the remains of her once- prosperous vegetables. I don't understand this country, she reasoned. I must have planted my garden too soon.

She heard the galloping horses, the whooping shouts, before the men came over the rise. Glancing up from the garden, she saw the logging crew break free from the timber and ride to the corral. They dropped their reins, leaped to the ground, and raced toward the lake. For weeks they'd been working in the woods, clothes sticky with pitch and sawdust, acrid with fetid smoke from the campfire, bodies encrusted with sweat, old salt, body filth, and now they wanted to clean up. Clara collected several bars of greasy, yellowish soap heavy with lye, caustic, handed it to the men, then stepped back as they dashed toward the water pulling off boots and socks as they ran.

She'd been expecting them, had been waiting every day for her husband's return, and now he was here to fetch the mail and share tales of adventure. And he looked strong and healthy, tanned, his body firm and muscular from the hard work.

Grown men shrieked like children when they hit the water, plunged beneath its icy surface. Some laid back and took a soak, others lathered up and washed their hair, scrubbed each other's backs, jumped, wrestled, splashed water and cavorted in the icy brilliance, created a flashback to when she and Charley dove into the old swimming hole at the Long Prairie River fully clothed after a hot afternoon of haying.

The loggers rubbed the caustic soap into their clothes, scrubbed at the pitch with gravel, rinsed them in clear water. Bubbles floated across the surface of the lake, shirts lay spread in the sunshine across the meadow grass like a gypsy camp, pants and underwear hung from the clothesline. Some shaved in the bunkhouse, others put on clean clothes and rode to Glacier Park for "the works" that included a haircut as well as an evening of bootleg whiskey and women. The cook drove the wagon into town to buy supplies for the rest of the summer; they would be leaving at daybreak for a new camp.

When Glenn left again for new territory, Clara replanted the garden with the last of her seeds, and the lonely hours merged into interminable, desolate days with little entertainment other than the spinning of fanciful tales that lacked an audience. She picked a few bowls of currants from bushes along the stream;

by late July serviceberry shrubs sagged with the weight of ripe, bluish-purple berries that promised thick, sweet jelly.

Afraid to venture too far into the timber, Clara gathered the berries in a dense thicket at the edge of the meadow. As she parted the branches to grasp another handful of fruit, the massive shoulders of a black bear heaved and rolled as he stood with his broad back toward her, his front paws raking the bushes, scooping leaves and berries into his mouth. She backed away, wondered whether to faint, backed farther away, then turned and ran for the cabin. She slammed the planked door and flipped the lock, braced it with her shoulder, thrust her full weight against it. Her rampant imagination felt the beast pushing back, heard him snuffling, growling, groping at the latch, ready to sample the sweetness of her flesh.

She rested her head against the door; the sound of chittering birds and waves lapping the lake shore forced her to realize the folly of her actions as she ventured a peek through the window where only the peacefulness of the meadow lay outside.

Clara's garden never survived; every month produced a killing freeze. In late July, a sliver of moon peeped from behind wispy clouds that raced across the night sky. The wind increased. It ripped down the draw, a blustering assault, the fearsome wind Glenn had frequently described.

She stepped outside, determined to lock the chicken house door. A powerful gust knocked her to the ground, kept her there. Unable to stand, she inched along on hands and knees, sometimes slid on her belly. Kept her eyes clenched against leaves and pine needles that stung her face, grit that lodged in her hair, riddled her scalp, heard the roar of the wind overhead, the lamentations of the trees as their branches churned, snapped, sailed overhead, tumbled across the meadow. She made her way behind the cabin, sequestered her meager flock, crawled back.

Abandoned on the shores of Lake Lubec during the summer of 1915, Clara experienced the loneliest time of her life. She couldn't see the roof of another cabin; Sadie only occasionally stopped by. Clara felt like the sole inhabitant of earth. She dared not venture too far because of her fear of wild animals. She had no gun, no means of protection.

Homesickness for her Minnesota family played havoc with her mind, a common affliction among isolated homesteaders. Lethargy and physical illness plagued her days. Her stomach burned, and she vomited with loneliness wanting a letter, wanting to hear something from her sister or a brother, wanting news from anyone. In Rudyard, Wilbert and Elmer had contacted her from time to time. They shared their letters from relatives in Minnesota, but at Lake Lubec she was totally alone and forgotten. When Glenn fetched the mail on his infrequent trips home, there might be a letter for her, but her family didn't write all that often. Perhaps they didn't think their news was important enough to mail since postage cost two cents a letter.

With despair as her companion, she watched the night lights of the Great Northern pass on the far side of Lake Lubec. She envied the passengers on their way East; she longed to be on that train headed away from the isolation of the log cabin where she had nothing to occupy her mind. And so August became September as she waited in solitary confinement.

The meadow and lower mountainsides radiated the brilliance of golden aspen intermingled with pines. Explosions of red sumac and serviceberry shrubs peppered the lower hillsides with bursts of color. Withered remnants of fireweed were the sole reminders of the magenta magnificence that once blanketed the upper elevations. On windless days the expansive valley of Lake Lubec lay pregnant with moisture-laden fog that waited in hushed expectation for the birth of a mountain shower.

Temperatures dropped, snow flurries fluttered. As Clara endured another night alone, the scream of a woman shattered her silent world. She bolted upright and stared into the darkness. She concentrated, listened and wondered whether she'd been having a nightmare when the woman's scream again pierced the night, but this time it was followed by hysterical cackles, low growls.

She leaped from her bed and checked the lock on the door; she braced herself against the imposing barrier as she prepared for an invasion, but no more screams followed, nothing tried to enter her haven of safety. Returning to bed, cowering under the blankets, hardly daring to breathe for fear of attracting the invisible menace that lurked in the dark, she passed the night listening for hostile noises and finally fell into a troubled sleep.

At daybreak she arose with trepidation and dressed for an icy morning in the mountains. A light dusting of snow covered the meadow when she stepped outdoors, walked toward the backside of the cabin. The devastation of a slaughter lay before her. Great puddles of blood-soaked snow, feathers, and entrails littered the ground around the remains of the rustic chicken house. A bloody trail and the spoor of a lone cougar led off into the forest.

Stunned by nature's brutal assault, she steadied herself on the stump that she used for a chopping block and surveyed the carnage with defeat. Her shoulders sagged beneath the burden of trying to survive in such a God-forsaken place with some semblance of sanity.

A distant sound from the bunkhouse caught her attention. Could it be? She cautiously approached the log building and peered around the door that stood ajar. In the dim interior she saw three hens and a rooster. Survivors of the debacle, their cackling and crowing penetrated the stillness of the morning in celebration of life. At that moment, Clara realized that she, too, might survive on the shores of Lake Lubec.

After that first light snowfall, Glenn returned home for the winter accompanied by his tall, angular friend Charlie Tobin.

Gangling arms swung from bony shoulders, extended several inches beyond the ends of his shirtsleeves. Striped overalls sagged on his fleshless frame, but his dazzling smile and hearty laugh proffered immediate charm. Although he was a builder by trade, Charlie had worked for Glenn as a logger all summer. Now he agreed to build a barn on the homestead where the crew had stockpiled logs.

They selected a site 125 feet west of the cabin on a slight rise where they excavated the floor and backside of the barn into the hillside. The barn, nearly twenty feet square, built of logs twelve inches in diameter and supported with heavier beams, could withstand the frequent storms that ripped down the valley from Marias Pass.

Charlie Tobin in later years.

Meanwhile, Clara hemmed long, gingham curtains to divide the cabin into two bedrooms and a living area. She enjoyed Charlie's easy-going personality and busied herself with cooking for the men, sewing quilts, and caring for her four chickens. During the winter Charlie built the barn and a large, sturdy chicken house for Clara; Glenn brought supplies from town, checked on his open-range stock, and caught up on his reading. Fascinated by politics and the state of the economy, he subscribed to five daily newspapers: *San Francisco Examiner, Chicago Herald and Tribune, Great Falls Tribune, Denver Post,* and *Seattle Times,* all of which came through the mail to Frank Pike's place, an adjacent homestead a half mile farther west.

In the area since 1904, Frank Pike's home lay nestled in a grove of trees up the pass near the railroad tracks where he could enjoy the view across the waters of Lake Lubec and watch the Great Northern wind its way toward the summit of Marias Pass. Frank, the postmaster for settlers who lived within a three or four mile radius, sold stamps and canceled out-going mail with his special stamp of Pike, Montana. Within the confines of his cabin, settlers gathered and gossiped while waiting for the train to deliver the mail, then watched as Frank waited at the edge of the tracks and exchanged mailbags in mid-air with the conductor.[1]

Clara's first winter at Lake Lubec in 1915-16, was brutal. In a twenty-four hour period on January 23 and 24, the temperature in the area dropped one hundred degrees from 44° F. to -56° F.,[2] but the cold winter months slipped away as the aroma of freshly baked bread and rich desserts kept the men close to home. She reveled in their warm-hearted compliments, participated in their lively conversation. After a few walks with her husband to collect the mail, she overcame her fear of the forest and willingly went alone in anticipation of receiving a letter from home. Sometimes the one-room school up near Frank's place hosted evening programs or dances. Claud and Sadie Dowen stopped by from time to time. Jack Hyde became a frequent visitor and exchanged news from Iowa friends with Glenn, and so the winter passed.

Waking with nausea each morning, Clara suspected that she was pregnant and voiced her concerns to Glenn as he and his crew prepared to leave for another summer. Recognizing her impending loneliness and her need for a proper diet, he surprised her with a Jersey cow securely stanchioned in the new barn.

The logging crew departed for the wilderness with Glenn's promise to return home more often than last summer, and Clara resumed her lonely vigil. Not to be defeated, she again spaded the soil of her garden plot and prepared it for planting. She collected the eggs of the three chickens until a dozen or so filled a nest, then set one hen to incubate the precious commodity. Morning and evening she milked the Jersey cow, churned butter, sold some of the milk to neighbors or gave it away.

In early June, cramps and false labor threatened the pregnancy as she maintained her daily routine alone. After months of anticipating the laughter and companionship of a child, she despaired of losing the baby. Back in Minnesota, distressed by the tone of Clara's letters with her vivid descriptions of a difficult pregnancy and loneliness, Emma decided to visit her sister for two weeks. She wrote a letter giving the date and time of her arrival in late June.

Clara waited impatiently, marked the days off the calendar and anticipated late night conversations about old friends. Her mind overflowed with questions and curiosity about her aging parents and about Lou, Fred, and Charley. She hungered for intimate details of Minnesota and the neighbors along the river. Without as much enthusiasm, however, she anticipated Emma's critical, unsolicited advice about her frontier lifestyle.

For Emma, the days on the train became tedious. In Minnesota every mile revealed something different, but on the plains nothing changed. She had grown up on a farm, she showed some interest in crops, but the North Dakota and Montana flatlands blended from one wheat field to the next for hours, days on end. She studied the bustling street of Rudyard, the site of her sister's disappointment, and she caught a glimpse of Wilbert's homestead as the Great Northern pulled out of town, but she spent most of her time reading and observing fellow passengers.

Emma stood nearly five foot nine. With her light hair gathered into a French twist and secured with ivory combs, she presented an austere figure in her stylish summer frock with its high neckline and fitted waist. The conductor instinctively knew that this was a lady who could not be expected to jump off the train, so he arranged for the engineer to come to a complete stop at Lake Lubec to allow her to disembark with grace. Running behind schedule, they didn't arrive until after sunset. The conductor collected her baggage and helped her down the steps, pointed out the shelter at the edge of the forest in the deepening dusk, and Emma made her way along the dark path to wait for Clara's rescue.

From the open doorway of the log house, Clara saw the undulating headlight of the Great Northern sweep the distant hillside as it broke free from the rise across the lake, saw the train slow as it proceeded up the grade, saw it stop briefly, move on again. She hoped Em was on that train as she'd written; she didn't like being out in the woods at night. She lit the lantern, pulled her shawl around her shoulders, and went to meet her sister.

With nerves on edge, Emma waited in the shelter. The mountains frightened her. Their silhouettes against the night sky obstructed her vision. Brilliant stars shimmered only enough light to stimulate her imagination as rustling leaves became stalking animals and the sounds of night birds chilled her blood. She kept thinking, Well, where is Clara? Is she sick? Did she not get my letter? In her uneasiness, the sound of approaching footsteps became predators in the darkness, but the flickering light from Clara's lantern bobbing toward her through the woods restored her faith in the U.S. Postal Service.

As the sisters made their way back through the sinister darkness, Clara chattered about her Montana life, and Emma watched for glowing animal eyes in the brush, listened for rustlings, for the soft tread of lynx, the low growl of a bear. They reached the cabin near midnight, and as Minnesota custom dictated, they shared a simple lunch of sandwiches and sweets before retiring. They reminisced about better times for a while, then Clara showed Emma a bed on one side of the curtain while she retired to her own side of the filmy partition and promptly fell into a dreamless sleep.

Emma studied the humble cabin with its open shelves, the wide spaces between the floorboards. It brought back memories of rough times in the Minnesota log house where the family had slept upstairs under the eaves, one room divided by curtains, frost-covered blankets on winter mornings, stifling heat in the summer. She couldn't understand why Clara would want to repeat a life filled with hardships.

In her meticulous way, she unpacked and arranged her garments on the shelf above the bed. She undressed, pulled the floor length nightgown over her head, modestly buttoned the front up to her throat, removed the ivory combs and brushed her fine hair, blew out the lamp, climbed beneath the patchwork quilt. She lay awake and alert; her sharpened senses detected the sounds of night creatures. Something furry rubbed against the outside wall, gnawed at the logs, stopped, rasped again. Mice skittered across the floorboards, played tag through the knotholes. The night symphony of the wilderness continued with the yipping of coyotes, the cry of the loon before she finally drifted off.

A woman's scream shattered the darkness. Emma bounded forward and ripped aside the curtain to Clara's bedroom. "Wake up, Clara!" she cried as she shook her sister to consciousness. "What is that? Something is going to come right through the bedroom window!"

Now experienced and unperturbed to cries in the night, Clara soothed her sister's fractured nerves. "Oh, that's just a cougar, a mountain lion. Think nothing of it. It can't get the chickens. They'll be all right. It can't get in here. Just go back to bed, Emma. Just go to sleep," she said as she rolled over, turned her back.

"Oh, my," Emma sighed as she returned to her bed. Fraught with unseen danger, the dark hours slowly eased toward daylight as she experienced her first night at Lake Lubec.

A gentle mountain rain drifted across the cirque concealing the lake in a gossamer mist as dawn stealthily invaded the eastern horizon. Beads of moisture lazily dribbled down the windowpanes unnoticed by the sisters who sat at the kitchen table exchanging bits of gossip until the clouds dissipated and shafts of morning sunshine streamed over the distant rise. They strolled out to inspect the garden that seemed to be holding its own against the elements. Emma admired the log barn while Clara milked the Jersey cow, then followed her through wet, pearl-tipped meadow grass on her way to gather eggs, feed the chickens.

Just before noon an enthusiastic Sadie Dowen came galloping on her horse toward the women. "We've been expecting you," she greeted Emma as she swung down out of the saddle, gave Clara a quick hug. "Claud's been out working for a fellow for a couple of weeks, and I'm all alone. Why don't you two come to my house for supper tonight? I'll fetch you in my buggy."

Clara remembered Glenn's vivid description of the road up to Sadie's place. "Oh, no," she answered feebly. "I haven't been feeling well, Sadie, and I'd better stay here to take care of everything. But you, Emma, you can go. It'll be kind of nice for you to see what's on the other side over there!"

Being a sociable lady of the Whiteville Methodist Church, a woman who took interest in her neighbors and one who enjoyed the hospitality of others, Emma said, "Oh, sure, Sadie. I'd like to come for supper and see your homestead. I'd like that." Surely there was nothing to worry about, she thought. Her usual suspicions were put to rest by Sadie's gracious invitation and Clara's eagerness for her to go. She expected that the homestead lay over the rise, perhaps just at the top of the hill or tucked away in a valley.

At four o'clock Sadie returned with her horse and buggy. They headed up a rutted trail past the barn and over the hill beyond Frank Pike's place; they plunged nearly a mile down the valley where Emma hung onto the buggy for dear life as Sadie encouraged the horse into a trot. This is the darndest road I've ever seen, Emma thought as she jostled from side to side. At the bottom of the valley the buggy rocked and jolted as the horse left the narrow road, splashed its way across the shallow, rocky bottom of Summit Creek, lunged up the opposite bank onto the primitive track that led up to Sadie's homestead. On the right side of the trail, a rock wall seeped water from moss-filled cracks; the left side dropped away into a bottomless canyon as the horse clamored and jerked its way up the steep grade. Terrified at the thought of plunging over the edge, Emma thought, I've never seen anything like this before in my life!

"Sadie!" she said nervously. "I could probably walk. This is kind of scary." She glanced at the treetops below her. "Let me get out and walk!" she begged.

Sadie laughed and said, "Oh my, no, Emma! This is too steep for you to walk up!" She whistled and luffed the reins in encouragement as the horse pawed and dug its way a quarter of a mile to the top of the grade. White-knuckled with fear, Emma clung to the side of the buggy and willed herself to be brave while rocks and gravel spilled over the precipice, rattled down the mountainside.

At the homestead, her knees weak with fear, Emma steadied herself for a moment after she climbed down from the buggy, but Sadie sprinted about and chattered as she led the way into her cabin. She opened the door to the tantalizing aroma of roasted chicken and fresh biscuits, and invited Emma inside.

The women enjoyed a leisurely meal and compared stories about frontier life. Emma relaxed and savored Sadie's good cooking and Western hospitality. For Emma, charmed by the cozy, decorated home with its frilly curtains and matching tablecloth, the hours passed too quickly.

"Well, I suppose we'd better get you back before too long

or Clara will be worrying about you. It's getting pretty dark outside," Sadie commented as she rose and cleared the table.

Oh, no! Emma thought. With the warm ambience of the cabin and interesting conversation, she'd almost forgotten about the horrendous trip back to Clara's. She reluctantly climbed into the buggy, girded herself against disaster, clutched at the sides as Sadie headed the rig downhill. The horse locked his front knees, nearly sat on his haunches as he slipped and slid, loosened gravel that cascaded before them, tumbled, clattered toward the bottom. Emma leaned back, braced her feet as though that might prevent the poor creature from sliding over the edge, but Sadie continued to laugh and converse with her guest without wasting a thought on the danger that lurked only inches away from the wheels. Going up and down that hill was an everyday experience for her. When they arrived at the safe shores of Lake Lubec, Emma wondered, How am I ever going to last for two weeks.

Clara's discomfort eased, the false labor became sporadic, stopped altogether. Emma tried to convince her to return to Minnesota with her on the train, but Clara didn't have the money. Besides, she'd have to face Lou's recriminations. "I told you so!" he'd say. "It's a good thing you're back here where you belong," and she'd have felt like a failure with her money all gone and a husband left behind. No, I can't go back, she decided.

Even though Clara had entertained Emma to the best of her ability and Glenn had shown her the beauty of the park on a trip to St. Mary's Lake, Emma described her trip to Glacier Park as the worst two weeks of her life. She couldn't understand how her sister could stand to live in such a place with its privations and severe weather. The tranquil, rolling hills of Minnesota had never looked so beautiful to her, but now Charley wanted to see Glacier National Park. Clara was overjoyed. Charley was her favorite brother; she'd taken care of him when he was a baby while her mother worked in the fields. She could hardly wait to see him.

She suddenly felt alive, rejoiced in the beauty of the red monkey flowers, the blue gentians, the shooting stars and columbines that nodded in the meadow, vibrant colors and gentle fragrances that had nearly been forgotten. She painstakingly picked bowls full of miniature wild strawberries, baked short-cake, whipped mounds of cream for Charley's favorite dessert. She baked bread, made a rhubarb pie, fluffed up his bed; prepared for a wonderful time.

Although Charley was nearly thirty years old, tall and broad-shouldered, Clara still regarded him as her baby brother, the special one who used to follow her around and listen to her stories. On the day of his arrival, Glenn bought a few groceries in Glacier Park and joined him on the train for the last few miles of his journey to Lake Lubec. Although Glenn had never met his brother-in-law, he recognized him from the Miller family portrait that Clara kept on the shelf.

"Now, Charley," Glenn said casually, "move your suitcases outside the door onto the platform between cars. We're going to have to jump off pretty quick here. You be prepared to jump."

Charley grinned and followed Glenn with his luggage to the back, but he didn't take Glenn seriously. He listened. He heard him say it; he just didn't believe it. Clara's letters hadn't mentioned jumping from the train, and he knew that Emma couldn't have jumped. This must be an example of Glenn's sense of humor, he grinned to himself as they stood out back in the open air and admired the passing scenery.

A few minutes later as they approached the lake, Glenn threw off the groceries and said, "Charley, come on, jump! Let's jump!" and he disappeared from sight. Unwilling to believe that Glenn had actually jumped off the train, Charley stood paralyzed on the bottom step and watched the ground pass beneath his feet.

Glenn ran alongside the train and yelled at him, tried to snap him back to reality. "Jump! Throw your suitcases off! Jump, Charley!" But Charley, hypnotized by the blurring landscape, maintained his firm grip on the suitcases and stared at the ground as the train continued west.

Glenn shouted again, "Charley, if you don't jump, you're going to end up in Kalispell! Jump, Charley, jump!" So Charley jumped, but he'd waited too long.

He tumbled down the steep incline near the snow shed. Head over heels he bounced and careened off the gravel as Glenn watched the horrifying accident unfold in slow motion. The tumultuous landing broke open the suitcases. Shoes, pants, shirts, and gifts littered the slope where Charley lay motionless on the ground.

Glenn thought, Oh, my land! He's broken his neck! How am I gonna explain this to Clara? He raced over to the inert body and checked for a pulse. He placed his ear near Charley's lips and listened to weak gasps. He said, "Charley, can you hear me? Can you hear me, Charley?" Charley opened his eyes and grinned. He gingerly moved each arm and leg, nothing was broken; he'd had the wind knocked out of him, but he was all right.

Subdued by Charley's rough tumble down the incline, they repacked the suitcases, collected the groceries, and silently followed the trail to the cabin with Glenn wondering why Charley wouldn't jump, and Charley wondering what kind of primitive country he'd come to see.

Clara impatiently waited for the Great Northern to come into view across the lake, then hurried across the meadow to welcome her brother to Montana. She plied him with his favorite foods for a week, but Charley's impression of the West and Glacier National Park was about the same as Emma's. Yet, for many years afterward, he told the story of his adventure in jumping off the train. It was the highlight of his trip.

Clara managed to reap a few onions and radishes from her garden, the deer ate the lettuce, but the first killing frost decimated the rest of her vegetables without mercy. Only the rhubarb continued to flourish. Silvery hues of summer aspens dissolved into vibrant flushes of saffron, the leaves chattering, rattling against each other in shivery, soughing breezes that drifted down from the western highlands. A purple haze furtively concealed the distant foothills; snow draped from the spine of Squaw Mountain like drizzled icing. Promises of colder weather. The blood-red leaves of wild strawberries carpeted the ground; clusters of Oregon grape added their mottled shades to the base of leafless shrubs as migrating Canada geese paused on the rippled waters, grazed in the meadow, a brief layover on their lengthy journey to a warmer climate.

Clara's pregnancy had been unpleasant. Now in her eighth month, clumsy and cumbersome, she continued to milk her cow and care for the chickens, but her energy waned. She lost her appetite, became listless and morose. Back pain disturbed her sleep; swollen ankles and fatigue plagued her days. Glenn, who had previously witnessed the birth of four children, became alarmed at her weakening physical state. He had already lost one wife after childbirth, so in early November he saw her aboard a train for Great Falls where he'd made arrangements for her to live with a doctor. Someone met her at the depot and cared for her until the birth of their son on November 26, 1916.

On December 12, Clara bundled her new baby, Glenn Charles, inside layers of blankets and boarded the Great Northern for the journey back to Glacier Park. She watched from her window as increasing winds whipped feathery snowflakes into a froth before delivering a blizzard that exploded out of the Rockies and held the land hostage. The temperature plunged below zero as glass-edged sleet borne on raging winds buried the frontier town.

Glenn waited for them at the depot, then guided his new family across the railroad tracks to the Log Cabin Inn. They remained entombed in the modest hotel where the inside temperature barely exceeded that on the outside, but accustomed to freezing winds that whistled up between the floorboards of her own cabin, temperatures that frosted the windows and iced the water bucket, Clara didn't notice any unusual discomfort. Friends of Glenn, fellow loggers and bachelor ranchers stranded by the weather, were also boarding at the Log Cabin Inn, so mealtime in the dining room provided the perfect opportunity for the new parents to show off their beautiful baby while the storm vented its wrath across the West for nearly a week.

When the blizzard subsided, Glenn, Clara, and Glenn Charles returned to their isolated cabin on the shores of Lake Lubec, and Clara wrote this letter to her Minnesota family.

Miss E.H. Miller   Pike, Montana
Long Prairie   Dec. 25th, '16

My Dear Sister

Your very nice leter was received by us quite a few days agoe we were very glad to get it.

And today it being Xmas day the baby got that lovely present from you: Glenn was to the P.O. and I was indeed surprised as he came home with a package. Ge, it just suits us fine its very pretty Glenn thot it just as pretty as could be. and you could not have thot of any thing more sensible then a blanket as it is: am very thankful to you fore it.

We are all well and happy hoping same to you all. Oh tell Charley I got his prety Xmas postal card yesterday. and I was very much pleased over it.

Yes its very cold out here now days too but no wind is blowing and hasn't fore the last week ore so.

Well I hope you folks all had a fine old time today. Glenn

and I were alone I am so glad we were as I spend most of my time with the baby.

I left the hospital Dec. 12 and I was in haste to get home before bad weather set in but I did not make it as in Great Falls it was mostly warm and when we got out to the Park here a blizzard was on and that was at near midnight but Glenn was at the depot and it was but a short distance over to the place we were to stay: and a nice warm room electric lighted every thing up to snuff bathroom toilet just as in the city I was surprised to find such at the Park. Well we were there about a week I had not a thing else to do but look after baby and myself. We boarded at the Log Cabbin Inn I guess its called the cooking was swell in all lines. my but I was just bugs to get home tho out here to Lubec as you see here I can wash and do just as I please all the time.

The baby is fine is growing every day. He sleeps a lot and wakes some too but is a lovely baby not mean and a cry baby he had a cold but is getting over it: I believe most everybody in the country has had a cold ore has one. Glenn is just now getting over with a bad cold a soar throat with it too I sure dont want baby to get it am glad Glenn is about over it.

Well I am glad now I did not come out to Minn. but we will come out this Summer all 3 of us. When its real warm.

Glenn and I thank you all very much fore that lovely honey its the best of any yet Glenn thinks. I have so much to tell you but will next letter.

So Bye Bye. Happy New Year

Clara

Clara adored her baby. At night he slept between his parents in the springy double bed and snuggled tightly against his mother's breast. During the day she kept him layered in blankets in a cradle near the stove. She rocked him and sang lullabies, she talked softly and soothed him with her voice. He didn't fuss; he didn't demand.

"Glenn Charles is such a good baby," she said proudly to her husband as she traced her son's delicate eyelashes and brows with her fingertip. "He snuffles when he wants to be fed, but he never cries."

Glenn looked up from his paper. "Yah, he's no crybaby, but Glenn Charles seems like such a big name for such a little guy. Let's just call him GC for short." Clara liked that; it made for less confusion between father and son.

She passed the winter months nurturing her precious one. Together the parents watched him pass from the infant stage to one of awareness and recognition of his protectors, but it was Clara who noticed every little nuance of development as he followed her with his eyes, raised his head from the blanket, and rolled over from side to side. She chuckled at his antics when he pummeled the air with jerking arms and kicking legs and smiled a toothless grin at her approach in anticipation of being held and cuddled.

GC, with his light, silky hair and blue eyes, promised to be a handsome lad. Within months his dimpled arms reached out for her love as he began to babble in response to her endless conversation with him about the weather, her thoughts. She carried him with her to milk the cow and tend the chickens; he was never far from her side.

When the logging crew left for the distant forests, Clara hardly noticed their departure as she continued to revel in the splendor of Lake Lubec with her son. As the last snow melted from the meadow, she plucked bouquets of graceful, yellow glacier lilies and shared their brilliance. She carried him to the edge of the creek that flowed into the lake and let him grasp at clumps of glossy yellow buttercups, then strolled to the lake shore and fed bits of bread to migrating mallards, teal, and canvasbacks. Late spring eased into summer. GC, a hefty six-month-old whose diet included mashed vegetables from his mother's plate, became her elixir of life.

During that summer of 1917 back in Minnesota with the crops planted and harvesting still a few weeks away, Lou decided to take a well-earned vacation and visit his sister Clara for a week. He'd listened to Emma's tales of horror about horrendous winds and frightening roads that dropped away into nothingness; too many times he'd heard Charley expound about his near-death experience of jumping off the train. Convinced that his siblings had overreacted to the adversities of the frontier, he decided to experience Glacier National Park for himself, to determine what it was really like, to put an end to the folderol of their outrageous stories.

He arrived in late July to assaulting, incessant screams of a baby cutting teeth. Nothing could calm GC as he suffered through rash, diarrhea, and painful gums. Knowing Lou's lack of patience with anything outside of his own pleasure, Clara tried to hush the baby, but her constant hovering only seemed to exacerbate the problem, and the maternal clucks and baby talk drove Lou into the wilderness. Desperate and determined to escape, he grabbed her fishing pole and trudged to the opposite side of the lake where he hoped to enjoy a few hours of tranquillity.

Without Lou's aggravating presence, Clara soothed GC's tormented body into a reluctant sleep while she went outside to do a few chores. A man's shout drifted across the water. She fed the chickens and tended the few puny vegetables in the garden; she smiled to think that Lou had finally found something to occupy his time. With his disparaging attitude toward her chosen lifestyle, she sincerely wanted him to enjoy this week in the West. A few more shouts piqued her interest as she walked down to the lake shore. She looked across the rippling expanse and spotted her brother across the lake. Only his upper body was visible. His lower body was submerged in quicksand, a gluttonous bog that lay camouflaged beneath a blanket of moss. Waving his arms above his head and shouting hoarse cries into the wind, Lou continued to submit to the oozing slime for his final interment.

"Oh, my gosh, he's going under!" she exclaimed aloud. She grabbed a bracing pole from her clothesline, hitched up her long skirt, and raced along the path. When she was directly before him, she hesitantly tested each footstep for firmness. Something invisible, heinous, sucked at her shoes, a camouflaged abyss anticipating another victim. She backed onto firmer ground, dropped to her knees, edged the pole toward her brother as he sank further into the muck, but it was no use. She flopped flat on her belly, extended her arms to distribute her weight over the unstable ground, thrust the pole forward trying to reach him. Viscous bubbles surfaced around her chest, gurgled and spattered an oily film onto her face, slimy moss lay on the surface, stank, made her eyes burn. She stretched the pole nearer to his clutching hands and wondered whether she'd have the strength to pull him out. "Help me, Clara," he croaked. "Don't let me die!" His desperate eyes sought refuge as his flailing arms reached, grasped the end of the pole.

She anchored the toes of her shoes into the mire, the muscles of her upper body strained to free him as he struggled, but she could only pull him from the devouring pit a few inches at a time. After each maneuver she backed onto firmer ground and readied herself for the next hoist. The stench of rotting vegetation, compost from past centuries, permeated the mountain air as she dragged him from the subtle clutches of the invisible quagmire.

Her strength and determination eased him onto firm ground. Clumps of muck seeped into the cavity; a thin membrane of oily residue, hues of shimmering rainbows, seeped across the surface destroying all evidence of the near-tragedy. On hands and knees he crawled toward the grassy bank where Clara lay on her back, one arm thrown across her eyes, her chest heaving, gasping for breath. He collapsed beside her, traumatized, contemplated his brush with death. They stretched out together, encrusted with filth, each of them reliving the terror of the past minutes. His panic gradually subsided, while only the soft sound of a mallard hen and her ducklings scuttling and scooping delicacies from the surface water disturbed the silence.

Remembering her baby back at the cabin, Clara roused her brother to his feet. Muddy and weak, emotionally shaken, he walked by her side as she scolded him all the way home. "Why in the world did you go fishing over there by the quicksand? The fishing is just as good at this end of the lake."

Lou caught the next train back to Minnesota. He welcomed the sight of his peaceful farm, the conveniences of a frame house and his Model T Ford. Emma and Charley were surprised to see him back so soon. They eagerly waited to hear about his experiences and opinions of Lake Lubec, but all he ever said was, "That kid bawled day and night. I didn't have a very good time."

After another successful season with his logging enterprise, summer eased into fall when Glenn bought a special gift for Clara. He appreciated her sacrifices for him, and her generosity toward the neighbors was unexcelled as she regularly gave away loaves of freshly baked bread, batches of donuts, or one of her famous pies. Remembering her abandoned organ at the soddy and her love for music, he frequently heard her singing lullabies to GC and humming familiar refrains as she worked around the homestead. A few weeks later, a delivery wagon from the Glacier Park depot rattled over the improved wagon trail that wound toward Marias Pass and deposited a talking machine at their door.

She couldn't believe that the beautiful piece of furniture was meant for her; she examined it from all sides. The tall cabinet was crafted of solid quarter-sawed oak with an oiled, hand-rubbed finish. It fit snugly in their cramped quarters where she placed it at the far end of the room between the beds. She smiled across the room at her husband as she stroked the satin-like finish, cranked the handle, and placed the needle on her chosen record. When the talking machine began to play, its sweet sound enveloped her in delight as she hummed to the music, swayed to the rhythm.

The talking machine generated much interest in the Lubec community as friends dropped by more frequently and hung around a bit longer. The new teacher at the Lubec one-room school, an Italian man from back east, brought with him a large collection of records. Upon hearing the quality of sound from Clara's talking machine and lacking one of his own, he immediately proposed a business deal to Glenn. "I need a place to live for the winter while I teach at Lubec. If I pay room and board, could I live here with you? You'd make some extra money, and I'd be gone all day and not be a bother to Mrs. Smiley," he said.

Glenn liked to make money, and Clara felt that having an Italian living with them might add a bit of culture to their lives. "All Italians love music," she commented as she agreed to the arrangement. She made up the extra bed, and the Italian schoolteacher joined them for the rest of the winter. He spent his nights on one side of the curtain while the Smiley family snuggled together on the other side. When the school session came to a close, their cultured boarder moved farther west and left his record collection for Clara.

The spring months of 1918 found Glenn preparing for another summer in the woods. As GC played in the dirt, followed his mother on her daily chores, and explored the edges of the meadow, Glenn fenced off the areas of quicksand.

Frequent letters from home told Clara of her mother's weakening condition. On May 6, 1918, at the age of sixty-nine years, Clara Marie Miller passed away, but by the time the letter of her death arrived, she was at rest in the Long Prairie cemetery. Hoping that a trip to visit Clara might help Charles Miller cope with his loss, the Minnesota siblings bought his train ticket to Glacier Park in 1919 and encouraged him to stay for a few weeks.

Clara's father arrived when the mountain meadow nodded and waved with a profusion of blossoming beargrass with its spectacular creamy masses of miniature flowers balanced atop tall, erect stems. Grass-like leaves created tufts of serene beauty as the lovely display welcomed him to alpine tranquillity. Pa helped Clara with her chores and tolerated GC's non-stop chatter as he toddled along behind the frail, old man with the long chin whiskers. Much to Clara's relief, Pa enjoyed the beauty of Squaw Mountain, the only member of her family to do so, while he passed the afternoon hours fishing on the safe side of Lake Lubec.

On GC's second birthday, Clara announced the impending arrival of another child. Once again she lacked pre-natal care as she entered the second trimester of a troubled pregnancy. She and Glenn shared the winter chores as he fed the young stock and she milked the Jersey cow, but while carrying GC during the icy snows, she'd taken two bad falls on the ice. She usually fluffed things off with, "Whatever happens, happens," but she worried about her unwavering discomfort.

In late April as she neared her ninth month, Glenn contacted Dr. Monroe in Kalispell, who agreed to let Clara and GC live at his home until the birth of the child. After a thorough examination, Clara was confined to bed; the lifetime of hard, physical labor was taking its toll on her health. Meanwhile, the care of GC fell to someone else in the doctor's household.

On May 20, excruciating pain marked the onset of labor. Cramps and contractions came in quick succession as the vise-like muscle forced the child into the world with remorseless haste as though wanting to rid itself of a despicable burden. The doctor cut the umbilical cord that lay coiled around the infant's throat, pushed the misshapen head into some semblance of order. Baby Melina spewed forth bellowing anger at being delivered under such duress; her body lay twisted, deformed. It writhed with jerking arms, splayed fingers; the left leg kicked and fought, but the right leg lay tightly curled against the left half of the abdomen. Motionless.

Dr. Monroe examined the baby at length, extended the deformed leg, felt the muscles, probed the joint, and concluded that it was not a structural defect of the hip, but one of a muscular nature; he could offer no advice to the distraught mother on how to correct the affliction.

Once Clara recovered her strength, Glenn arranged to meet her at the jumping-off point when the train came east from Kalispell. She boarded the Great Northern with her suitcase, GC, and baby Melina. Deep snow concealed the ground; it had been another brutal winter.

In the mid-morning swirl of yet another snowstorm at the top of the pass, Clara placed the baby on the seat and slid the suitcase out the back door onto the coupling platform. Several passengers had watched her board the train with her two little ones. Now they wondered why she was moving her suitcase outside, bundling the baby in blankets, buttoning the little boy into his heavy leggings and coat, pulling the wool stocking cap snug over his ears.

They watched her stand up, slip into her heavy coat, tie a wool babushka over her head, knot it under her chin. She lifted the baby from the seat, balanced her in one arm, took GC by the hand, and walked toward the back of the car. They watched with interest, wondered in silence. One Good Samaritan said, "There's no need to get ready yet. We're a long ways from Glacier Park. Just sit down awhile. Just sit and wait for a few more minutes."

"We're a-gonna jump off here pretty quick," Clara said as she kept moving toward the back.

The passengers looked at each other in alarm. The conductor entered the car. "Conductor!" someone shouted. "Stop that woman! She's going to jump off the train!"

"I'm coming, I'm coming," he said as he continued to walk toward the back of the car. "The train doesn't stop here, but it slows down so the local settlers can jump off."

Amused by the startled faces of fellow passengers, Clara set their minds at ease, "Mr. Smiley is waiting in the deep snow. If he doesn't catch the children when I throw them off the train, at least they'll have a soft landing!"

The passengers craned their necks searching to see the husband waiting beside the tracks; some stood up for a better view. The conductor braced the back door open then turned expectantly as Clara handed him the baby. The train slowed. She stepped outside the car, lifted GC, and threw him into Glenn's waiting arms. With a deft move he deposited his son into the snow and turned in time to catch the bundled baby that Clara tossed in his direction just before she hurtled herself and the suitcase into the white softness below. Jumping off the train isn't such a challenge anymore, she admitted silently as she stood and brushed the fluff off her clothes. Fellow passengers shook their heads in disbelief and continued east toward civilization.

Feathery down danced on the wind as Glenn retrieved her bag; little GC clutched at the handle and dragged along behind. Clara tucked the baby against her body inside her long coat to protect her from the wind-whipped flurries, and the family trudged off through the woods.

Pushing onward through the cold and the wind, Clara consoled herself with warm thoughts of Minnesota. How lovely it would be back home with wild violets and grassy carpets of the wooded pasture. Memories of greening fields filled with the song of meadowlarks, lush marshes teeming with life amongst the reeds, and the sweet smell of blossoming fruit trees brought a smile to her lips. But reality loomed before her as they neared the family homestead in late May of 1919.

Melina's birth defect became Clara's top priority. When she changed a diaper, she lifted the baby by the crippled leg and stretched it out, then strapped the leg to a board so it couldn't curl back. Several times each day she massaged the joints and muscles with warm olive oil. Month after month Clara continued her self-prescribed physical therapy and, eventually, the atrophied muscle straightened and grew.

With Glenn's return to the woods, Clara was unable to milk the cow and take care of the outdoor chores with one child in her arms and another running alongside, so GC became Melina's baby-sitter. Clara impressed upon him the importance of his duties for those few minutes every morning and evening while she was out of the house. Although less than three years old, he comprehended the depth of his responsibility and gravely followed her directions.

Black bears frequently strolled between the house and the barn, she caught an occasional glimpse of a grizzly in the meadow where they grazed on grass and sedge just as the morning frost turned to dew. Once she watched a sow and two cubs wrestling and playing across the lake, the sheen of their fur glistening in the sunlight, and it was her greatest fear that GC might leave the house and come face to face with a bear, but her fears went unfounded as he faithfully sat by the cradle and watched over his sister.

His self-imposed obligations continued long after Clara settled the children into bed for the night. He mulled over the day's activities; he worried about unfinished chores before falling asleep. Each night he called from his bed across the darkness of the cabin, "Ma, did you get the diapers off the line?"

"Yah, GC. I put them away. Good night now."

"Ma, did you lock the chickens up?"

"Yah, GC. Everything is fine. You go to sleep now."

"Ma, did you put the buckets inside so they won't blow in the lake?"

"Yah, GC. Everything is safe. Let's go to sleep."

In late fall as herds of elk moved to lower elevations and migrating waterfowl paid their final farewell to the shores of Lake Lubec, clouds descended and shrouded the valley. Once again, concerned about the density of an evening's fog and cautioning GC not to leave the baby, Clara lit the lantern and stepped into the wafting apparition that ebbed and flowed before the flickering light. She hurried through the milking and barn chores in order to get back to the children.

As she stepped from the barn with her bucket of milk, the kerosene lantern cast back reflections of itself against the mist-filled barrier. The uncertainty of direction plagued her as she shuffled over uneven ground toward the milk house. Holding the bleak light at arm's length, straining and peering into nothingness, she continued forward only to realize that she'd gone too far. Frantically, she held the light higher as she pivoted and searched; a shadowy corner of the milk house loomed in its periphery.

Depositing the milk in the cooler and gathering her bearings, she took a few tentative steps blindly searching for the cabin, but the chilling specter of panic assumed the authority of the night. It exuded its dominance and enfolded her in its impenetrable veil. Illusions of light summoned her forward even farther from the milk house until she became totally disoriented.

Frightened by his mother's lengthy absence, GC fidgeted and stared at the door. "Ma," he whimpered.

He pushed a chair to the window and climbed up to search the outside darkness, but saw only his reflection with its terror-filled eyes. Ma might be in trouble and need help, he reasoned.

Determined to rescue her, he struggled into his jacket and opened the door. Baby Melina began to fuss. He rushed back to her cradle for one final check. "Never leave the baby alone in the cabin," he could hear his mother caution. GC looked out at the murky darkness. He looked back at the baby. He decided to take her with him.

She thwarted his frustrated attempt to wrap her in blankets as she writhed and struggled to get free of his clumsy mauling. Piteous cries rose from the cradle as he wrestled and subdued her in preparation for their journey into the night.

Clara listened, but heard nothing. The uncertainty of direction muddled her mind as she groped and stumbled in circles. What if I fall into the lake, she wondered. What if I miss the house altogether and wander off into the meadow? What if GC leaves the baby and gets lost in the fog? The consternation of her predicament brought her near hysteria as she reeled forward and pawed the air in a desperate attempt to grasp anything that lay hidden in the turbid mist.

A stump reared its ugly head from the white shrouds. She grabbed for security; it was her chopping block. Knowing that the cabin lay a few feet up the gentle slope, she inched her way forward until its massive logs appeared in the glow of the lantern. She followed along the rough walls toward the front of the cabin; light from the open door shimmered before her. Had GC wandered into the night? How would she ever find him?

"GC!" she cried. "Where are you?"

She rounded the corner and confronted the gaping doorway. Over near the cradle GC staggered and reeled under the weight of baby Melina clutched in his arms. His worried blue eyes looked up in relief as he continued to falter under the heavy burden. "We was coming to find you, Ma," he said.

Frost-nipped foliage fluttered to earth concealing the forest duff in preparation for the interminable, frozen months ahead.

Cords of firewood rested against the windward side of the cabin to absorb the myriad of storms that descended into the valley from Marias Pass. Sleet and snow straddled the driving gusts of wind earlier than usual. Bears and marmots drifted into hibernation; elk continued their passage to warmer areas. From the polar regions of the north, tumultuous blizzards played hide-and-seek as they chased each other in quick succession around rocky sentinels of the national park wilderness. The mercury plummeted; ice-filled clouds obscured the weakening winter sun as Glenn gathered his range cattle nearer the homestead. He staked a heavy rope between the house and the barn to guide the family to the animals in the event of an arctic assault, and together they gathered enough provisions to endure an extensive time of seclusion.

Although heavy snow usually held off until January, November of 1919 delivered tempests that gathered momentum in the Canadian Rockies, concealed the slopes of Squaw Mountain and buried the shores of Lake Lubec in glacial drifts of white splendor. The ice-shrouded boughs of the evergreens and reflections of the sky from the waters of the spring-fed lake offered the only relief from a colorless prison that lay outside the cabin walls. Claud Dowen frequently wandered through in search of his cattle, Glenn trekked to Frank Pike's post office to gather his papers, and Clara ventured only as far as the barn.

The Smiley family prepared for Christmas. Glenn cut a broom handle for the body of a hobby horse for GC; Clara fashioned a horse's head from brown gingham. She shaped the ears with bits of wire; tufts of yarn created the forelock and mane, black buttons became eyes. Glenn attached the head to the body and fastened a twine halter to make it complete. From a stuffed cotton sock, Clara made a doll for Melina with embroidered features and stringy, yarn hair. On December 24, Glenn and GC cut a tapering, subalpine fir for the family

Christmas tree. Its unadorned beauty softened the stark symmetry of the interior log walls.

Entranced with the festivities of the holiday season, three-year-old GC helped Clara bake and decorate glossy-iced star cookies to hang from the branches. Glenn helped him make long strings of popcorn and draped them with care. Clara hung red apples from the tips of stout branches while she and Glenn shared Christmas memories of days long past, harmonized with familiar carols from the talking machine. Melina, now seven months old, sat bundled in her cradle as she watched the family activity and basked in GC's attention as he shared his treasured ornaments before hanging them on the tree.

Being fully engrossed in Christmas preparations, neither parent noticed the abrupt change in the weather. Morning had dawned calm with a few pink fish-scaled clouds scattered across the sky, but northwesterly winds in the early afternoon presented them with dry, powdery snow that fell at an alarming rate. The increasing wind scooped great arms full of down from the breast of the earth and scattered it into the shoveled pathways; it obscured the barn from view while Glenn gathered stove wood from the side of the house. "We'd better get our chores done early tonight, Clara," he cautioned as he filled the wood box. Clara watched the children while Glenn fed the young stock, then she milked the Jersey cow and fed her chickens before returning to prepare supper.

And the howling wind continued to build. Glenn's sharpened senses detected a rasping strain overhead, a grating irritant, a power struggle between metal and wood. He periodically examined the rafters and roof joists while he helped GC fasten shiny, tin candle holders to the last barren boughs. His uneasiness prevailed at the severity of the bestial storm. Polar gusts battered the massive door, wrenched its hinges. That mighty protector from the tempests of Montana now quaked with fear before the wrath of Mother Nature.

Clara nervously watched it vibrate as she tucked ribbons and pine cones into the evergreen centerpiece on the holiday table. She started to prepare Christmas Eve supper. She grated potatoes and onions together, added an egg and a heaping spoonful of flour for potato pancakes and plopped the mixture into a frying pan of sizzling bacon grease. She sliced the bread, scrambled some eggs, then called her family to the table. They ate in subdued silence while roof boards drummed against log rafters.

Clara gathered the dishes for washing, and Glenn tried to concentrate on his newspapers, but the wrenching tumult overhead allowed no peace. Frightened by the roaring wind, GC huddled beside Melina's cradle. "We're a-gonna be all right. Don't worry," he reassured her with a quivering lip, but she was impervious to the fear that afflicted the rest of the family.

A broadside blast issued its final assault; the walls whimpered as the storm moved in for the kill. Glenn saw a rift between the ceiling joist and the rafters where dizzying spirals of snow crashed the party. He leaped from his chair and shouted, "We've got to get out of here! I can see that the roof is going to blow off!" Bone-wrenching moans erupted from stressed log walls, obliterated his voice as the intensity of the wind increased. "Who knows, maybe the whole cabin will disintegrate. Quick! Get some clothes together, get some blankets wrapped up!"

Clara bundled GC into his outdoor clothes and swaddled Melina in layers of baby quilts as Glenn doused the fire and kerosene lamps. The situation became critical. With the baby muffled tightly against her chest and belted inside her long wool coat, Clara grabbed some blankets. Glenn carried GC and latched the cabin door behind them as they confronted the furor of the storm.

"Now take a good grip on this rope," Glenn shouted into the wind as he guided Clara's hand into position ahead of him.

"Come on now, let's go! Don't let go of the rope! Lean into the wind! Come on, get moving!" he shouted as he gently maneuvered her toward the barn. Clara maintained a death grip on the lifeline with one hand while the frenzied wind ripped at the blankets clutched in her other arm. With Glenn nudging gently from behind, she groped along the rope and stumbled through the trackless wilderness as she led the way to safety. Behind them the cabin wailed in misery as it succumbed to the appetite of the enemy.

Bermed into the bank of the hillside, the barn nestled below the impact of the Christmas storm. Body heat from the animals provided warmth. Fumbling his way through the dark interior, Glenn found a comfortable area in the manger of the Jersey cow, scattered clean hay where the family nestled together on soft blankets and rode out the storm.

The next morning a peaceful calm reigned over the land. "Hello! Are you in there? Is anybody here?" The voice of Claud Dowen awakened the family. Crystalline sunshine streamed into the barn as he opened the door. Glenn and Clara roused themselves from the manger, their hair matted with straw and chaff, sat up and recalled the events of the past evening. Stumbling toward the doorway, they met Claud, who motioned toward the cabin. Below them, four log walls lay open to the sky, a blemish in the white, virgin wonderland while the roof lazily drifted across an unfrozen area of the lake.[3] The distant hammering of a woodpecker echoed from the forest, broke the stillness; a snowshoe rabbit eased his way from behind the woodpile and loped across the meadow.

Clara, disoriented from lack of sleep, observed the devastation in confusion; snow-covered household debris protruded from the diamond-studded meadow. She clutched Glenn's arm for support and began to cry. "What in the world are we a-gonna do? It's the middle of winter!"

Claud looked at her in surprise. "Why, you folks come on

up and stay at our place," he offered. "We'll get a new roof on in no time, and Sadie would like some company." He turned to Glenn, "Now we'd better dig out that sleigh and get the horses harnessed so Mrs. Smiley and the little ones can get up to our place where it's warm." No disparity of wealth existed amongst the

Sadie Dowen

settlers in the inhospitable environment of Lake Lubec; community-minded, they helped each other in times of illness, bad luck, or poor judgment without expectations of retribution.

Grateful for Claud's generosity, Clara checked on the children, then wallowed down to the gaping walls where she dug through the snow to collect diapers and clothing. The two men shoveled out the sleigh and hitched up the team. As Clara milked the cow and fed the chickens, she wondered how long she'd be away from the comfort of home.

Glenn carried GC from the barn while Clara collected baby Melina and tucked the blankets tightly around them in the sleigh. Claud's saddle pony had already broken a trail through the snow making it easier for the team of horses as they followed him back up the dreaded hill to the Dowen cabin. Sadie prepared Christmas dinner, and the Smiley family accepted their frontier hospitality.

During the winter of 1919 and 1920, endless blizzards swept across western Montana isolating the people, killing the stock. The Lubec community lost great numbers of open-range cattle. Lacking the intelligence to seek shelter, they stood shivering and starving, their backs hunched against the cold, their eyes frozen shut and crusted with ice until rescued by their owners or attacked by starving wolves, wolves too weakened by the devastation of winter to kill the animals, simply chewed off their tails, left them mutilated, foundering in the snowdrifts. Other ranchers found carcasses of their cattle with clogged nostrils, suffocated with particles of sleet and snow from swirling winds.[4]

The loss of the roof had disrupted the snugness of the Smiley cabin. During its exposure, the fluctuation of temperature crumbled the chinking between the logs. Biting winds continued to nip away at bits of plaster and sand; it fell onto the cabin floor where Clara swept it through the cracks in the floorboards. Although she securely blanketed the children into their beds near the stove in the evening, she found their comforters covered with a light dusting of snow each morning. Unable to tolerate the frigid conditions of the cabin any longer, she solved the problem in her own way, stirred up a dishpan full of thick pancake mix and plastered the cracks shut.

Warm chinook winds frequently followed ice-age conditions. The upper layers of snow melted away and offered a break from the monotonous winter before another storm reclaimed its grasp upon the frozen land. In late spring with another impending storm at hand and heavy snow already beginning to fall, Clara heard a shout outside the door, opened it a crack, and saw Claud Dowen hunkered over his saddle pony, his beefy shoulders encased in a sheepskin coat. Snowflakes collected on his collar, a wool scarf covered the bottom of his face, his hat pulled low on his head. He asked if she'd seen any of his cattle in the area; they'd been out for several days and he wanted to get them closer to home. She hadn't seen them, so he rode up the ridge to where the Great Northern had built a snow shed, a slanted timbered roof nearly two hundred feet long over the railroad track to protect it from avalanches sliding off Squaw Mountain. Sometimes animals sought refuge inside the shed, and that was where Claud continued his search.

As he approached the snow shed, he could hear terrified cattle, thirsty, starving, bawling inside the shelter. He dismounted and tethered his horse in a grove of pines to protect it from sheets of snow that whipped across the roof. Icicles hung from the eaves of the snow shed, hung toward the ground, reached up from the earth, frozen stalactites and stalagmites, fingers of ice reaching toward each other for strength against the wind. He entered the dim interior, allowed his eyes to adjust to the darkness, then herded his cattle toward the entrance where snowflakes as large as teacups concealed the atmosphere, an opaque veil of dull gray, shrouding, churning, tumbling.

Claud felt vibrations beneath his feet that rippled up his legs, spread throughout his body, realized that the Great Northern was barreling down the pass, bearing down without mercy. He turned, frantically searched for an escape from the snow shed, stared blindly toward the shrieking blizzard as the massive engine, encrusted with layers of frozen snow like a behemoth from the ice age, exploded into the shelter, splattered him and his cattle against the wall and between the rails.[5]

Sadie persevered alone, but the sheds for the young stock remained empty, and she needed money. Two miles west of her log cabin the railroad had built a beanery, a place where its workers could eat and relax, play cards and play pool. They employed Sadie as a waitress; she rode her horse to work and back. However, the loneliness was overwhelming. When a local rancher began to court her, she readily accepted his advances. They married shortly thereafter and moved to California.

Glenn had homesteaded and logged at Lubec for ten years. He'd "proved up" on his homestead in 1919 and registered it in Clara's name, but he'd always wanted to own a business in the town of Glacier Park. In 1920 with enough money to begin his quest, he approached John Lindhe, the owner of the Glacier Park Trading Company. Most local ranchers, homesteaders, loggers, and trail guides bought their supplies from John's store, so Glenn proposed that they operate a meat market together. John, a tall, husky man, studied his friend through round, gold-rimmed glasses and nodded his plump head in agreement to have the meat market built on land behind his trading company; he would manage the business if Glenn would provide the beef. Being a man who rushed through life, he walked fast and talked fast, John wanted the meat market in operation immediately to cater to tourists arriving from the East, so Charlie Tobin began construction on the building, and Glenn prepared to butcher his cattle before he headed to the logging camp.

Unaffected by her husband's business ventures that kept him

The Glacier Park Trading Company and John Clarke's Studio on Armistice Day, 1918. Photo courtesy of Collections of the Glacier County Historical Museum and Archives, Cut Bank, Montana

away from home during most of the summer, Clara attempted to grow another garden and managed the homestead in his absence. She had the children to watch and barn chores to do. She sold eggs and butter to her fellow homesteader Mrs. Market, and showered all of her neighbors with altruistic surprises from her oven. Sometimes she rested on her hoe and gazed out to the roof that floated on the waters of the lake. Still traumatized by the severity of the Christmas storm, she worried about summer gales that might blow GC into the lake. Unwilling to confine him indoors on windy days, she attached a long section of rope outside the cabin door. On days when the wind whistled around outside corners, GC donned his heavy wraps. Carrying his toys to the door he'd announce, "I'm ready, Ma. Tie me up!"

Twice a day Clara milked her Jersey cow. First, she tied its tail to its back leg with a piece of twine so she couldn't be switched in the face, then she washed the udder. She lowered herself onto the three-legged milk stool, spread her legs, and balanced the milk pail between them. Her long fingers encircled two engorged teats and began the rhythm of milking, the forefinger squeezing and pulling followed by the rippling of the other fingers downward until the little finger forced the white froth into the pail splashing and foaming, first one hand then the other. She stripped each teat to get the last of the cream then grasped the other two teats.

The cow tossed her head and bellowed, then kicked Clara onto her back where she lay sprawled on the barn floor. Surprised, she attempted to stand, but pain in her knee kept her down. Her fingers prodded and explored the surface of the kneecap; she could feel a vertical crack. Sitting with the throbbing leg extended before her, she agonized about what to do next. GC was tied to his rope, so calling for help was out of the question.

She placed her hands far behind her on the barn floor, bent

the knee of her good leg and brought it up next to her body, raised herself off the floor, and shifted her torso backward to her hands while dragging the injured leg. Continuing to repeat this procedure, she winced her way over the rough spots as she eased her way out the door and crossed the open area toward the cabin.

Alarmed at seeing his ma coming backward along the ground, GC ran toward her as far as his tether would reach. "What's wrong, Ma?" he cried.

"Oh, it's nothing," she answered. "The cow kicked me, but everything's a-gonna be all right. Go into the house and see if you can reach Mr. Smiley's tall bottle of horse liniment on the shelf. See if your rope is long enough to get to his red neckerchiefs, too, and bring them out here. Go along now," she urged.

The consuming pain continued as she dragged herself across the open area around piles of horse manure and bounced off hummocks of grass. The dead weight of her useless leg pressed down on the heel of her oxford and gouged a trail to the door sill where she pulled herself to a sitting position and examined her knee.

The skin wasn't broken, but the engorged purplish-black flesh lay misshapen. GC silently watched as she smeared the knee with liniment and massaged it into the flesh. Easing the two halves into place, she tied Glenn's neckerchiefs around the kneecap. GC gathered small boards, leftovers from the new roof, for splints. She tied them to the sides of her leg with strips she tore from cotton flour sacks for a brace. No tape, no aspirin, no painkillers offered relief; she relied on her own sense of survival and knowledge of first aid, and hobbled through her chores with the aid of a walking stick.

Left vertical column, top: Local Blackfeet in traditional dress; **2nd photo**: Squim, trained to pull cart in background; **3rd photo**: GC at 4 and Melina at 2; **4th photo**: Glacier Park, 1931. **Middle column, top**: the new Glacier Park Hotel; **2nd photo**: Entertaining tourists; **3rd photo**: Band leader Ed Prader; **4th photo**: Clara's potato patch. **Right column, top**: Tricks for tourists; **2nd photo**: Watching the diggers—is the woman with Clara the bad renter?; **3rd photo**: GC training Squim; **bottom**: Clara, Iowa Smiley, and the children.

PART IV

Vignettes of Glacier Park

"From 1892 until 1911, the town was called Midvale. In 1911 it was changed to Glacier Park. By 1920 there were 300 to 400 permanent residents. Most of them made a living by cutting stove wood for neighboring towns during the winter. Those who didn't have a business or string of horses were Bootleggers in the summer."[1]

After the establishment of Glacier National Park in 1910, the construction of Glacier Park Hotel, and the new train depot in 1912, the small town of Glacier Park began to grow. The Glacier Park Hotel, a majestic log structure built of Douglas fir and cedar from the Pacific Northwest, offered a touch of class to the community where genteel folk from Boston, New York, Chicago, wealthy cities in the East, could relax in cushioned willow lounge chairs, sip tea before expansive plate glass windows, admire glaciated ramparts that lay off to the north and west, or stroll outside where they could mingle, have their photos taken with Blackfeet natives adorned in their best eagle feather headdresses, beaded leather leggings, moccasins, local Indians employed by the hotel who spent their summers living in traditional teepees on the hotel grounds.[2]

East of the railroad tracks lay the dust-choked street of a one-horse town, a collection of frame buildings, the local business district. Following rumors that the new highway to Kalispell might pass through that part of the community, Glenn bought a block of property from Tom Dawson and his wife Isobel in 1921. The new property, strategically located between Washington Street and Meade Street diagonally behind the Glacier Park Trading Company, was the intended site for his new store. He registered it in Clara's name; she owned it free and clear.

Dan Boyington's Log Cabin Inn offered modest rooms and meals for local folk, John Lindhe's Glacier Park Trading Company supplied them with groceries, and Glenn's meat market built behind the Glacier Park Trading Company provided steaks and roasts, but on the main street next door to Lindhe's store, The Emporium, a weathered, frame building constructed in 1918, attracted cowboys, fur trappers, and loggers, hardened men of the frontier who caroused with painted ladies, whispered obscenities at shadowy tables, danced to the strains of a frontier orchestra, groped and squeezed in the obscure light of kerosene lanterns. A sordid place where lonely men relieved their thirst with illegal whiskey smuggled down from copper stills secreted in mountain ravines, where bullet holes penetrated rough, slivered walls, where palmed aces, loaded dice helped tinhorn gamblers line their pockets. Roughhewn cowboys on untamed broncos plowed the street into clouds of dust, swaggered down board sidewalks that shuddered beneath the clamor of boots, dangling six-guns, jangling spurs.

Michael Shannon, an old logger, reputed to be the first man to take a log drive over the White Water Rapids of the Flathead River into Columbia Falls, also arrived in Glacier Park searching for a place to make money, a place to spend his final years. For reasons unknown, The Emporium was confiscated by the law and old Mike bought it at a sheriff's sale, installed electricity, and cleaned up the place where the western spirit was kept alive without gamblers and brawls.[3] He changed the name to "Mike's Place," and made it one where tourists and locals could dance six nights a week. During late summer afternoons he encouraged cowboys to add a bit of local color for the tourists by riding their bucking broncos out front, broncos with colorful names like Deadman's Folly and Nightmare, exhibitions that ended with cowboys passing the hat amongst the Eastern dudes while the orchestra played, luring customers inside to whet their thirst, to take a spin or two around the dance floor before they wandered back up to the big hotel. On Sunday night old Mike brought heavy planks into the dance hall, laid them across rounds of wood for benches, then draped a white cloth against the wall and showed silent movies of Hoot Gibson, Ken Maynard and Charlie Chaplin.

During that summer Clara abandoned her garden; the family moved their belongings to a small log cottage nestled under the pines on the fringe of Glacier Park on the road to Looking Glass Pass. Glenn continued his logging and supplied fresh beef for the meat market, but Clara and the children boarded the Great Northern and spent several weeks in Minnesota at the family farm where Emma had remained as housekeeper after the death of her mother; she welcomed the extended visit of her sister's family. Meanwhile, Charlie Tobin moved to the homestead and cared for the animals while he built a four room log house for the Smiley family on Clara's new property in town, facing Meade Street on the corner of Meade and Dawson. The Smiley family moved into their new home on February 5, 1922.

With a block of land for development, Glenn hired Charlie to construct two log cabins for rentals facing Washington Street, plus a large chicken house in the center of the block. In the evenings after supper, before heading back to the homestead, Charlie lowered his loose-jointed frame into the rocking chair and invited the children to sit on his lap while he read stories to them. His throaty laugh and twinkling eyes encouraged mischief; they thought he was a member of the family.

Most frontier women raised a few chickens. Clara was no exception; raising chickens gave her great satisfaction. Even in the most dire circumstances, hens could survive on bugs, seeds, and natural foods while providing eggs and meat for the family. Each spring she ordered several dozen buff Orpington chicks from back east. They came through the mail in flat, cardboard boxes with round perforations along the sides where peeping beaks begged for freedom and downy heads protruded to take a look around. She sold some as fryers, the others she kept as laying hens and sold eggs to the neighbors. Then in 1923, Charlie constructed a log barn on the corner of Meade and Glacier, and the beloved Jersey cow moved to town. Neighbors wandered over to buy milk and butter, to share a bit of gossip as Clara toiled in her treasured vegetable garden near the chicken house.

Although Glacier Park lay a mere six miles from the homestead, it encompassed a different weather window, one in which hardy vegetables and root crops such as turnips, rutabagas, and carrots grew profusely. Gardening was her passion, where the steady grating of her hoe accompanied the placid, serene music of children's laughter, chickens clucking after a beetle, bees dancing in the depths of wildflowers, as she tried to make up for the lost years at Lake Lubec.

Gunshots, the whine of bullets, shattered the tranquility of a May afternoon. Clara glanced up from the garden, searched for the children, saw them playing over near the house, heard the distant thunder of galloping horses. A neighbor rushed over, eager to share the gossip. "Clara, did you hear that racket?" she asked. "My husband said that J. J. Smith was coming into town today on business, so the sheriff got a posse together and waited for him over by the depot. They were going to arrest him for breaking into boxcars during the winter. Some of the men hid on top of railroad cars and some of them laid on their bellies on the ground behind the tracks. They didn't want to shoot him dead, but fired over the top of his head so he'd know it was hopeless and give himself up, but he turned around and galloped right back into Lubec Valley!"

Clara pursed her lips, wondering about Smith, who once paid visits to her husband in the late evenings at the old log house. For years the community of Glacier Park had speculated about J. J. Smith, the one-eyed outlaw whose hideout lay concealed in the hills above Lubec. No one knew from whence he came nor why. Some claimed that he'd been trained as a doctor, but he endeared himself to the local folk when he occasionally boarded and robbed the slow freight train as it wound its way up the pass, tossed off clothing and food, then distributed it at night to destitute families, a Robin Hood of the West. However, his knowledge of the back country made him too dangerous for the sheriff and his posse to hunt…or so they claimed.[4]

And the settlers in Lubec protected their own. They rescued neglected children, scrubbed them with caustic soap, combed the nits from their hair, returned them to their parents with words of advice, gifts of food, remained tight-lipped about the camouflaged stills in the ravines, and proclaimed their ignorance about J. J. Smith whenever the sheriff made inquiries. And thus, under pressure from the Great Northern Railroad to catch the outlaw who kept robbing the train, the sheriff had gathered a local posse, set the trap for Smith, made a half-hearted attempt to placate the demands of the railroad barons back east.

On June 27, 1922, Glenn came home from logging, wandered into the kitchen in search of his wife. "Clara," he said, "J. J. Smith was killed in an ambush up near Two Medicine Lake where he was preparing to head out over the mountains. Took a bullet right through the neck. The second bullet cut the rope to his pack horse."

She turned and asked hesitantly, "Was it the sheriff?"

"The first report was that he was shot by a government detective while resisting arrest, but it turns out that he got in a duel with Deputy Sheriff Joe Danens." J. J. Smith, the one-eyed enigma who always carried a six shooter on each hip, died as an outlaw to some, but died as a hero, a man with a friendly smile and a generous heart to the local folk who welcomed him into their homes late at night in the hills near Lake Lubec.[5]

Did Clara worry that her children might get caught in the cross-fire of unsavory characters who rode into town? Probably not. Although things occasionally got out of hand, life in Glacier Park was usually quiet, a place where neighbors watched each other's children, where Clara needn't worry about bears, quicksand, or a howling wind blowing them into the lake.

And why did Glenn register the land deeds in Clara's name? Perhaps because of their age difference, if he felt that she'd outlive him. Perhaps since he'd already provided for his older children, he wanted to leave his second family secure without inheritance taxes or the contesting of a will. He was an astute businessman, one who gave careful consideration to every decision concerning money.

In 1924, while a new Mike's Place was under construction to replace the one that had recently burned down, Glenn sold the meat market and hired Charlie Tobin to build him a store. Located on the corner of Dawson Street and Washington Street, it lay diagonally across from the old meat market.

The store, a building approximately 16' x 20' with upstairs storage, contained mostly grocery items. Glenn offered credit to no one; he named it the Glacier Cash Grocery.

As customers entered the store, shelves lined the left wall. Directly in front of them, a long counter supported a glass display case, a heavy brass scale, a gleaming nickel-plated cash register, and a butcher paper dispenser. A spool of cord string dangled above it. Suspended from a hook in the ceiling, a stalk of bananas caught the shopper's eye. A nearby table displayed ham, bacon, and summer sausage, meats that kept without refrigeration. Boxes of apples and five gallon containers of coconut, dried apricots, raisins and dates made a colorful display. Shelves of canned goods, a panoply of colored labels, covered two walls; stacks of overalls, jackets, gloves, and work socks lay in the corner.

The Great Northern delivered the merchandise, but Glenn needed a means of transporting the barrels, boxes, and pack-

The Glacier Cash Grocery as it looks today. The Brown House contains the original display counters, cash register, ledgers, piano, potbelly stove and antiques. The owners sell their own pottery, and art by local artists. In the Smiley tradition, they also rent rooms to tourists.

ages from the depot to his store, so he purchased a used flatbed truck. It had seen hard use over the years—with paint-chipped wood-spoke wheels, a one-man cab maimed with a warped wood door—but it was more convenient than using a horse and wagon.

Two other general merchandise stores served the community of Glacier Park. The Glacier Cash Grocery, however, marketed commodities that no one else offered. The spacious glass case on the counter displayed Clara's home-baked bread, a crusty delight that sold out almost immediately. "Oh, boy," Glenn exclaimed as dollar signs flashed across the cash register. "We're onto something good here. No one else can provide home-baked goods!" In addition to the delicacies from Clara's oven, they sold fresh eggs and garden produce.[6]

Glenn also dealt in firewood. Behind the store, stockpiles of logs provided fuel for his stoves and cordwood to sell, both of which involved a lot of cutting and splitting. When customers couldn't pay their rent, Glenn escorted them to the woodpile, and they worked off their debt.

Shortly after the completion of the Glacier Cash Grocery, the family moved its living quarters in the spacious room above the store on a temporary basis; an outside stairway provided access. Near the back of the store, Clara's cook stove consumed vast quantities of wood and kept the groceries from freezing. The broad side of the building caught the brunt of the winds that hurtled down out of the mountains; canned goods frequently tumbled from the shelves after powerful gusts shook the walls, but they were easily restacked, and the business became an overnight success.

Housing was scarce in the small community of Glacier Park, and the Smileys' cottages were in big demand by both local families as well as people passing through. In the summer, tourists rented the log cabins at inflated prices. In the winter, Glenn leased them to local families and charged only what they could afford. Meanwhile, additional space was being attached to the side and back of the store. He believed in having something to rent. "It pays the freight," he said.

Glenn relied on the steady income from the rentals during the off-season; he was a no-nonsense landlord, demanded his rent money on time to meet his own expenses. Renters came and went, but one long-term renter who worked at various jobs in the area was late with the money. With the husband frequently absent, Glenn approached his wife. "You know, you've been living here for several months, and now you're behind in your rent. I want it today."

"Well," she said hesitantly, "I'll have to speak to my husband about that."

The rent money didn't materialize. Glenn watched for the husband to come home, then walked over to the house, rapped on the door, waited. A burly, barrel-chested man swung the door open wide, studied his landlord through bleary vision; his bloodshot eyes matched the plaid of his shirt. Glenn confronted him, "Your rent money is a week late. If I don't have it by Monday morning, when you come home from work Monday night your belongings are going to be set right out there in the street. Now I mean that!"

Mellowed by the first few drinks of the weekend, the man folded his arms, leaned against the frame of the door, responded with a chuckle, "Oh, Smiley, you wouldn't do that, would you? To a hard working guy like me?"

Glenn answered, "Try me."

Monday morning arrived without rent money. GC and Melina, witnesses to the unfolding drama, tagged along when Glenn paid a visit to his friend Albert "Shorty" Hynes who lived across town. Shorty, a rotund little man with a swarthy complexion and hook nose, had a reputation around town as a hard worker. Neighbors suspected that he still had his first dime after he built a new house, then rented it for cash while he lived out back in the woodshed. Always looking for an easy way to make money, Shorty especially enjoyed working at the Smiley place where he could get a free meal.

Glenn heard the thud of an ax, rounded the corner of the weathered woodshed. Unaware of his audience, Shorty balanced a round of wood on the chopping block, raised the ax over his head and brought it down dead center splitting the round into two parts, half falling off the edge while he reached for the other half and threw it over his shoulder onto a pile before picking up the next round to be split. Splinters of wood, clusters of sawdust, lay glued to the pitchy filth of his bib overalls. A flat carpenter's pencil protruded from the top pocket, a ring of keys rattled from the hammer loop on the side. The armpits of his stained shirt, rank half-moons blackened with hard work and sour sweat, sagged toward the unbuttoned side opening of the overalls. Glenn interrupted the rhythm of his work. "Hey, Shorty, ya want a job?"

Shorty stood up, buried the ax in the chopping block, pushed back his wide brimmed hat exposing plump cheeks and shrewd, dark eyes. Tufts of greasy dark hair curled over his ears concealing the back of a stumpy neck. "Sure! Whatcha got?" he asked as he anticipated some extra money in his pocket.

"Ya know that renter in my big log house? He's a week behind in his rent, and I told him last Friday that if I didn't have my money by this morning, he'd find himself out on the street. And that's what I meant. I want you to get yourself a helper, and I want everything in that house moved out. Everything!"

With a rental of his own, Shorty understood Glenn's position; there was no need for an explanation. He found himself an assistant and accompanied Glenn back to the log house where he entered into the job with enthusiasm while anticipating a tasty dinner at Clara's table. He might even be able to get a cup of coffee and a couple of donuts if he worked it right.

For two hours the men stacked furniture and family possessions outside on the dusty street while neighbors observed with interest, watched the distraught wife. She wailed, wiped her nose on her apron, ran back and forth between the Smiley store and her house, consoling her children, frantically trying to stop the men, pleading with Clara to get Glenn to reconsider his brash decision, begging Shorty not to humiliate her, but Shorty could already taste a chicken dinner with gravy and dumplings at Clara's table, and he wasn't about to risk losing that. "I do what I'm paid to do," he announced as he pushed past her to deliver a chair to the street. News of this eviction had probably reached his own renters by this time, would set a good example of what would happen if they missed a payment to him, he thought to himself as he entered the house for another load.

Upset by the crass decision of her husband even though she suspected that the renters had been stealing her chickens, Clara tried to convince him to reconsider. "Mr. Smiley, think of those poor children. Where are they a-gonna go? There's no other place to live around here." She pleaded with him. "It's not their fault. Maybe you'll get the money next week."

But Glenn was an adamant businessman, a man of his word. "Well, I told him that he had to bring me the rent this morning or his furniture and everything would be out in the street, and that's exactly what I meant," he said as he continued to stock his shelves and wait on customers.

The renter returned home to an empty house, saw his furniture stacked outside, watched the flutter of curtains in nearby windows as neighbors anticipated a bit of local entertainment. Glancing through the paned windows of the store, he saw his wife talking to Clara while Glenn lay stretched out on the daybed reading the daily paper. Angered by the audacity of Smiley's behavior, he barged through the door. "What in the world is going on?" he roared.

Glenn briefly lowered his newspaper, glanced up and said, "That's your stuff. Get it out of there."

The wife leaped to her feet and pleaded with her husband to pay the rent. The children tugged on his belt and begged for reassurance that they wouldn't lose their home; he shoved them aside and slammed the door on his way out. Glenn returned to his reading while Clara commiserated with the homeless wife without offending her own determined husband. The Smiley children waited and watched.

A half hour later the belligerent renter returned. "Here!" he grunted as he thrust the money toward Glenn. "Now you help us move the stuff back in before dark!"

Glenn set the newspaper aside, sat up and methodically counted the money as he spoke. "No, you get it in any way you can. I'm not helping you. And from now on, if the money isn't here on time on the first of the month, you can expect your furniture to be back out there in the street."

Clara welcomed the rising sun from the rows of her garden where she worked at first light. Her long skirt fluttered in the brisk mountain breeze as she stirred the soil around her potatoes and pulled pesky weeks from the vegetables. She bent over to thin the carrots and separate the radishes as she worked her way along the rows. When confined to the store on rainy days, she'd gaze through the window at the garden and tell her children, "My hands just itch to get out there with my hoe."

Fresh vegetables provided a steady income. GC and Melina pulled the radishes and lettuce and brought them into the store where Glenn gently eased them into a bag so that two bunches filled the space. When Clara took care of customers, she packed the produce deep into the sack and gave them three or four bunches of vegetables. The thought of anyone going hungry distressed her, so her customers received twice the normal amount.

A major re-organization followed the completed remodeling of the store building. The north addition, a room as large as the original store, became the new business area, while the original store became the family's living space. The outside steps were relocated to the interior of the building with access from the front entryway; Glenn partitioned off three rooms upstairs. The addition at the back of the store provided three more rooms; the south bedroom contained two beds for the family, and the other two rooms, the middle one with an outside entrance, were rented by the night. Glenn now had three houses and five rooms to "pay the freight."

For three dollars a night, a man could rent a bed. That meant more laundry for Clara. She didn't have a washing machine, so she scrubbed the sheets outdoors on a washboard, rinsed away the suds in tubs of clear water, and hung them on the clothesline. During inclement weather, she hung ropes across the interior of the store and dried the sheets at night. When time permitted, she returned to the garden, but Clara's home bakery lured the most customers to the store.

When she could no longer meet the demand with her regular size cook stove, Glenn purchased the commercial stove from the kitchen of the Barrett Hotel on the west side of the tracks. The black steel monstrosity presented a problem. After removing the stove pipes and all detachable parts, it took several men to carry it into the store where it devoured entire rounds of wood in its cavernous firebox. Massive ovens baked ten loaves of bread and five pies at once.

Like so many frontier families, the men handled the financial affairs and the women did the work. Clara's life was no different. She lifted and dumped fifty-pound sacks of flour and sugar into large metal storage tins with ease. She set her yeast foam for bread before going to bed, and roused herself out at 4 A.M. to stir together a mixture of ingredients that weighed nearly thirty pounds. She kneaded, folded, tucked, and rolled the sticky mass until it became firm. Returning it to the large, oiled metal dishpan, she covered it with a clean cloth, placed it near the warmth of the stove to rise, and tended to her outside chores. She gathered the eggs, fed the chickens, and milked the cow. She hoed a bit in the garden and returned to the kitchen to punch down the dough.

Then she made pies. Glenn ordered gallon tins of apples and berries. She had rhubarb from the homestead. She relied on lard, flour, salt, and water for the crusts and filled them with succulent combinations of fruit and spices. She tucked them beneath upper crusts fluted around the rim to seal the bubbling juices within, while a quick swab of cream and a sprinkling of cinnamon-sugar added the final enhancement as she slid them into the giant oven.

Dumping the elastic bread dough onto the floured table surface, she divided it into ten parts and formed each section into a loaf that she oiled and placed in individual loaf pans for the final rise before baking. Sometimes she prepared molasses cakes and simple fruit cakes to be baked along with the bread. When the steaming pies came out of the oven, the rounded loaves of bread and cakes went in, and Clara cleared the work table for her next project.

While two three-gallon metal dishpans of lard melted and heated on top of the stove, she prepared the batter for several dozen cake donuts. With deft strokes of the rolling pin, she leveled a mound of dough to a thickness of a half-inch on the kitchen work table and used her metal donut cutter to cut them to shape. As the pans of grease began to bubble and roll, she dropped a donut hole into the cauldron to test the temperature, then set about frying the delicate dough.

Her rich batter contained only enough flour to hold the dough together. When she lifted a donut to drop it into the churning fat, it stretched by its own weight until a donut of huge proportions draped before her. The edges of the golden circles sizzled and crackled as they slid, one after another, into the grease and caromed off the sides of the pan until the surface could hold no more. She turned each one and browned the other side while the smell of hot cinnamon and sugar engulfed the kitchen. When she finished frying one batch, she repeated the process until mountains of donuts nestled together under a dusting of sugar in the front showcase. Steamy brown loaves of bread and moist cakes emerged from the oven and added their own enticement to the heavy warmth that permeated the store. Being a clever businessman, one with a flair for marketing, Glenn opened the front door, encouraged the aroma to waft through the streets.

Clara's Donut Recipe

1¹/₄ cups sugar	1 teaspoon salt
1 cup milk	2 teaspoons baking powder
4 eggs	4 cups of flour, then add enough
4 tablespoons melted fat	more to make a soft dough,
2 teaspoons vanilla	up to 5 cups total
(or 1 vanilla and 1 cinnamon)	

Beat eggs and sugar together until light. Add milk and melted fat. Sift the dry ingredients together and add them to the mixture. Make a soft dough.

Roll out about ¹/₂ inch thick. Heat grease to 360°.

Cut out donuts with a donut cutter and drop into hot grease. Turn donuts when they are brown on one side.

Dust lightly with cinnamon and sugar if desired.

Her pies sold for thirty cents each, her sugared donuts sold for thirty-five cents a dozen; one donut and a cup of coffee made a meal. For customers with children, she contributed three or four extra donuts to the bag. When children came into the store alone without money and longingly gazed at the mouth-watering delicacies inside the glass showcase, she presented them with a sample of her baked goods and sent them on their way.

A multitude of unemployed men passed through Glacier

Park in the mid-20's. Clara's generosity to the neighbors was a well-known fact, but Glenn's reputation for never turning a man away from a meal was carried across the West in the boxcars of the Great Northern. Some vagabonds rode the rails for adventure while others actively sought work, but all of them developed an appreciation for Clara's home cooking.

If the traveler looked hungry, Glenn filled his belly then escorted him to the woodpile; they weren't given a hand-out. Some of the travelers stopped over for a day or two every time they passed through. Some of them stayed for several weeks at a time because Glenn assured them of employment. He might not let a man go hungry, but he didn't believe in a free lunch.

John Smith from Rochester, New York, a man in his mid-thirties, became a long-term customer every summer when he rented one of the upstairs rooms and took his meals with the Smiley family. He was tall, husky, and eager to work, and Glenn took advantage of his strength when heavy lifting was involved. His slicked-back pompadour and clean good looks appealed to Clara, and he kept the family amused with his happy-go-lucky personality and keen sense of humor. He entertained the children and admired the garden, but his favorite place was in the kitchen listening to Clara's stories and smelling the goodies about to come out of the oven. He felt obligated to sample the quality of her baked goods, then rewarded his good judgment with extra desserts after meals.

He stayed in contact with the family during his absences, but his letters were addressed primarily to Clara.

January 22

Dear Friends:

just a line to let you know that I arrived home OK, but will be back with the first flock of ducks in the spring. so be shure and have lots of cakes and pies backed when I arrive...

how is the children getting aling ask glen if he has got any more stoves to move haha how is every body at the park. I suppose they are all waitting fer the park to open up to flim flam the duds...

Well Frends, their isent much news just at present so will close hopping to hear from you soon

yours Truly
John Smith

Another letter soon followed.

March 3rd

My Dear Friends:

Received your most welcome letter...and was very much suprised to hear that their has ben so much sickness around Glacier Park.

the people around this part of the country has all ben lucky. as far as sickness is conserned every body has ben feeling fine but me and I've had the montana blues several times. so you see that isent very serious and I probely will get over it OK.

...I was wondering if they are goeing to work on that new road this spring...If they are let me know and probely I will come out this summer...I could almost taste some of your good old home made pies and cakes. Belive me.

yours Truly
John Smith

The store catered to the dudes from back east who strolled down from the big hotel across the tracks; its rustic exterior fulfilled their expectations of the wild frontier. Toward the end of the summer when business slacked off, an occasional tourist wandered in, gawked at the gas lanterns hanging overhead, the potbelly stove with its Grecian urn, the open barrels of dried fruit, stacks of clothing, the talking machine, and commented, "Isn't this a quaint little store! Oh, my, are those fresh donuts?"

Melina knew that they were holdovers from the day before, but she watched her father's response. "Oh, yah! They're just barely cool," he said as he moved to fill their order.

The Glacier Cash Grocery catered to the local Blackfeet families. When their lease money arrived on the first of the month, the family store welcomed them with a mouth-watering cauldron of spicy beef stew bubbling and simmering on the back of Clara's stove. The enticing bouquet of herbs encouraged them to spend money as they browsed amongst the merchandise. When their orders were filled and paid for, orders that always included some of Clara's donuts and molasses cakes, Glenn served them each a free bowl of succulent stew, a mosaic of garden vegetables and hearty chunks of meat. The business arrangement worked well.

Summer in Glacier Park lasted a mere three or four months. Wood smoke, the pungent, veiled fragrance of a drowsy community, curled from the chimneys, drifted upward, lingered briefly in the intimate hush, and heralded the arrival of killing frosts and winter weather. To preserve heat, they closed off the east bedroom that opened into the store. In the family bedroom Glenn and GC slept in one bed; Melina and Clara slept in the other. Clara always referred to her husband as Mr. Smiley, he simply called her Clara. The parents displayed no affection toward each other, the children received no hugs, no kisses. It was not the family's way, but the children knew that they were loved.

The dark season with high winds and heavy snows confined them to the store as snowdrifts ten, twelve, fifteen feet high cut them off from their neighbors except for the white-walled alleyways each family shoveled to the toilet, the barn, out to the narrowly-plowed streets. During whiteouts, students were held captive at school until rescuing parents, snow-shrouded bodies like abominable snowmen, bundled their children in layers, clutched them by the hand, and blindly guided them home through the labyrinth of narrow pathways while the storm raged in its attempt to bury the town, to batter the residents into submission. But for the family battened down inside the homely shelter of the Glacier Cash Grocery, the smell of buttered popcorn filled the air, the talking machine cranked out their favorite tunes, Glenn and GC concentrated on a game of checkers while Melina played school with her dolls, those naughty children who never got their lessons quite right.

When the storm subsided and relinquished its hold over the land, the people dug their way out and persevered in their struggle against Mother Nature. The steady rhythm of snow shovels, scooping and dumping, cleared concealed pathways. Squeaking boots crunched the frozen snow like splintered glass in the sub-zero air. The children tumbled outside, climbed the highest banks, dug snow caves and sat inside like Eskimos in a hunting lodge, played fox and geese with their friends while Clara made snow candy, a caramel concoction of brown sugar, syrup, water, and butter. She cooked it to the hard-ball stage, then cooked some more until drips fell from the spoon in long, hairy threads, floated on the air. She took the pan outside, drizzled the dark brown sweetness onto the clean snow creating animal shapes that snapped, crackled, sank into the snow where the children lifted them out with their mittened hands, held the delicate glassy shapes in the air, and devoured the creatures one leg at a time.

Clara's heavy baking schedule eased off to a few days each month. Her garden lay buried beneath its white, protective covering, and she fed her chickens special feed to encourage more eggs during the winter months with their short daylight hours. She used the extra hours to sew. She made patchwork quilts and pillows; she bleached white flour sacks for dish towels and embroidered them with designs. She sewed new dresses and mended the family clothing. She gathered boards, fine wire mesh, screws, and nails and helped GC build rabbit traps like she and Charley used to make, took him to the fields, taught him how to set and bait the traps. Shortness of breath and chest pain occasionally left her lightheaded and weak, but she dismissed it as unimportant and didn't tell the children as the calm of winter allowed her to regain her strength.

The five daily newspapers arrived regularly. While Glenn lay on the daybed behind the potbelly stove, tended the store, and read the news of the world beneath the mantled glow of the gas lantern, GC and Melina sat nearby engrossed in the funny papers. The family didn't maintain any kind of schedule, and most nights they stayed up together until well past midnight until they wandered off to bed one by one.

Time Will Help You Glacier Park

I've traveled all its worth
Many times around the earth.
I've traveled by ships and by wheels,
I've been far above the eagle's squeals.
I've traveled in the sun and in the shade
In the most beautiful places God ever made
And after all my traveling around,
At last I've found
A place I like the best,
So here I built myself a cozy little nest.
And I feel like my neighbors do
So carefree and so contented always ready to tell
Living interesting stories, letting it out
Why we all are happy as a lark
To be living in Glacier Park.
Well making a long story short
When the good old summertime ends,
You will realize that you met your dearest friends
That you idolize and love the dearest on earth.
Memories that are so sweet
Gained in Glacier Park's cheerful street.
Believe it or not you will
find the best people right in Glacier Park.
They cheer the very atmosphere,
and you can't forget their handshakes and wonderful
smiles.
That's Glacier Park.

Clara A. Smiley

Top horizontal row: Scale, cash register, and Smiley family personal account.
Second row, left: Clara tending her chickens; *center*: Glenn's meat market behind John Lindhe's store; *right*: Melina, age 9.
Third row, left: Glenn's log pile where men passing through could chop wood to pay for their food; *right*: The first log house built for the Smileys in Glacier Park—the barn is in the background.
Fourth row, left: Ledger page showing the prices of meat; *center*: GC; *right*: GC and friends clowning around.

PART V

Voices of the Children

The children regarded their parents very differently. Glenn read whenever he had a spare moment, Clara fascinated the children with original stories, but seldom glanced at the written page. Glenn had a keen talent for making money; Clara would give away her last possession if she had the chance. She boasted about the children's musical achievements in her letters to Emma even though she, herself, no longer wasted time on such frivolous activities.

In the sleepy, midwestern town of Center Point, Iowa, S.L. Smiley, Glenn's father had been an upright member of the community where he operated a hardware store, speculated in land, made good money, and built a large Victorian home. A carefree childhood like his own was what Glenn wanted for his children. Drudgery described Clara's formative years as the

Miller children became slaves to the land, victims of a father's ambition to achieve prosperity in the new country. And so for very different reasons, Glenn and Clara wanted their children to live a life without restraint, without want. It was a new generation.

At Christmas, Glenn selected the largest Christmas tree he could squeeze into the living quarters. They decorated it with popcorn and cranberry strings and little ornaments created from candy wrappers. The parents showered their children

Stuart Leslie Smiley, father of Glenn Cecil, and Edna

with gifts. They each had a Flexible Flyer for sledding with their friends, GC had a multitude of toy cars, Melina mothered fifty-two dolls. Glenn bought them a miniature cardboard store with display cases and pop-out shelves. In the winter they played "store" assuming different roles while imitating local customers and their parents. "I've got a check coming in next Tuesday, so I'll pay you then," answered by, "No, no, I gotta have the cash today." Conversations of everyday life.

Glenn adored his two children; their possessions knew no end. They each had a dog. They raised goats, rabbits, canaries, and homing pigeons, and he organized a rodeo for them and their friends every 4th of July. When GC got his first Indian pony, Diamond, Melina had to have Snipacasnooze, Snip for short.[1] What one child had, the other child wanted as well. They pastured their ponies in a nearby grassy field where Joe McGregor, the colorful owner of the Bison Creek Dude Ranch, kept some of his horses.[2]

They both had saddles back at the house, but preferred to ride bareback with a halter. They galloped along the wagon road out to the homestead, hair blowing in the wind, voices shouting, hooves pounding along the dusty road resonant with the smell of warm pine needles, past the whispering aspens, over glaciated hills mottled with pink carpets of moss campion, urging their sure-footed ponies ever onward down to the log cabin to visit Charlie and to collect rhubarb for Clara's pies.

Melina rode her beloved pony Snipacasnooze every day. Sometimes she rode as far as Heart Butte with her father, she frequently rode out to Lake Lubec.

Each year the children's summer explorations on horseback went farther afield as they prowled on the fringes of civilization, hunted for treasures, discovered old grave markers, found brick chimneys and residue of forsaken homestead shacks, rusted stoves, enameled pots riddled with buckshot, camphor tins and liniment bottles. They peered through the windows of deserted cabins where, in one derelict shanty, they spied an upright piano, lonely and abandoned, begging to be adopted. They rode home at breakneck speed, slid off the backs of their ponies and dashed inside the store where they babbled about the treasure, interrupting each other, their volume increasing with excitement. Glenn listened somberly, then rode back with them to take a look for himself.

The three explorers wiped the dust off the window and shaded their eyes against the reflected glare as they studied the treasured instrument at length. Covered with dust, encased in spider webs, it lacked a few ivories, but looked solid enough. "Oh, please, Daddy," GC begged, "won't you buy us that piano? We really want it!"

Without realizing that mice and moths had feasted on the felt hammers, he located the absentee owner, agreed to pay $100, and moved it to the store. A piano tuner came on the train from Great Falls to renovate its interior, to replace missing keys, and returned home a richer man, but the children loved music, Clara was thrilled, and Glenn felt that he'd made a sound investment in his children's happiness.

Although Clara had enjoyed playing her organ back in the soddy and had left her piano in Minnesota with Charley, she couldn't teach her own children to play. She simply didn't have the time, so a local music teacher came to the house, and the children practiced diligently under Glenn's watchful eye.

The inseparable duo gallivanted on their ponies with their Indian friends through the warm months of summer. A gallop southeast of town to the shale banks of the Two Medicine River provided daring adventure where the riverbank sloped to the tumbling waters below. Urging their sure-footed ponies over the precipice, the mounted band of urchins watched loose shale cascade before them as they plummeted into the canyon where the animals waded across the river, or if the water ran deep, swam across while the mighty riders encouraged them onward. It might have been dangerous, but no one cautioned them.

Being preoccupied with baking, the chickens, and gardening, Clara was only too glad to have her husband do the parenting of her children. On hot summer days, dust-caked sweat smeared their bodies like a renegade tribe of little people decorated with Mother Nature's war paint. Hot and miserable with stringy hair standing straight up from her forehead where sweaty palms pushed clinging strands out of her eyes, Melina became the liaison between the motley gang and her dad.

Midafternoon, hot and humid without a breath of wind. Glenn relaxed on his daybed reading his newspaper behind the potbelly stove that stood cold and serene. Melina galloped to the door, threw one leg over Snip's neck and slid to the ground. She entered the store, sidled up to him, snuggled close to his side in spite of the sweltering heat. She took his hand in her own as she earnestly gazed up into his face. He glanced down at her sun-bleached hair, dirty face. She oozed the sweet, pungent smell of a sweaty child, radiated heat like a furnace.

"Well, what's up?" he asked.

She tried to be casual. "Daddy," she said, "we want to go swimming. We found a good spot at the bend of the Two Medicine River where the water runs deep. Can we try it?"

He solemnly studied her eager face as he thought it over. Finally he agreed. "Yah," he said. "You could do that. You know, there is a whirlpool there, and it sucks anything under that tries to swim there, and we never see them again," he paused, "but if you want to go, you go."

He returned to his newspaper while Melina contemplated the situation, envisioned herself spinning out of control, being sucked into the churning funnel, disappearing into a deep, black hole under the water, probably to the center of the earth. As an afterthought, he put down the newspaper and continued, "Just tell me who you want to feed your horse after you're gone."

"I don't want anybody to feed my horse!" she said. "He's mine!"

"Well," he continued in his conversational way, "You'd better leave word with me so someone can take care of your horse, because if you go swimming there, you're not coming back. You'll be drowned." He commenced reading the newspaper once again, and the thoughtful messenger left the store with no further interest in swimming at the bend of the Two Medicine River.

Like all kids, they tried to make money. There wasn't a shortage of money; they could have all of the money they wanted. All they had to do was put a little slip of paper in the cash register to let their parents know how much they'd taken; there were no restrictions on them. But they wanted to earn their own money.

In March they trudged over the snow banks from house to house selling packets of garden seeds. People looked at them like they were crazy. Garden seeds! Are you out of your mind? their eyes said as they shut the door. The two salesmen shrugged it off. Their ma raised a garden; they couldn't see why other people didn't do it.

Next came Cloverine Salve. Told people it would cure chapped lips, heal a burn, dry up a cold sore, impetigo, flea bites, poison ivy. Buy some salve, receive a colorful poster picture to hang on the wall, decorate a bedroom, perk up the kitchen. That was a hot item. They earned a Brownie camera, then a telescope, but the neighbors finally tired of the Smiley kids standing on the doorstep with the latest product from a magazine ad or the funny papers. They'd come to the store and say, "Glenn, keep those kids away from us. They're always bothering us to buy something!" but he believed in free enterprise and usually sold the complainers a pair of gloves, a hunk of cheese, perhaps a few donuts before they left.

GC, ambitious and conscientious, hauled wood for the neighbors every night after school. He drew up an individual contract for each customer, had them sign on the dotted line, and for a dollar a week he kept their wood boxes filled. In the middle of winter when darkness came early, Melina helped him meet his deadlines...for a fee, of course.

He took meticulous care of his possessions; he kept each

item in a special drawer, on a shelf, in a box under the bed, never threw anything away. He managed money carefully, kept himself on a budget. He raised turkeys and ducks that he sold at a profit, he bred canaries and sold them to the neighbors. After Glenn helped him register his own brand, SIA, he bought a second pony (for speculation) named G. Whizz. Later on, he invested in a buckskin mare without involving his parents. His sidekick Melina witnessed the bill of sale.

Melina liked to make money, too. During her seventh summer, she got her first regular baby-sitting job. "We'll pay you twenty-five cents an hour to take care of our little girl while we go to Mass," they offered.

Melina sized up the two-year-old; she wasn't a crybaby or a tattletale. She played with her every day anyway, so she decided that she might as well get paid for it. "Do we have to stay in the house?" she asked in her business-like way.

"No, you can take her outside," the mother said.

Every Sunday morning Melina arrived at the appointed time, barefoot, wearing her usual faded bib overalls and a cotton shirt. She played with dolls, stacked blocks, entertained her charge until the parents left for church. When the coast was clear, she pushed open the creaking screen door, checked in all directions to be sure that the adults were out of sight, then led the child outside around the corner where Snip waited patiently for her return. Hoisting the toddler into the saddle, Melina climbed up behind her, fastened the little fingers around the saddle horn, held her around the waist with one arm, and galloped off toward the open field. Riding horseback while baby-sitting a two-year-old was a great way to make money.

The job lasted for several months until a new baby joined the family. When the couple asked her to baby-sit for both children, Melina knew that her baby-sitting days on horseback were over. "Well," she said, "it's gonna cost you more money."

"Why?" the lady asked.

"You paid me twenty-five cents an hour for one child, but now I'll have twice as much work. It'll cost you fifty cents."

Two blocks from the Glacier Cash Grocery, a red brick school served sixty students in two rooms. It also housed a stage and a gym where community meetings were held in the evenings. The Indian children, Blackfeet and Cree, far outnumbered the white children. The differences between their talents and hers perplexed Melina as she sat at the table with her legs wrapped around the chair legs while concentrating on a drawing assignment for the teacher. She chewed on her eraser and contemplated the mystery.

"Ma," she finally asked, "why can Billy Big Spring draw so good? His horses look like real horses. Mine look like they're creatures from outer space or something. And when the Indian boys play basketball they always run faster, jump higher, and shoot better than anyone else. Why is that, Ma?"

"Oh, that just means we all have different talents, Melina. They probably aren't as good at music as you and GC," she answered.

Melina accepted that without comment; none of her friends played the piano, but she had another question.

"Ma, what's a picnic? Every year the new teacher promises us a picnic at the end of the year, and we never have one. What's a picnic?" Because of the remoteness of Glacier Park and its isolation in the winter, new teachers arrived and left with frequency. To reward the students for their hard work, every new teacher made the same promise to have an end-of-the-year picnic, but they didn't know about the local weather. The school year generally ended around May 20, and the longed-for event usually produced a snowstorm, heavy rain, or hurricane-type wind. Melina had been promised a picnic for three years; she wanted to know what she was missing.

"Oh, it doesn't amount to much," Clara answered as she

continued with her work. "You just make a bunch of sand-wiches, then go sit under a tree and eat."

Melina frowned. "Is that all? It doesn't sound like much fun to me," she said as she returned to her drawing. She never participated in a school picnic at Glacier Park; she never felt a sense of loss.

But she loved everything about school. She played school for hours on the long winter weekends, organized her fifty-two dolls, arranged them into grade levels across the bed where she instructed them in the finer points of reading, writing, and math, although that was not one of her favorite subjects. After one particularly enthusiastic lesson, she ran out to the day-bed and grabbed Glenn by the hand. "Daddy, come and visit my school. I'm the teacher and my students are all waiting for you!"

He looked at the somber arrangement of studious dolls as Melina explained her teaching techniques. "These are the older grades at this end of the bed. I write their assignments on the chalkboard and they work quietly while I go to the little dolls over there and teach a reading lesson, then while they copy in their workbooks, I go back to the big kids!"

Her eyes sparkled with excitement. "When I grow up, Daddy, I'm going to be a teacher, and I'm going to teach right over there at my red school. And at the end of every month I'll bring you a big sack of money!"

He chuckled as he listened to her enthusiasm, ruffled her hair with his hand. "You just do that," he said.

Mike's Place continued to gear itself to family gatherings and became the cultural center of Glacier Park. Every summer Ed Prader and his five-piece band, the evening entertainment at Mike's Place, rented one of Glenn's log cabins where they could practice without disturbing the neighbors. Ed, the pianist, prac-ticed on the children's piano, sometimes the entire band held an afternoon jam session in the store causing the rafters to rock and canned goods to bounce from the shelves while tourists crowded inside for a free show. On Saturday nights Glenn took the children over to Mike's Place to hear Ed's band play, a band with class, one that wore matching jackets, white shirts and bow ties, a band that raised the social level of the community, showed the dudes from back east that this was no hick town.

With his mustache trimmed and thinning hair slicked back over the bald spot, Ed turned the cuffs of his shirt back over the sleeves of his jacket. He sat on the piano stool, arranged his feet on the pedals, and loosened up. He rolled his shoulders backward and forward, lolled his head from one side to the other to relax the neck muscles, stretched his long tapered fingers, exercised them, limbered them up in mid-air, admired their dexterity, gave the count, and the music began. Melina squeezed herself onto the end of the bench closest to him where she could watch the blur of his hands while her fingers danced on her knees. If only I could learn to play like that, she dreamed.

"How do people know where to put their feet when they dance?" she asked one evening. Thus, the dancing lessons began. Clara cranked up the talking machine, placed the needle on the record while Glenn taught the children to waltz, two-step, and polka. In late evenings when business slacked off, the parents danced with their children, practiced for weeks gliding and bouncing, counted out the steps, and circled around the potbelly stove.

What were Clara's thoughts about her husband's business dealings as he confronted delinquent renters, forced hungry men to work for their meals while she clandestinely gave food away, allowed customers to pay later? And what about the children who watched the goings-on with wide eyes, who imitated their parents when they played store, who made judgments of their own?

*Glenn Cecil's sister Edna and his mother Iowa Smiley astride
their horses at the Lubec homestead*

One time when Clara asked Melina to deliver a loaf of warm bread to a neighbor, the woman said, "Tell your ma that I'll pay later."

Melina shrewdly looked at the woman and knew that she never paid. "No!" she retorted as she jerked the bread away. "Gimme the quarter now or the bread goes back to the store."

The Glacier Cash Grocery tried to anticipate the needs of the community as Glenn stockpiled baled hay and grain in the barn, sheltered pigs, horses, and young stock for a fee and sold sacks of feed to the owners. The barn held rope, harnesses, hardware supplies, and a plethora of goods a settler might want without venturing a trip to Browning.

Glacier Park experienced a booming economy as tourists flocked by the thousands to visit the new national park with its majestic scenery, trail rides, big game hunting, hiking and fishing. Engineers finalized their plans for the completion of the highway over Marias Pass, an engineering feat that would deliver even more tourists to their doorstep, while the Glacier Cash Grocery counted dollar signs rising in the East.

Late at night in the fall of 1927, men shouting and a commotion behind the store stirred Glenn from his sleep, a whiff of smoke brought him to his feet. He pushed aside the curtains; a dark, rosy glow illuminated the bedroom, a dreaded scenario. "The barn is on fire!" he shouted hoarsely as he shook Clara awake, struggled into his clothes, searched for a missing shoe that he held in his hand.

The children leaped out of bed and stared at the burning building, hypnotized by tongues of flames flickering between the logs. Disoriented and disheveled from sleep, Clara pulled a dress over her nightgown; she sat on the edge of the bed unable to catch her breath, dizzy, an arrhythmic pulse in her temples as memories of the prairie fire flashed before her. The swirling smoke, the choking ash, and crackle of the flames encompassed her once again, a nightmare resurrected. What if the winds change and blow the sparks toward the store, she worried. What if the entire block goes up in flames? But a more immediate emergency rose to the forefront. "We've got to save my cow!" she cried as she moved toward the door.

With Glenn in the lead, the family raced out to the barn to rescue the animals. Choking masses of smoke poured from cracks, erupted through the roof. Animal screams ripped through the night as distraught neighbors broke the door lock, attempted to rescue the beasts and appease the fire. Being a primitive town, Glacier Park had no equipment to fight fires. They had no hoses, they had no organized plan.

Some of the renters plunged into the smoky interior to release their horses. Glenn covered his nose and mouth with a neckerchief as he dashed forward in an attempt to free his young stock and Clara's cow, but it was too late. Death-screams from dying pigs echoed into the night, horses broke loose from the barn with blazing backs while men tried to smother the flames with their coats. The nauseous stench of burning flesh was borne on the wind; the impending death of innocent creatures silenced those who witnessed the furor. With the barn totally engulfed in flames, the clouded sky over east Glacier Park reflected a crimson radiance and illuminated the holocaust below while the hysterical Melina hid her face in the folds of her mother's skirt, occasionally peeked at the inferno as the ravaged building collapsed upon itself sending sparks and embers hundreds of feet into the sky.

Mrs. Hickson, a neighbor and close family friend, wrapped her arms around Clara's shoulders and tried to move her and the children away from the intensity of the heat. The wrinkles around her eyes deepened as she squinted to fend off the heavy smoke. Towering flames reflected off her gold tooth as she watched open-mouthed at dazzling sparks floating overhead. Hugging the threesome tightly, she consoled them with the pretension of calm. "Don't cry, Clara. Mr. Smiley's all right, and some of the animals have been rescued," but she, herself, felt weak with despair for the family's loss.

Long time friends from across the tracks swarmed to their aid, but the intense heat and incredible fury of the flaming winds forced the rescuers to retreat when they realized that all was lost. The massive logs of the barn fueled the unappeasable appetite of the surging flames; all they could do was watch.

Six horses had been salvaged, but for several days the smoldering, charred remains of the young stock and pigs continued to emit the stench of death. Dying embers smoked from the depths, feathery clouds of ash hovered and swirled through the town. Clara avoided looking at the pyre as she mourned the passing of her Jersey cow that lay buried somewhere beneath the twisted mass of blackened timbers. She harvested the last vegetables of the season; she dug potatoes and pulled rutabagas with abandon, hoped that hard work might help allay her grief while the children averted their eyes from the devastation, looked the other way when they rode past on their ponies.

Glenn hired a crew of men to clear the site. Masking their noses with heavy kerchiefs to avoid the malodorous fumes that rose from the rubble, they used picks and shovels to claw their way through charred carcasses and burned timbers, loaded the debris onto heavy wagons and buried it outside of town.

Times were changing. The automobile had replaced the horse and buggy; there was little demand for hay and feed. Local farmers could provide beef and pork, several neighbors sold milk and butter, so Glenn decided not to rebuild the barn, left the corner lot empty and barren, hinted that maybe someday he'd build a house on that site, another rental to "pay the freight."

Glenn's interest in politics began when he first moved to Lubec. His former business partner, John Lindhe, served a term as county commissioner; his longtime acquaintance, John Coburn from Cut Bank, served two terms in the State Legislature and, in 1928,[3] Glenn became increasingly involved as he registered voters, attended rallies, and campaigned around the community for the Democrats.

His dog, Duke, a massive, long-haired mongrel, perhaps a cross between a boxer and a St. Bernard that he'd rescued beside the road some years before, accompanied him on his rounds. Duke's loyalty was admirable; he seldom left Glenn's side, but he was old and arthritic, and the early October snows were taking their toll on his health as he hobbled along beside his master.

Glenn studied old Duke twitching in his sleep near the stove. "Ya know, Clara," he said softly, "I think I'll put Duke out of his misery. He's been such a good old dog, but the rheumatism in his hips makes it hard for him to get around. He limps when he follows me to the post office." The children listened in silence.

Clara looked at Duke's time-worn body quivering and jerking on his blanket; his body had the stink of sickness. She could smell him across the room. "Well, maybe you should," she agreed.

From his bed, Duke watched Glenn with rheumy eyes, waited in calm anticipation for a command. Clara acknowledged that he had always been a one-man dog, but she added, "He's always made me feel safe. I'm a-gonna miss him."

Glenn passed the morning hours stocking shelves and doing small jobs around the store as he contemplated Duke's weakening condition. Finally convinced that he was embarking on a mission of mercy, he put on his jacket, removed the rifle from the rack. With Duke limping along behind, he stepped outside into the frosty air and walked east toward the horse pasture. Clara and the children watched from the window as he paused from time to time, patted Duke on the head, allowed the dog's aching bones to rest, then continued on. She turned away, pondered how to console her husband on his return. He loved that old mongrel.

At a fair distance from town, Glenn stopped. "Stay, Duke!" he ordered. Glenn backed off, unsteadily raised the rifle to his shoulder, and aimed. Duke's wagging tail distracted him. Glenn lowered the weapon.

"Come along, boy," he said as he scratched Duke behind the ears and moved farther from town. Twice more he raised his gun to relieve Duke from his suffering, but he couldn't do it. The devotion that gazed from those warm, brown eyes filled him with guilt whenever he shouldered the gun, and he finally returned home with his faithful friend limping along behind.

Listening for Glenn's return and anticipating her husband's sadness, Clara worried about his grief, shed a few tears as she waited. She turned as the outside door opened. From the kitchen she watched him replace the rifle on the pegs while Duke staggered to his bed. She smiled and returned to her work.

The presidential race between Al Smith and Herbert Hoover commanded Glenn's undivided attention for months. He was an Al Smith man, a Democrat, a party man, and voted a straight ticket. He contacted eligible voters on the fringe of the wilderness. He set a schedule of events for himself and abided by it, even though the weather became nasty, and he caught a chill. Not one to submit to illness and regarding all doctors as quacks, he pushed himself to exhaustion as he plowed his way through snowstorms and freezing temperatures. The urgency of a Democratic sweep was foremost in his mind.

On Saturday, November 3, Glenn came home earlier than usual accompanied by Charlie Tobin who had come in from Lubec to stay a few days with the family. He wanted to attend the local rallies; he enjoyed election hype. Glenn felt chilled. He hugged the warmth of the stove and sneaked sips of whiskey from a hidden flask. GC sat near Charlie, made small talk with him, and hoped Ma wouldn't catch Dad drinking because it would mean war. One time she scolded so angrily about the effects of booze that Dad disappeared for two days, so he kept the secret to himself and swore Melina to silence.

Bustling about in her busy routine, Clara noticed her husband's unusual behavior. "What's the matter with Mr. Smiley?" she asked Charlie as he prepared to go downtown.

"Oh, nothing. He caught a little cold. Smiley's gonna be all right," he answered cheerfully.

Clara approached her husband and felt his forehead for fever as he sat and shivered. "I'm not feeling very well, Clara. I think I'll sleep in the spare bedroom where I won't disturb the family. Will you make me a bowl of oyster stew? That might make me feel better." Apprehension clouded her mind. Glenn had never been ill nor had he ever slept away from the family.

A wary Melina watched him lie down on the bed in the spare bedroom, one they used as a summer rental. She'd never seen him like this. "Who's going to pump up the gas lantern for us tonight? How will we see?" she asked, hoping to maintain the family's evening routine.

"Oh, I'll do it later," he said as he crawled under the covers, but he didn't get up later and he didn't finish the bowl of oyster stew Clara served to him in bed. She watched with a worried eye. He loves oyster stew, yet he only ate half of it. Golly, there's something really wrong with him, she decided.

When Glenn awoke the next morning, churning, snowy winds were whipping the atmosphere into buttermilk. Feverish and weak, he swung his feet over the edge of the bed and sat quietly gathering his strength as he assured the family that he felt better after his night alone. Clara begged him to stay home, but he ignored her pleas. The urgency of the upcoming election made it imperative that he recruit a few more votes for the party, but he returned home earlier than usual. His cold had worsened as he traipsed from place to place and shivered his way through impromptu speeches in support of Al Smith. His lungs ached; short raspy breaths couldn't alleviate the pain that rippled through his chest, convulsed through the muscles of his arms. He closed his eyes and rested on the daybed while the disturbed children sat nearby, frightened at seeing him in his debilitated state.

In the kitchen, Clara somberly shared her concerns about Glenn's condition with Mrs. Hickson whose healing powers were well known in the area. Mrs. Hickson turned in her chair. Heavy creases at the corners of shrewd eyes deepened as she observed the sick man from a distance. He sat on the edge of the daybed with sagging shoulders, chest caved inward, arms hugging his body. He was unshaven, his eyes were closed, his mouth drawn down. He blew his nose into a square of white cloth, a raspy cough from deep in his chest loosened yellow viscous slime that he spat into a tin can. Mrs. Hickson mentally rummaged through her medicine bag of roots and herbs searching for the right concoction. She rose from her chair and approached him. Her long, black braids hung before her as she bent over the ailing man; she studied him with a practiced eye, listened to his labored breathing. "Mr. Smiley," she said, "you don't look very well. Let me make a mustard plaster for your chest. It will draw out the pain; you'll feel a lot better."

"No, I'll be just fine," he weakly responded as he waved her away.

The children had been invited to an evening party across town, but they were reluctant to leave the house. They sat close to their father and watched for signs of improvement. The hidden flask appeared more frequently as the keen bite of its contents calmed his fevered mind, anesthetized his pain.

Clara had never seen him sit on the daybed without something to read. Sometimes he read until 2 A.M. "Mr. Smiley," she asked, "wouldn't you like your newspapers to read?"

"No, I'm just fine, but I think I'll go to bed now. You kids go to your party and have a good time. You go ahead now," he said as he struggled to his feet, shuffled into the bedroom for another night of seclusion.

Clara fluffed the pillows and offered him hot soup. She didn't like the sound of his rattled breathing; she sat near his bed and talked about the election with him. The children reluctantly attended their party, but their hearts weren't into silly games, and an hour after they arrived, Clara fetched them home. Glenn's condition had worsened. There was no light in his bedroom—only rhythmic, labored rasps of breath revealed his presence. Bewildered by the darkness of the room, the children tiptoed to his bedside and wished that he would get up, that he would get well and sit out on his daybed where they always spent the evenings together, but the shivering body beneath the blankets made no attempt to rise.

The heavy, planked door of the Glacier Cash Grocery opened as a fellow campaigner stomped out of the darkness into the somber gathering and brushed snow from his jacket. His great bulk blocked out the lamplight of the store as he stood in the bedroom doorway. "Hey, Smiley, how's it going? You've gotta be well to help with the election. Remember the rally tomorrow night. We need you there!" his boisterous voice boomed.

From the darkness of his bed, concealed beneath the visitor's shadow, Glenn answered, "Oh, yah, I'll be fine." His promise to get better set the children's troubled minds somewhat at ease, but Clara wasn't so sure.

On Monday, November 5, the day before the election, Glenn returned to the campaign trail despite the fact that he felt worse. Duke staggered to his feet and followed him into the cold. November promised to be a miserable month. The outside temperature had plummeted, and seven inches of snow covered the ground, but that didn't deter him from his mission. An evening rally was scheduled at the school, and he felt obligated to get the voters out for this last-ditch effort to elect the Democrats to office, but at 3 p.m. he returned home and collapsed in bed.

Confused by his behavior, Melina and GC watched with troubled eyes. Going to bed in the middle of the afternoon was unheard of. "What's going on, Daddy?" they asked as they sat beside the bed.

"I don't feel well," he replied. "It's just a bad cold."

Clara bustled around the bed and tucked him beneath the quilts, but he didn't want to be bothered. "Oh, I'll be all right. I just want to be here by myself," he said. "Just don't bother me." He continued to medicate himself with sips from the flask. Its soothing comfort helped him rest and numbed the pain in his chest. The children continued their watchful surveillance and kept him covered as he slept.

At 6 p.m. Clara lit a kerosene lamp and set it beside the bed, then brought him a steamy bowl of chicken soup. In a weaker state, he sat up and swallowed its healing broth, then collapsed back onto the pillow. "I feel pretty rough," he murmured. A morose foreboding spread its shadow over the somber family; the children continued their vigilant attendance and listened for each breath to assure themselves that he was improving. Clara removed the soup bowl and stood outside the bedroom door in the hollow gloom of the store.

The gas lantern wasn't any dimmer than usual, but tonight, deprived of Glenn's unrestrained laughter, she felt like she was spiraling into darkness. Ever since that April day when she'd jumped off the train in her wedding dress and followed her new husband to the shores of Lake Lubec, she had abandoned her desire for independence and relied on Glenn for her strength. Now, thirteen years later, she had to make a major decision alone. Thus, Clara confided to the children that she intended to telephone the doctor and that everything would be okay once he arrived, but the children both knew that calling a doctor was the last hope.

Disregarding her husband's belief that all doctors were quacks, Clara pulled on a heavy coat and stepped into the biting November wind where she walked through the darkness to the Log Cabin Inn and telephoned for a doctor to come from Browning. He promised to arrive on the train at 9:30 P.M. The children remained at Glenn's side. GC talked to him and gave him sips of water; Melina held his hand. Sometimes the patient opened his eyes and smiled.

At 9:45 P.M. an elderly doctor emerged from the darkness. He removed his hat and coat, opened his leather bag, and began to examine the patient. Glenn opened his eyes and recognized the intruder. "What do you want? What are you doing here?" he said. "I don't want you here!"

"Well, I'm going to try and help you," the doctor replied as he placed his hand on Glenn's forehead and felt for fever. Major and Mrs. James Monteath, close friends who lived across the street, owners of the first hotel built in Glacier Park,[4] stood at the foot of the bed and watched the examination. Clara had stopped at their house on her way back from the Log Cabin Inn and asked them to join the family. It would make her feel better to have close friends at hand. Old Duke made thwarted attempts to sneak into the room to lie by the bed. He crawled on his belly to make himself inconspicuous; he seemed to sense that something was terribly wrong, but the visitors expelled the smelly mongrel to the store, finally put him outside.

At 10 P.M. some of the fellows from the rally came back to the house with Charlie to see why Glenn hadn't attended. They crowded into the small room, gathered around the bed and talked about the meeting. The doctor reached into his vest pocket and withdrew a gold watch at the end of a braided chain. He snapped open the filigree lid and checked the time. It was getting late, and he had to catch the next train back to Browning or spend the night at Glacier Park. Snapping the cover shut he returned the timepiece to his pocket and interrupted the discussion. "Well, I think I'll give him a shot so he'll sleep well tonight. He'll probably be all right in the morning."

Glenn's face flushed. He raised up. His head pounded, his pulse throbbed as he croaked, "Oh, no! I don't want a shot. I don't want a shot!" The children had never heard him so distressed. His panic alarmed them. Clara desperately wanted him to get well, but his undisguised terror at getting a shot made her question whether she'd made the right decision by calling the doctor.

"Oh, he's just trying to help you, Smiley," someone said.

Disregarding Glenn's wishes, the doctor prepared a hypodermic needle from a vial and approached the bed with his thumb on the plunger. Glenn shouted, "No! I *don't* want a shot!" as he sat up and shoved the doctor backward against the wall.

Violence was not part of her husband's nature; the confrontation confused Clara. The stress of the past few days and now his terror of the needle was too much. Pain constricted her chest; she couldn't catch her breath, she clutched at her throat and gasped for air.

Not to be challenged in his line of duty, the doctor barked, "Hold him down! He has to have this shot, and I don't want to break the needle!"

The men saw for themselves the seriousness of Glenn's illness; he was delirious and since the doctor said it had to be done, they moved to the bed and held down his arms and legs as commanded. The children watched in horror as their father kicked and fought to wrench himself free, but it was to no avail, and the doctor administered the shot in the night.

"I've done about all I can do," he said to Glenn as he put away the needle, packed his black bag and snapped it shut. "You'll sleep now."

Seeing Clara's stricken face, he reassured her. "He'll be just fine in the morning. I'll be in touch with you in a couple of days." Quickly retrieving his hat and coat, he departed into the winter darkness to catch his train. It was 10:45 P.M.

Apprehensive about the commotion caused by the doctor, the children watched their father for signs of improvement. Since no one in the family had ever been examined by a doctor before, they didn't know what to expect. Momentarily, Glenn raised his head and listened to the thinning crowd talk about the rally, then fell back onto the pillows gasping for air. In his weakened state he motioned Clara to come closer. She rose from the chair and bent over his body. Tucking the quilt around his shoulders she looked into his face and strained to hear his throaty whispers. "You be sure to get out and vote for the Democrats tomorrow," he murmured. "I don't expect to be here."

Her chest convulsed. She slumped to the floor and lay motionless.

"Quick, get her a cup of coffee!" someone shouted.

"No!" Charlie answered. "In her condition she'd choke to death. She hasn't fainted, this is an angina attack. I've helped her through them before." Charlie knew what to do. He raised her to a sitting position on the floor and began swinging her arms, jump-starting her back to life. Within a few minutes her breathing returned to normal, and the men helped her onto the chair, but in the frenzied activity to revive Clara, no one noticed the frightened children clinging to each other in the mistaken belief that both parents were dying.

At 10:55 P.M., oblivious of his surroundings, Glenn closed his eyes one last time and took a labored breath. His spirit was gone, he'd given up. Surrounded by those he loved, he drifted more deeply toward a comatose state, and within the half hour, he was dead.

Charlie felt for a pulse at Glenn's throat, pressed his ear against his chest, listened for a heartbeat. Too stunned by the sudden tragedy of the evening to shed tears, the children stood mute at the bedside, held hands, refused to believe the worst even when Charlie pulled the sheet over their father's face.

Mrs. Hickson, always nearby in troubled times, placed a comforting hand on Clara's shoulder. Shorty Hynes stared at the floor quietly absorbed in his own thoughts as he fiddled with his hat; other friends had departed with the doctor. Clara wanted to be courageous for her children, but the stress of the past week and fear of another angina attack left her feeling drained. She remained on the chair to gather her strength. "Charlie," she said at last, "will you take the children across the street to the Monteaths'?"

Mrs. Hickson, a widow herself, said, "Shorty, let's wait out here and give Clara some time alone with her husband," as she urged him toward the bedroom door.

Thankful for the time alone, Clara remained by the bed in muted shock. She swayed, gently rocking on the edge of the chair not seeing the shrouded body, but remembering the lovely times long ago when they'd shared the beauty of the full moon rising above Lake Lubec, reflected from diamond ripples that lapped the shore, and the time he'd surprised her with the beautiful talking machine, and the time he'd built that wobbly chicken house for her baby chicks even though he didn't know what he was doing.

Never again would the store echo with his laughter as he joked with friends. She'd miss how his bright eyes danced with pride over their children's accomplishments. She recalled the evening when he'd bounced into the room after a school program and said, "Oh, Clara, our kids played their three piano duets "Flying Pigeons," "Melody," and "Chatter" beautifully. Our kids never made one mistake, not one!" She remembered how Mrs. Matermach, GC's teacher, had stopped by the store on her way home to compliment them on their children's achievement, and how Mr. Smiley required them to practice in front of an audience regularly, remembered how anyone who shopped at Smiley's store might be subjected to listening to his kids play the piano.

"Oh, Mr. Smiley," she cried out, "it's a blessing to be in your heavenly home where everyone is healthy and happy, but how am I a-gonna raise your two kiddies all by myself?"

Waves of anguish washed away the memories of lovely times drowning her in reality. Mrs. Hickson returned to her side and gently led her out and closed the bedroom door. "There will be time for mourning later, Clara, but now we need your help. Arrangements need to be made. Charlie and Shorty will go to the Log Cabin Inn and telephone for the embalmer to come from Browning tomorrow. You and I will select burial clothes for Mr. Smiley and clothes for you and the children for the next few days. Is there anything else?"

Clara wiped away tears, remembered a promise she'd made years ago, and sniffled into her handkerchief. "Mr. Smiley told me that he wanted to be buried beside his first wife in Center Point, Iowa, and I gave him my word." She paused; resented the unfairness of it all, but once again stood straight and tall in her grief. "Charlie, will you contact his mother and sister and make arrangements for the casket to be sent on the train?"

"Okay," he said, "but someone should accompany the body to Iowa. I think I should stay here with you and the kids."

Shorty volunteered. "I'll go, Clara," he said, "and don't worry about the chores or the store. I'll take care of that for you until I leave. You don't need to worry about a thing." Shorty's ambition and attention to detail set her mind at ease. One less thing to worry about, she sighed. After making arrangements with the undertaker, Glenn's two friends returned to stay with the body. And so the formalities began.

Mrs. Hickson, herself a stylishly dressed woman, selected proper clothes for the family. Clara swallowed the strangling lump in her throat and lifted Glenn's brown suit from the closet. She held it against her cheek longing to feel the strength of his body within, but it eluded her; he'd only worn it a few times. She tenderly brushed off the collar and removed lint from the sleeves. She selected a long-sleeved shirt and his favorite tie remembering how he always liked to look good. Expending her last bit of energy, she rubbed a shine on the brown leather shoes and placed them on the bed beside a new pair of socks and garters. With the burial wardrobe complete, she turned to the arms of her friend who led her away to her own home.

It was well past midnight when Mrs. Hickson retrieved the children from the Monteaths' where they'd fallen asleep in front of the fireplace after a cup of hot chocolate. "Tonight you'll sleep at my house. I have a nice bed waiting for you," she said as they walked the few blocks in the winter air. From her home, they would be unable to see the casket delivered, a decision she and the men had agreed upon beforehand to avoid more trauma to the family.

Watching his mother sob, GC said, "Brace up, Ma. Come on, brace up! Things are a-gonna be all right!" but in his heart he was unsure, and that night the three of them nestled together in a double bed, their arms and legs intertwined sharing the burden of their loss.

Election Day, November 6, 1928, dawned. Clara's determination to vote overcame her grief as she and the children walked hand in hand to the polling place at school, moved forward one step at a time, a lonely journey through empty streets hardly noticing the snow flurries that played on the wind. The children bolstered her with their strength as the desolate trio entered the building. She felt Glenn's presence when she voted a straight Democratic ticket, knew that he would have been pleased.

After responding to condolences from fellow voters, the family returned to Mrs. Hickson's where they withdrew from the public eye for the rest of the day. That night they shared a bed at the Monteath home, and again they sought strength from each other as they lay entangled beneath the quilts.

On Wednesday morning, November 7, Charlie, his face etched with sadness, arrived to escort the family to view the body. A swirling wind blew down from the mountains sculpting the snow into bony, white fingers that stretched across streets and vacant lots. Clad in her mourning clothes so carefully selected by Mrs. Hickson, Clara wore a black ensemble that matched her woeful demeanor. The children were in their best school clothes. Being the man of the family, a responsibility almost beyond his endurance at the age of eleven, GC supported his mother's arm and guided her with assurance he didn't feel. He wanted to cry out, to purge his system of its grief, but his new role, as he saw it, dare not show weakness. Melina clutched Charlie's hand, and the somber foursome forged their way in silence to the school two blocks away.

The stage area, concealed by dark curtains away from the classrooms, provided an appropriate setting for the sad event. They could hear Mrs. Rice, the Sunday School teacher, playing hymns on the piano as they entered the room. Glenn's brown, metallic casket lay open as people from the community passed by and paid their last respects to the man who had touched their lives. They couldn't believe that a vibrant member of the community could die so unexpectedly; it made them realize that the line between life and death was tenuous indeed. Clusters of folding chairs quickly filled with mourning friends who came to console the family and share stories about their good times with Glenn.

Charlie led Clara to the casket where she viewed her husband's body. He looks so lifelike, she thought as she examined each familiar feature. Dressed in his brown suit, he appeared younger than fifty-six. His dark hair hadn't turned gray at all except at the temples. And his complexion was rosy and natural. Clara felt thankful that he looked relaxed and peaceful after his illness. She hesitated at the casket not wanting to say goodbye. "He's with his Heavenly Father now, Charlie. Some day we'll all be together again where there is no sickness, no hard times, and no…" Tears flowed once again as Charlie led her away to a chair near friends. He, too, felt dazed by the loss of his best friend.

GC and Melina held hands and studied their father's body. He looked so natural. Melina refused to believe that he wasn't coming back. "He's just asleep," she murmured. "The doctor said that he's going to get better."

But her fragile window of hope shattered when GC put his arm around her trembling shoulders and said softly, "Nah, he's not a-gonna come back any more. He's gone. He really is dead."

His blunt statement brought her face to face with days of denial. Her eyes flashed terror as she turned and grabbed his shoulders; she shook him violently with both hands and bawled out like a wounded animal, "But who is going to take care of us?"

GC didn't respond. He didn't know the answer.

Mournful hymns droned in the background as people spoke in hushed voices. Unable to bear repeated condolences any longer, the children waited outside in silence. Their father had been the pillar of strength for the family. A future devoid of his nurturing guidance chilled them with fear, a frigid premonition far colder than the wind now descending upon them as they waited alone on the steps.

They watched six men carry the casket out of the school and place it on the back of their old flatbed truck; Shorty drove it to the depot. Clara and dozens of friends filed out of the building. The children walked beside her as the shivering crowd moved up the street in a solemn wave of mourning. The northwesterly wind whined. The temperature dropped. People pulled their coats snug to their bodies and held onto their hats as the somber procession made its way to the depot for the last goodbye.

The train hadn't yet arrived from Kalispell; Clara's friends crowded inside the small waiting room to comfort her. Other passengers waiting to return east observed the casket outside on the platform where GC and his nine-year-old sister stood like solemn soldiers; they wanted to spend the last few minutes close to their father. And so did a faithful friend. Old Duke, hobbling with arthritis, emerged from the blowing snow and dragged himself across the tracks. He whimpered beside the casket as the children patted his head and consoled him. They comprehended the depth of his grief; it matched their own.

The crowd heard the whistle of the Great Northern long before it came into view. They spilled onto the platform and waited in the deepening snow. Clara stood beside her children and watched the men move her husband's casket to the edge of the platform. It was storming just like this when I brought my new baby home and Mr. Smiley took us to the Log Cabin Inn, she wept soundlessly. She waited as they lifted the casket aboard; the doors slid shut. Shorty Hynes consulted her one last time. She slipped him some money, then he boarded the train to accompany the body of his friend back to Iowa. After eighteen years, Glenn was going home forever.

Clouds of steam erupted from the engine of the Great Northern as it prepared to depart. The whistle blew as the massive drive wheels began to turn, and the conductor called out one last time, "All aboard!"

Clara watched the train pull away. Devastated that she would never see her husband again nor be able to visit his grave, she excused herself from the gathering of friends and returned to the depot where she sat alone on the oak-slatted bench.

Eager to get home before the blizzard struck in full force, the crowd dispersed while the children remained on the platform and waited until the last car of the Great Northern passed by. Duke dropped onto the tracks and limped behind the caboose. Following his lead, Melina and GC began to run after the train as though they could catch their father and bring him back, but Melina fell behind.

Panicked and grief-stricken, GC chased behind the train. With his arms pumping wildly, he pounded on through the driving snow until he was breathless and fell to his knees. "Oh, Dad!" he cried out in torment. "Please don't leave us! Oh, Dad, what are we a-gonna do?" Then all of his pent-up fears of the last week broke the barrier of despair as he collapsed in sobs between the rails of the Great Northern.

Melina had never seen her brother cry; confused and apprehensive, she waited for his return, then gently held his hand as the train faded from view. Emotionally spent, absorbed in their fear, the children returned to the depot to lead their mother home. Clara, engrossed in her own thoughts, patiently waited for them, watched them pit their strength against the heavy, glassed doors as they fought their way inside out of the wind.

They are such fragile kiddies, she thought to herself. How

am I a-gonna raise them alone? She wiped her eyes and attempted a weary smile as she stood to join her children. With their arms wrapped around each other, the family stepped into the snowstorm and made their way back to the store...a lonely, abandoned trio and a grieving, crippled old dog.

Saddened by the death of his friend and needing some time alone, Charlie drove the truck back to the store where he stoked the potbelly stove and waited for Glenn's family to arrive. He piled Glenn's newspapers off in a corner and tidied the area around the daybed; it would be easier on the family if they didn't see his personal items scattered about.

Somber and subdued, the children entered the quiet interior of the store. They looked around at the shelves and canned goods, they looked at the daybed where their father had relaxed with his newspapers and waited for customers, but the place was deserted except for Charlie, who welcomed them home with a big smile as he continued to set the table with donated food from the neighbors.

Overwhelmed by the task ahead of her, Clara asked for advice. "What am I a-gonna do now, Charlie? I have the three cabins and the rooms in the store to rent. Then there's the garden and my chickens to tend. The store and bakery is almost a full-time job. I can't manage all of this by myself." She paused and considered the hard facts. "I have wood to chop and two kids to raise. Gee whiz, it took both of us to run this business. I can't do it alone."

Charlie considered her options; there weren't many. He'd asked himself this question a hundred times and could find only one solution. "Why don't you write to your brother Charley and ask him to come for a while. He's not married; he could help out until you get back on your feet."

Melina interrupted the conversation. "We don't know him. Why don't you live with us, Charlie?" she asked hopefully.

Charlie smiled at her eagerness. "I can't do that, but I will stay here for a few days until things settle down. And I'll come into town and spend a night with you once in a while. Would you like that?" The children were relieved at his willingness to stay; they felt vulnerable without a man's protection.

They returned to the routine of school and achieved some escape from the loneliness that encompassed their waking hours, but GC suffered alone. He was nearing his twelfth birthday, an impressionable age. He was neither little boy nor young man; he couldn't cry nor could he make major decisions, but he could see their lives crumbling. Without the strength of his dad, he wondered how they'd survive.

Clara found herself trapped in the store with memories of her husband. She visualized him reading on the daybed, playing cards with Melina, and talking to customers. She listened for his footsteps to come through the door as he shared good news about a letter from home or a new business venture or the latest gossip from downtown, but the familiar voice had been silenced, and the children found her crying at the table when they came home for lunch each day. Her face remained blotched and swollen, friends found it difficult to cope with her inconsolable grief. She wrote detailed, tear-stained letters to her Minnesota family explaining the dire circumstances in which she found herself, and they discussed it amongst themselves.

Back in 1927, discontent at being under Lou's control, Emma had withdrawn her life's savings and made the down payment on an eighty-acre farm five miles from the home place that she named the Lake Breeze Poultry Farm. Daily farm chores and caring for her aging father, who suffered from prostate disease, prevented her from going to Glacier Park. Charley was soon to be married, and Lou was reluctant to leave the milking and winter farm chores to his brothers, so it was decided that Fred and his wife Grace would leave their two children with relatives and go west to console Clara. They arrived two weeks after Glenn's death.

The children had never met Uncle Fred and Aunt Grace, but they were thrilled to have some family support to ease their mother's grief. It was Fred's first trip to Glacier Park, and even though Clara had hoped Charley would come, she welcomed this brother to her home. Fred, always the passive brother, relaxed quietly on the chair with his arms crossed and listened to Clara's fears. The children liked his gentle ways. During the day he chopped wood and did outside chores while Grace tended the store, and Clara worked in the kitchen. Always ready for a good time, Grace entertained the children with games in the evenings while Fred listened to Clara's problems and tried to help her make decisions; it was a time of rejuvenation for her troubled mind.

Fred, however, became the troubled one. His Minnesota life, surrounded by the stability of family and friends, contrasted sharply with Clara's life in Glacier Park. He observed the freedom of her children. They ignored Clara's suggestions and did as they pleased. They rode horseback with the Indian children, stayed up until the wee hours, and maintained their own agenda answering only to each other. He and Grace considered the children to be a bit less than civilized as they understood it in a Minnesota way of thinking.

Fred sat with his sister and pondered her future. He shook his head in concern and bewilderment as he wondered how in the world she'd raise those two unmanageable children. Finally he said, "This isn't a very good place to raise kids, Clara. Here on the reservation, I mean."

She agreed with him, but at least she had a store and rentals for independence. She would stay and create a new life with them. Filled with apprehension about her decision, Fred and Grace returned to the civility of the family farm; they had done their best to advise her.

Realizing her inability to do the work of two people, Clara waited for Ed McManman to come into the store. Ed, an elderly bachelor who had lived in the area for years, might be willing to help her. The Glacier Cash Grocery always stayed open until 9 p.m., and late one evening just before closing time, Ed came into the store for a loaf of bread.

She greeted him warmly. "Golly, Ed, we haven't seen you for a while, and I've been wanting to talk to you about working for me. Since Mr. Smiley passed away, I just can't do all the work around here. I can't pay you any money, but if you'll take care of the store and wait on customers for me, I'll give you free board and room."

Melina and GC didn't approve at all. Ed, an irritable old man, didn't like kids. In return, they didn't like his looks. Overweight and flabby, he had a flat, bald head with a fringe of white hair around the ears, and they suspected his age to be near seventy, but old Ed was nearly destitute and accepted the offer even though he didn't care for those two kids who stared at him from the daybed.

Clara had always preferred her chicken chores and baking to meeting the public; Ed's presence allowed her to pursue those interests. Clara felt kindly toward him, and considered him to be harmless. She was unaware of the fact that his personality irritated customers, and that he aggravated her children with his constant criticism.

"Ma," GC said, "let's get rid of old Ed. Let's just live alone again. He's grouchy to us, and he isn't any fun."

"Yah, Ma," Melina added. "He wears those heavy twill pants that are about hundred sizes too big then holds them up with suspenders. He's got big gaps all the way around. I'll bet he could stick a pillow inside and still have room left over!"

"No," Clara answered. "Ed is an honest man, and he's a good help to me. You just try and be a little nicer to him."

Christmas came and went. Without Glenn to lead the festivities and buy gifts, the holiday passed with little fanfare. And so did Duke. His appetite diminished. His shaggy coat hung in matted disarray revealing a spiny backbone and flesh-less ribs. Lying at the foot of the daybed near the warmth of the potbelly stove where he'd lazed away the years, he mourned alone and ignored while the children played with their own dogs. On a January afternoon, a primitive instinct beckoned him away, lured him out toward the pasture away from the family, away from the frontier town, and he never returned.

The children weren't grumbling about old Ed so often; neither were they acknowledging his presence, but Clara no-ticed that customers weren't frequenting her store the way they had in the past. Maybe the children are right about Ed, she thought. I'll have to pay closer to attention to what goes on, but Ed's help gave her time to do as she liked, and she quickly relapsed into her former belief in the goodness of the old man.

One evening the children sat at the table playing cards with Leo Hickson, one of GC's friends. Without customers to dis-tract him, Ed couldn't mind his own business; he interfered with their game by peering over their shoulders, kibitzing and inter-rupting their fun with sarcastic criticism. From a distance he caught a glimpse of something shiny. He shuffled over behind Leo's chair and looked down toward the object now reflecting light from the lantern. Suddenly his brittle voice crackled accus-ingly, "Say, Leo, is that a gun in your boot?"

The card game continued. "Yah, it's a gun," Leo answered as he claimed a trick.

Old Ed moved closer. With his hands on his knees he bent over for a better look, his great pants gaping open before him. "What in the world are you doing with a gun? It's not a real gun, is it?"

Melina glanced down at the boot resting on the rung of her chair and saw the silver handle of a small gun. "Yah, it's a real gun," Leo answered as he played another card.

Perturbed at being ignored, Ed turned belligerent. "Let me see that! I don't believe that that's a real gun!" he scoffed.

Leo reached down and casually removed the gun from his boot. Without a backward glance he handed it to the bothersome old man in hopes that he'd leave them alone. Not wanting to miss the action, Melina pushed her chair back away from the card game and stood to examine the gun herself, her face only inches from the muzzle.

Clara entered from the kitchen and was astonished to see Ed pointing a gun toward Melina. Before she could speak, Ed said, "Yah, that looks like a real gun all right," and he pulled the trigger.

The shot reverberated throughout the store as the card players lurched back and Clara cried, "What in the world is going on here?"

Blood dripped from Ed's left hand while he clutched the smoking weapon in his right hand and looked at it in surprise. The air thickened with the pungent smell of burnt gunpowder. "What do you think you're doing? You could've killed Melina!" Clara gasped as she grabbed a towel and wrapped it around his hand to staunch the flow of blood.

"Are you all right, Melina? Are you sure you're all right?" she asked in alarm while sponging up the blood on the floor.

"Yah, I'm fine," Melina answered.

Unconcerned by the commotion, Leo retrieved his gun from Ed's shaky hand and slipped it back into his boot while GC shuffled the cards and dealt a new hand; the game continued.

Clara's quick inspection revealed that the bullet had gone through Ed's forefinger and lodged in the knuckle of his middle finger. Blood seeped through the towel as she scolded him, then pressed money into his pocket and urged him to catch the next train to the hospital in Cut Bank. Old Ed lost the use of his finger; he lost his job as well, but the cash register in the Glacier Cash Grocery once more sang their favorite song as former customers found their way back.

Without Glenn's management skills, delinquent renters continued to reside in her cabins. Clara allowed them to stay; her conscience couldn't condone turning them out without a home, and they took advantage of her big-hearted tolerance of their shortcomings while they stole armloads of wood from her woodpile.

Clara had to admit that the family evenings were more peaceful without Ed interfering in everyone's business. Once or twice a week Charlie came for dinner and played cards with GC. He read stories to Melina and embellished them with foolishness until peals of laughter empowered the children to believe that there could be life after death.

Chewing on a straggly strand of hair, Melina's eyes sparkled with mischief as she grinned into Charlie's face. "Will you marry me, Charlie?" she asked. "Will you wait until I grow up and marry me?"

Charlie chuckled at her merriment. "Sure, I'll marry you, but I'm gonna be an old man by that time!"

Charlie's calming presence enabled Clara to meet her responsibilities without duress; she no longer wept for what might have been. Glenn had left a void in her life that would never be filled, but she felt stronger and more able to deal with the unknown. She knew that the children missed him terribly, but they were finding solace in those who loved them.

Sometimes the two adults sat by the stove and reminisced about their early days at Lake Lubec with Glenn; he'd rescued each of them from a life fraught with adversity and taught them to laugh again. On other evenings when Clara sat alone beneath the golden glow of the gas lantern, she talked to her husband. She described his children's achievements, she composed verses, verses reflecting memories of better times.

Sweet Memories

Alone today I went for a walk,
And it seemed as though I heard you talk
While I stood beside that water so clear,
Just like we used to do years gone by, my Dear.

Amid the green grass and blooming wild flowers
Memories of those happy, bygone hours
Overwhelmed me, and I reached out my arms
To capture your visions in heavenly charms.

Just then the huge shade trees
Bowed gently in the summer breeze,
And the lowly whispering of their leaves,
Shook my heart that always grieves

For you, my only beloved one.
I hope my day's work will soon be done
When I say my last prayer and close my eyes
To awaken with you, my darling husband in Paradise.

Forever lovingly,
Clara A. Smiley

The frozen months of January and February slipped away as the children waited on customers and stocked the shelves after school in hope that their mother wouldn't hire old Ed again. Laughter and gossip flowed from the store as neighbors sat around the stove until the late hours of the night. Clara's storytelling skills, buried beneath years of hard work, surfaced once more as she spun creative tales for her guests.

In the spring of 1929, Clara received a letter from Lou and Fred encouraging her to sell her Glacier Park business and buy the Max Kienberger farm adjoining theirs. The price was reasonable at $75 an acre. They would help her with the crops, she could raise poultry and garden produce. She knew that without Glenn's help with the Glacier Cash Grocery, she couldn't make it. He had been the businessman, she had done the hard work; they'd been good working partners, but she couldn't swing it alone.

Envious of Emma's farm, Clara now had the opportunity to follow her lead. GC was a strong, ambitious young man who could help with chores, and Melina was tall for her age. It presented an opportune time to make a change, so while the children were at school, Clara journeyed to Cut Bank and listed her property with a real estate broker.

Although the children didn't remember Emma from their summer visit in years past, they corresponded with her in a pen pal sort of way; it brought happiness to their mother. Emma responded.

Osakis, Minn.
March 22—'29

Dear Melina,

Your nice newsy letter was in the mail box waiting for me Sunday morning. I was very glad to get it…

Yes I can play a few games of cards, but not as many as you can. ho learned you how to play all those games? I can play cinch, seven up, smear, rummie. I have played 500, but a long time ago, don't think I could now. It's kind of a hard game. One trick is all I can do.

Am glad that your weight is just right. I weigh 200 pounds. Too bad about Mrs. Hixson falling into the snow bank. The next time they see a snow bank they must think "the longest way round is the safest way home."

No, my chickens do not lay many eggs. 33 are the most I have had in one day and I have 140 chickens. Your chickens beat mine. I do not feed mine special for laying. I think they lay more in the summer if they don't lay so many in the winter.

GC must have a fine dog if you can hitch him up and he will pull a load.

…I am going over to the mail box tomorrow morning and will then mail this. How far do you have to go to get your mail? We have to walk half a mile to the mail box. Grandpa is very anxious to see you and GC. Every time I bring home a letter he'll say, "Well, I wonder if Clara has sold."

…Write me another letter like the last one soon

Aunt Emma

The children felt ambivalent about the move to Minnesota. On one hand they would be living near family; they might even be able to go to Iowa and visit their father's grave. On the other hand, the only life they knew was in Glacier Park.

"What will happen to our horses when we move, Ma?" GC asked. He and Melina couldn't imagine a life without horses.

Clara smiled. "Gee whiz, that won't be a problem. We'll have lots of room for your horses on our farm. When I sell out, I'll rent a boxcar on the train, and I'll take back your horses and dogs, all your rabbits and pigeons and canaries. Even my chickens. Everything we own will go into that boxcar."

"Ma," GC said, "I'm worried about my baby turkeys, raising them here then selling them to be butchered. Can we send my turkeys back to Emma?"

"Oh, yah," she answered, "Emma won't mind a few more turkeys, and then when we get our own place, you can have them back again."

Osakis Minn.

April 1 -29

Dear GC,

Your turkeys got here in just fine shape. They reached Long
Prairie Wednesday afternoon at six oclock. That being too late to
go and get them, uncle Lou went down and got them Thursday
morning.

The road is very muddy where I live…so he took them to
his place and took them out of the crate and put them into a
shed where they could eat and drink. Saturday afternoon he
brought them over here. I turned them into the house yard, it
has a woven wire fence around it and my turkeys were outside of
the fence. You can not mix strange turkeys with out first sort of
introducing them, by having them in a separate enclosure where
the home flock can see them, but can not molest them.

When time to go to roost came they began to look and act
sort of uneasy and I let them out of the yard and when they got
over to where the chickens were then they were happy. They
went right into the chicken coop with the chickens. My chickens
are buff orpington just like yours. Your turkeys are very tame, eat
bread right out of my hands. They are just as tame as mine, I am
glad of that.

Where did you get them, are they Montana grown? Am
very glad you sent them out here rather than to sell them to the
butcher. They are very nice turkeys and I will mark them so that
I can tell you just what they will do. If your mother does not sell
the place, you better give us a visit, am sure we would all be glad
to see you and Melina.

Aunt Grace and Uncle Fred told me what a nice big boy you
now are. Now that your father is gone you must always try and
be a perfect little man. I am kind of looking forward to the time
when you come to Minnesota to stay, may be your mother
will have good luck and sell her place…

Lots of love from Aunt Emma

Dreams of buying the beautiful farm next to her brothers filled Clara's days. To the children, she described the two-story house with its wraparound porch and gingerbread trim. She extolled the expansive lawns beneath the shady elms, the large garden between the house and the barn. Chicken coops and machine sheds hovered at the perimeter of her descriptions, a corral sprawled behind the barn where they'd milk the cows outdoors during the heat of summer. Meanwhile, the daily routine at the Glacier Cash Grocery dragged on, but now the raucous cacophony of returning crows announced the arrival of spring, and the garden had to be prepared and planted. "I want our property to look real nice if a potential buyer comes to look at it," she told the children as she prepared for another day with her hoe.

June brought thousands of tourists to Glacier Park. With the sleeping rooms in her store all rented, Clara's income increased dramatically, but extra laundry added to her burden. There weren't enough hours in the day for her to bake bread, operate the store, tend the chickens, nurture the garden, chop wood, and care for the children. John Smith arrived from New York and stayed for a while; Shorty Hynes helped when he could, but the bulk of the workload fell on her shoulders as she rose before dawn and seldom retired before midnight.

A plain middle-aged couple from places unknown arrived in late June and stayed for two weeks. They rented the only bedroom with an outside entry where they could come and go as they wished. Clara liked long-term guests because she didn't have to wash the sheets as often. They kept to themselves and enjoyed the beauties of Glacier National Park, but they couldn't help but notice the long hours of labor that Clara endured alone. Wanting to linger longer in the brisk mountain air, they offered to mind the store for her in exchange for their room until she found a buyer. Clara gave a silent prayer of thanks and eagerly taught them how to stock shelves, take reservations and rent rooms, package goods, and greet customers who streamed down from the great hotel across the tracks to savor a bit of the Old West with the locals.

Every afternoon at 5 P.M., two blocks around the corner at Mike's Place, local cowboys continued to entertain the tourists just as they'd done for years. Out in the street they rode bucking broncos, wrestled a few steers, and lassoed pretty ladies in the circle of onlookers. After the show, the cowboys passed a sweat-stained hat amongst the appreciative audience from back east, who generously parted with their dollars. GC and Melina faithfully attended the daily fiasco of frontier entertainment where they cheered for their favorite cowboys and mingled with the crowd before heading home for supper.

When they arrived at the store after another spectacle of cowboy shenanigans, the two renters greeted the children from behind the counter. Perplexed as he studied them in silence from the doorway, GC finally asked, "What are you doing back there?"

"Your Ma hired us to mind the store for her this summer, so she can have more time to work in the garden," the man answered as he wiped off the counter with a towel and rearranged the baked goods in the display cases. "We're gonna help you folks out." He continued stacking the remaining donuts in one corner while he moved the last apple pie out near the cash register where customers could smell the caramelized cinnamon that lay on the flaky crust.

The children hadn't paid much attention to the couple before, but now that they were going to be around, they took a good look, and they didn't like what they saw. The woman stood less than five feet tall; she was shorter than GC and Melina. Her mousy, brown hair was cut short like a man's; it grew straight up from her scalp like pig bristles on a brush. Heavy, black eyebrows bushed above glasses as thick as the wax atop jelly jars, and thick lips couldn't conceal the overbite of broad teeth that protruded from her mouth. Her husband, short and nondescript, sported a big belly, the type of man who could disappear in a crowd. When he spoke to GC, his eyes flickered down at the floor, over the shelves, or above their heads. His shifty eyes troubled them.

They found their mother hoeing her many rows of potatoes. She didn't hear them come up from behind until they called her name. "Ma," GC said with Melina trailing behind like a shadow, "what are those two renters doing in our store?"

Clara detected concern. She straightened and smiled at her handsome son. He had his father's fair good looks and sense of duty. "They're a-gonna help us out for a few weeks," she said. "I need time to work in the garden, and you two shouldn't have to spend your summer working in the store. You should have time to play with your friends before we move away."

"But Ma, we don't know those people," he answered. "They're strangers."

Clara leaned on her hoe and studied her children. They're always suspicious of people's motives when they try to help me, she thought. Melina even criticized Shorty as being a skinflint when he wouldn't buy her an ice cream cone downtown, but hadn't he sacrificed his time to escort Mr. Smiley's body back to Iowa? She recalled GC's anger when he caught the neighbor lady pilfering wood during the winter, but he didn't understand how that lady had brought food for them on the days after Mr. Smiley's death. She couldn't understand their suspicious nature.

"I don't like their looks, Ma," Melina said remembering the man's evasive eyes as he mumbled about his new duties in the store.

"Now Melina," Clara answered, "you can't judge people by

their looks. We can't all be born good-looking. Now you two go and play."

The children returned to the store and sat on their father's daybed until Clara came in to cook supper. They watched every move the couple made; they didn't miss a thing. Early the next morning they galloped on their ponies out to Lake Lubec where Charlie lived in their old cabin. They knew that he would listen to reason.

GC described the scenario in town. With exaggerated drama, Melina enhanced the unsightly portrait of the intruders with a few deft brush strokes of her own, then grabbed Charlie's arm with both hands and pleaded, "Oh, please, Charlie, you've just got to come into town and live with us. Something awful is gonna happen!"

He patiently listened. "It's not my place to tell your ma what to do, and you know that I can't come and live with you. Just look at all I have to do around here," he said, but he, too, felt disturbed by the children's anxiety and promised to come into town sometime in the next few days to check on the situation.

Clara's garden drew her like a magnet during the warm, daylight hours as she hoed her way up and down the rows; she diligently worked to meet the demand for fresh vegetables from her customers, and the first week passed blissfully in her mind.

Unease gnawed away at the children. Their father had always dressed so smartly in a long-sleeved shirt and trousers when he tended the store. These people were an embarrassment to them. Even when doing her chores and hoeing in the garden, their ma looked better than those strangers.

During the second week of their employment, the children again brought up the subject. "Ma," GC said, "every time I come into the store those people are eating our food. Today I saw him cut a big slab of cheese and eat it. And she's always gobbling your donuts."

Clara tried to be patient. "Now, GC," she explained, "all they're getting from me is a free place to stay. They take all their meals downtown. It can't hurt if they have a little snack once in a while. My goodness, look at what a help they are for me. He drives the old truck to the depot and delivers all of the supplies to the store. They stock the shelves, wait on customers, and rent out the rooms. What more do you expect of them?"

Melina retorted, "I expect them to look better. What do the customers think when they see a woman with a hairdo like that? And all she ever wears are those blue bib overalls and a man's shirt with the sleeves rolled up to the elbows."

"And they're always whispering," GC added. "When they aren't eating, they've got their heads together whispering. What is there to whisper about? I don't like it." He paused, then added, "And I don't like it when they sit on Dad's daybed and read our papers. If they're working, they should stay behind the counter or go out and chop wood."

Enlightened by her children's possessive comments, she smiled and said, "Oh, GC, they're not taking your father's place just because they relax on his daybed and read the papers. And if it will make you feel better, I'll ask them to do more work around the place." The children wondered what other kind of work those impostors could do; they were too short and fat to do much.

A few days later when the children arrived home for supper, they found Clara behind the counter tending the store; she seemed distracted as she wiped fingerprints from the display case and polished the cash register to a sheen. "Where's your helpers, Ma?" GC asked.

Without looking up from her task she answered, "They went to Browning this morning to buy a few sacks of chicken feed, and they haven't returned. I was a-gonna go myself and do my banking, but he told me that loading those heavy sacks of chicken feed was too much for a woman."

She set the polishing rag aside, justified her decision quickly to quell her unease, "Gee whiz, they've been watching the store for nearly two weeks. When he offered to do the shopping and banking for me, I thought they might like to have a few hours off." She looked at the children for reassurance, but her sunny optimism about people's good will began to dim when she observed the skeptical glance that flashed between them. She walked to the window and searched the empty street hoping to see the old truck heaped with sacks of chicken feed. Deepening twilight obscured all but the dark silhouettes of neighboring buildings where dim lamps emitted feeble light onto the street. Goose bumps prickled at the back of her neck as unwanted truths wrestled with weakening hope. They should have been back a long time ago, she admitted to herself.

What Clara refused to acknowledge, GC blurted out. "They stole our money, Ma! They didn't want to buy your chicken feed; they wanted the money you were a-gonna put in the bank! How much did you send with them?"

Clara's chest constricted with the blatant truth. She fought to catch her breath. "Nearly $800," she whispered. The children were appalled at losing such a fortune; they couldn't imagine that much money.

"Maybe they missed the train or the old truck wouldn't start," Clara suggested feebly. The children's incredulous stares brought her to her senses. "Let's go check their room," she said finally as she removed the lantern from its hook above the counter and led the way toward the door.

The trio hurried behind the store to the back bedroom. Clara rapped on the door and waited. She turned the doorknob with foreboding. Please let their clothes be in here, she prayed as she pushed her way inside and held the hissing lantern above her head for a better look, but a vacant room with an unmade bed met their stricken eyes. The couple had smuggled out all of their belongings, stolen the family's money, and boarded the train with hundreds of other tourists departing from Glacier Park for places unknown. How could they do this to me, she thought, but self-incrimination assailed her once again with the truth. She'd selfishly ignored the warning signs that even the children had begged her to see. The seductive lure of the land, her consuming desire to experience its sensuous touch, its scent of life, had once again resulted in catastrophe. Visibly shaken by the turn of events, the family returned to the store where Glenn's imagined presence haunted her with disdain; she'd better sell and get out.

In late July, a potential buyer came on the train from Shelby to examine the Smiley property. Its size and location, one block away from the main part of town, met his requirements for a new motel he planned to build; he wanted to cash in on the hundreds of motorists coming to Glacier Park every year. He returned several times. He liked the idea that the entire block was deeded property, so he agreed to buy it for the asking price of $20,000.

"I'll have the money together in just a few weeks," he said, "and then we can close the deal."

That was the plan the way she explained it to her children.

Would Clara have married Charlie and remained in Glacier Park if he'd proposed? A moot question since Charlie enjoyed the company of a half-empty bottle, and Clara was dead set against alcohol. She had a fiery disposition when it came to whiskey, and many a time Charlie had witnessed her wrath, like the time when he and Glenn arrived home in an inebriated state and Clara hurled a heavy pottery bowl across the room at her husband's head, missing him by inches, hit the wall, bounced across the floor.

Because of his encounters with her temper, it's highly unlikely that Charlie would have ever considered marrying her in spite of his love for the children. Some years later, however, he married a nurse, newly arrived from New Jersey, and purchased the Lubec homestead from Clara. They remained close friends of the family for many years.

At long last Clara had a buyer for her property, and the Minnesota relatives breathed a sigh of relief. With Melina entering fifth grade and GC entering seventh, Clara wanted them to avoid a mid-year upheaval, so she arranged to take them back to Minnesota on the train in August. They would live with Emma and Grandpa until she returned with the money from the sale of her property.

The idea of living with strange relatives didn't appeal to the children. Grandpa had come to visit them in Glacier Park two summers before, and even though he had whittled them each a new pair of skis, they remembered him as a surly old codger without a sense of humor. Uncle Fred and his wife had been nice enough to them on their visit, but the children knew Emma only through her letters. They couldn't remember much about their trip to Minnesota seven years before.

"How long do we have to stay there without you, Ma?" Melina asked.

"There's this perspective buyer, and just as soon as he gets his money together, I'll move back. But I want you to enroll in school now. We'll leave in mid-August, so you two start your packing. You decide what to take, but it can only be a few of your favorite things."

"Can we take our horses?" they begged.

"No, Lou has horses on his farm that you can help take care of," she said. Once again she explained the plan. "When I move back, I'll bring your horses with me along with the dogs, all your pets, and all your toys. Now you take just what you think you'll need until I get there, and do your own packing," she instructed again.

"Ma," GC pleaded, "I just have to take my canary birds. They'll be all right on the train. Please, Ma."

His eyes pleaded for understanding. Raising and selling canaries had been his hobby for two years. "Okay," she smiled. "Emma has a big house. She won't mind those birds."

The children's friends helped them pack and sort their toys. On the day of departure, GC and Melina walked over to Joe McGregor's pasture and hugged their beloved horses one last time. Unable to imagine life without Snip, Melina held her mother's hand and cried all the way to the station while GC suffered in silence. What am I doing to my children, Clara wondered. First they lost their daddy, and now I'm taking them away from their friends, but she'd made the decision to sell, and she knew that it was a good decision even though the children were too young to understand.

Shorty delivered their luggage to the depot on the old truck. He agreed to take care of her chicken chores; the store would be closed until her return. As the lonely whistle of the approaching train echoed from the hills, a forlorn GC blinked back tears. "You know, Ma, I think that we should all stay here. We'll just wait until you sell. Then we can go back together and buy that farm."

"No," Clara answered remembering Mr. Smiley's stories of when he'd taught school for a term in Iowa, "your daddy would have wanted you to start school on time. He said that it was very important to be there on the first day."

They boarded the train with a menagerie of boxes and luggage in addition to four canaries in two separate cages. Clara carried a covered wicker basket filled with baked goods. Her personal suitcase contained only a few changes of clothes; she planned to return in two weeks. The children couldn't fathom such a radical change in their lives. There was a certain element of excitement about it, but they hated to leave their friends, and leaving their horses was the worst sacrifice of all. They placed the canary cages on the shelf above their seats and settled in for a long trip to an unknown place with unknown people.

Knowing that she had a buyer for her property and that Shorty would take good care of it in her absence, Clara surrendered to the rocking motion of the Great Northern as the comfortable seats and rhythm of the wheels lulled her to sleep across the northern plains of Montana. She drifted in and out of dreamland envisioning a tranquil life on her new farm, a pastoral nirvana rising from the banks of the Long Prairie River in central Minnesota.

On a hot August afternoon Aunt Grace met them at the train depot in her Model A Ford. Their luggage overflowed from the recesses of the car; Aunt Grace would have to make another trip to the depot to retrieve the remaining boxes. Clara, dressed flamboyantly with a large flower-strewn hat, sat up front, and the children scrunched together in the back seat with their caged canaries as Aunt Grace sat forward, her back straight, spine like a ramrod, clutched the steering wheel in both hands and took off in a cloud of dust. The passengers got jostled around, jerked and slammed over washboard roads, ground and churned their way from soft gravel verges where Aunt Grace strayed when she talked too much, steered too little. Thankful for the cooling breeze that blew through the side windows, they bounced over rutted one-lane country roads, emerald tunnels between forests of cornfields, stalks eight feet high with rustling leaves, honked at dogs that nipped at the tires, scattered flocks of delinquent chickens, and made their way toward the Lake Breeze Poultry Farm, Emma's pride and joy, located near Osakis Lake.

Emma turned the seven cows out to pasture. She'd finished the evening milking, washed the separator, submerged the milk cans in the cold water tank, and secured the handles to steel hooks until the morning milk truck came to deliver them to the creamery. Twilight of Minnesota dog days, oppressive heat. Humidity, which could be sliced with a knife, draped over the land, pressed its weight against her skin.

Flies exploring the bloodied hatchet droned around the chopping block where she'd lopped the head off a chicken earlier in the day. She closed the hen house door, checked on the geese and ducks for the night, bolted the barn door, and turned to see Grace's Model A churn through the sand where the end of the driveway met the gravel road. With wheels spewing clouds of fine silt that hung in the air, it came to an abrupt stop near the back porch where Pa sat whittling.

Clara and the children piled out of the car. Emma waved to her sister then observed the disheveled duo where they stood clutching their canary cages. Skinny children with wild, darting eyes. She wondered whether she'd been too generous in offering her home for a few weeks. Fred and Grace had warned her repeatedly about their undisciplined lifestyle, but she couldn't turn back now when her sister needed the support. A family takes care of its own, she sighed inwardly as she approached the weary travelers; her dog Fanny ran forward to sniff the visitors, wrapped herself around GC's ankles.

Grandpa Charles Miller remained on the porch, folded his jackknife, slipped it into his pocket. He reached for his cane, stood up for a better view and studied Clara's unkempt offspring from the reservation with apprehension. He wasn't so sure that he wanted them living under his roof. That boy looks like a troublemaker the way he keeps kicking up dirt in the driveway, and the girl has shifty eyes, he noted to himself. Clara unloaded their luggage. Grace departed without further comment; no one showed enthusiasm about their arrival.

As Emma approached the wary family, the children sized her up. Her letters had been full of love, but she presented an imposing bulwark of authority like they'd never seen before in a woman. Her towering body, husky and powerful, lay concealed beneath a limp, flowery dress that sagged to her ankles. She walked toward them with slow deliberate steps, each foot placed directly in front of the other as though walking a tightrope, the flat heels of men's brown leather gaiters scraping the dust, furrowing it to the side, leaving a trail of scuff marks as she approached. Ivory combs held silvered blond hair away from her face; rivulets of sweat coursed their way from her forehead, temples, over plump cheeks, disappeared into wattles beneath her jaw. A sour odor emanated from her flesh, caused the children to draw back not wanting to be touched. She seemed pleasant enough, she must like children since she'd once been a teacher, they thought, but she had a firm, no-nonsense way of speaking when she greeted their mother.

Melina remembered Grandpa Miller from his visit to Glacier Park without fondness. Glaring down at her from the porch he looked strict and stern with hard features and white, bushy chin whiskers. He wore a flat, battered hat. Short, wide suspenders pulled the waist of his pants toward his skinny chest. She could see the tops of his high shoes, a double knot at the end of the laces. His bony fingers tightened around the grip of his cane, shook it toward her in a threatening gesture. She kept her distance and remained silent, concentrated on the distant gobbling of the turkeys, noises of the barnyard off in the distance. A lazy breeze unburdened itself of the emanation of dog days...slimy moss, a mucky swamp, dead fish, stagnant sloughs. GC set his canary cage aside, squatted down and played with Fanny, wondered whether he might go look at the turkeys, maybe find his own, but decided against asking, withdrew into his own thoughts, ignored those around him, pretended that he didn't care.

Emma finally smiled. Her eyes were warm, crinkled at the corners when she welcomed the exhausted children to her home, a white two-story farmhouse set back from the road nestled in a grove of elms, a house with high ceilings, spacious rooms. Hollyhocks reached as high as the windows, phlox and snapdragons concealed the foundation. A green lawn lay between the house and the manicured garden. She helped carry their luggage inside, laid out towels and washcloths beside the cistern pump and encouraged them to wash up. She and Pa had already eaten supper, but she offered an evening lunch of fresh milk, homemade bread, and honey, a real treat for two hungry youngsters who had been living on pastries.

It was nearly 9:30 P.M. when they finished eating; Emma cleared the table and escorted them upstairs to their bedrooms. She believed in ten hours of sleep for growing children.

Clara was well aware of her sister's adherence to routine, and wondered how her free-spirited kiddies would cope as she silently watched Emma march them off to bed. Oh, well, she thought, it's only going to be for a few weeks. She saw no need to accompany her children upstairs; they knew how to take care of themselves, so she remained at the table and talked with Pa about his old neighbor, Max Kienberger, whose farm she planned to buy.

At home in Glacier Park the entire family had shared one room. Here at Emma's farm, Melina and GC each had their own bedroom with a bed and a dresser. A fragile, kerosene lamp offered a warm glow. Eager to crawl into a real bed again after the cramped quarters on the train, Melina slipped into her nightgown, curled up, listened to snatches of conversation at the foot of the stairs, but the spacious room with its high ceilings intimidated her; she missed the coziness of their cramped quarters at the store where she could hear GC's breathing and feel her mother's warm body.

Always a worrier, Emma listened for sounds from upstairs as she sat at the table and exchanged gossip with her sister. Melina's lamplight reflected into the upstairs hallway.

"I wonder if there's something wrong with Melina," she

said as she indicated the light. "Could she be sick from the train ride?"

Clara glanced up the stairs. She knew that Melina was drawing pictures or reading the funny papers she'd brought along on the train. "She's all right. Just let her be," she said as she went back to her conversation with Pa.

Emma couldn't relax. That tired child needs her rest, she thought. Tomorrow she has to start school. Emma returned upstairs to Melina's room. "What's the matter? Is everything all right?" she asked as she leaned over the bed.

"Oh, yah," Melina answered. "I'm fine."

Emma said, "You haven't turned your light out."

Accustomed to a home where the parents stayed up most of the night, the children didn't know what it was like to go to bed in the dark. "Well," Melina yawned, "we don't turn the lights out in Montana when we go to sleep. We let them burn all night."

That's a lot of foolishness, Emma thought. She tersely replied, "Well, you're in Minnesota now, and we sleep with our lights off!" She blew out the lamp and returned downstairs leaving Melina wide-eyed in the dark, apprehensive.

Clara left early the next morning when Charley fetched her to examine the farm she planned to buy. Conscientious about her new duties with the children, Emma cooked a hot breakfast and prepared them each a lunch of sandwiches, hard-boiled eggs, cookies, and fruit that she packed in shiny one-gallon syrup cans with tight lids. She inspected the backs of their necks, examined the insides of their ears. The children brushed their hair, she checked for clean fingernails, handed them each two pencils and a tablet, a clean handkerchief to be tucked into a pocket while Grandpa watched in silence. He didn't trust those two hooligans.

Emma prepared the car for the two-mile drive over the narrow, country road. She hadn't learned to drive until she was forty-five years old, and she didn't take any chances. First, she added water to the radiator. Then she took a little gauge and checked the pressure in all four tires starting at the front and working her way around. "Glenn Charles," she said, she enjoyed the formality of his name, "get out the tire pump and pump this back tire up. It's down two pounds."

She adjusted the choke, and prepared to crank the engine. "Let me do that," he begged.

"No, you're not strong enough yet," she answered. "It might snap back and break your arm. You operate the controls."

Glenn slid behind the steering wheel; Melina climbed into the back seat. They watched Emma crank the handle around and around, the chassis rocked from side to side. Her head bobbed up and down in front of the car, but the motor wouldn't catch. She stood up, her face florid, two hundred pounds of disgust gasping for breath. Pearly beads of perspiration lost their grasp, seeped toward her jowls, dripped into the dust as she reached toward the crank, and swore at Charley for selling her that miserable aggravation.

Glenn patiently waited anticipating her next move. "Pull the choke all the way out, Glenn Charles!" she called as she cranked the handle again; her head bobbed faster and faster as though playing a game of peek-a-boo behind the radiator.

The motor turned over once, twice. She shouted above its gasping voice, "Adjust the choke, adjust the choke," and the engine roared to life, rocked the old bucket of bolts with a spluttering cough, an attempt to catch its breath within the confines of gasoline fumes, then finally settled into a gentle pulsating twitch.

Glenn slid into the passenger seat on the right, and Emma eased her great bulk behind the steering wheel. She adjusted her long skirt, pulled it above her ankles, leaned to the side peering into the darkness under the dash, found the brake. She grasped the steering wheel in both hands, raced the motor, and released the clutch. The old car shot forward, snapped their necks like a slingshot. Without letting up on the gas, she negotiated the turn out of the driveway, churned the wheels in the loose sand, climbed onto the narrow, dirt road, and chugged toward the country school, District 53, where she enrolled the children for the 1929-30 school year.

Adjustment to the new school presented problems. All eight grades, a total of thirty students, shared one room with one teacher. Each wide desk accommodated two students; it was very different from the red brick school in Glacier Park with its two separate rooms for primary and intermediate grades. Unaccustomed to strangers in the community, their classmates treated them like invaders from outer space. No one spoke to them, no one invited them to play. Confused by their reception, they ate their lunches in isolation behind the woodshed and worried about the future.

The local farm boys ridiculed GC's felt cowboy hat, a gift from his father, his treasured possession. Wearing it gave him strength, provided him with courage, helped him through the hard times of hostility and confusion. He silently suffered the loss of his father and dreaded the departure of his mother, but he kept his misery locked away. He adopted his given name of Glenn instead of GC since there could no longer be confusion between father and son, but he couldn't decide on the spelling. Sometimes he spelled it with one *n*, sometimes with two as he struggled for his identity.

Clara sensed a remoteness about her son, but couldn't determine the cause of his distress. He enjoyed milking Emma's cows and feeding the pigs. He liked to go fishing with Charley, and Lou took him to the movies, but there was an undercurrent of resentment she couldn't fathom, and one that her son was unable to share. She watched him struggle with his homework, suspected that he might be lagging behind academically. Emma's clever tutoring will soon get him up to snuff, she decided. It never entered her mind that he didn't have a friend.

The stifling environment of her family's obsession with perfection jolted Clara's memory of why she'd been so desperate to escape sixteen years ago. They hadn't changed. If anything, they were more dogmatic than ever. How will my kiddies cope while I'm gone, she wondered.

She played cards with Pa and quietly observed while Emma taught Melina how to iron. Emma insisted that broadcloth shirts be starched, then sprinkled and kept damp in a basket. The wood fire had to be kept at a certain temperature to heat the irons exactly right; they had detachable handles, so as one iron was being used, the next one was heating. Melina ironed with determination trying to attain Emma's standards of perfection only to hear Emma say, "No, Melina, anything that's worth doing at all is worth doing well," then she'd redampen the shirt, roll it up, and put it back in the basket to be re-ironed. Clara watched with exasperation, but knew that she dare not interfere if the children were to live here. Thank goodness, she'd be back to rescue them in a few weeks.

At the end of two weeks, Clara prepared herself for departure. She dreaded leaving the children behind, but that had been the purpose of the trip, that and deciding to purchase a farm. She knew she had to be strong for their sake; she couldn't risk another emotional scene like what had happened after Mr. Smiley's death, and besides that, she'd soon be back. Melina won't have to meet Emma's expectations, and GC can be his own boss with the animals, she thought. The brothers will help me plant and harvest my crops, but the children and I can farm just the way we want without their interference. I won't have rents to collect nor a store to run. I can spend as much time as I like in my garden and raise chickens without thieves invading my coop. Although she was no longer a young wisp of a girl, deep inside her matronly body an impish spirit longed to be free once again to soar with the larks and smell the freshly mown hay of her own meadow.

Yet, she worried. She hadn't been alone since that first agonizing summer at Lake Lubec. Would she be able to cope without the melee of rambunctious children slamming the door, shouting and caterwauling, tattling and wrestling with their friends? What joy could there be without hearing the children pound piano duets or watching them race their ponies down Washington Street, each of them determined to win? But it's only for a few weeks, she reassured herself once again.

The children now walked the two miles along the dusty road to school, but on the day of Clara's departure, the sisters drove them. GC and Melina, quiet and forlorn, settled into the back seat of Emma's car while she cranked the engine; their ma sat up front. At the school, the despondent youngsters climbed out of the back seat and hesitated. They didn't want their mother to leave nor did they want to live with Emma and Grandpa.

"When are you coming back, Ma?" Glenn asked.

Clara smiled and tried to placate their anxiety, "I'll be back before you know it! Just as soon as I get my money I'll be back, and we'll buy that farm next to Lou's where we'll grow a big garden and have lots of chickens. You'll have your rabbits and pigeons. You can even raise cows and pigs of your own, GC."

She turned to Melina. "Do you remember those swell apple trees that you and GC planted all in a row at our place? Do you remember how fast they grew, and then how that neighbor let her rabbits loose, and they chewed off the bark and killed them? We're a-gonna plant wonderful apple trees here on our farm, and we won't have to worry about the neighbor's rabbits getting loose, either!"

"What about our horses, Ma?" Melina asked for the hundredth time. Just once more she needed reassurance that Snip would soon be part of her life again.

"I'll have Joe load those horses in the boxcar for me with

lots of hay and water. Then when I get back here, we'll put them right into our own barn. You can ride down to the river or gallop to Clotho or over the hill to Gutches Grove to get groceries from the store," she said with excitement. "Gee whiz, we'll have a wonderful life!" There were no tears, no hugs, no painful goodbyes as the children tried to imagine happier times on their own farm.

Charley and his wife delivered Clara to the train station. Charley, delighted at his sister's decision to move back to the family, waited at the depot until the Great Northern disappeared from sight, then returned to the Lake Breeze Poultry Farm where he and his wife enjoyed Emma's cooking and compared strategies on how to raise those two children.

Clara settled into her seat for the long journey home to Glacier Park and reflected back to the first time that she'd headed west on the Great Northern. How times have changed, she smiled to herself as she reviewed her plans for the future. Little did she know that she wouldn't see her children again for eight years, nor would she ever return to the rolling, verdant hills of Minnesota.

After moving to Lou's place, GC, age 12, and Melina, age 9, were each expected to hand milk seven cows twice a day to pay for their room and board. In addition, Melina was excused early from school every day in the spring to empty the sap buckets on the maple trees so Emma could make maple syrup to sell. Lou and his brothers farmed with three teams of horses and an old tractor. GC also worked in the fields with the men.

PART VI

The Depression

During the Depression millions of Americans struggled to survive as they moved around the country in search of employment. Farmers of the Midwest who had managed to survive the first years of the Depression were assaulted by several years of drought followed by high winds that produced the Dust Bowl. Mountains of sand covered their fields, and they, too, piled meager belongings into decrepit vehicles and abandoned their past lives. Cruel propaganda campaigns lured them to California where they believed that employment in the fields and orchards was a surety, but there were no jobs, and they suffered indignities and deplorable living conditions worse than they'd ever imagined.

Now acclimated to the balmy Minnesota days of late summer, Clara shivered and pulled the sweater more tightly around her body as drizzling fog welcomed her back to Glacier Park. Pearls of mist dampened unruly strands of fine hair at the nape of her neck as she straightened her hat, grasped her suitcase, and hurried toward the ambience of her kitchen and a comfortable bed. A plethora of spider webs, a gossamer veil draped and misshapen with beads of moisture, barricaded the doorway as she brushed them aside and fumbled in her pocketbook for the key. Chilled hands forced it into the keyhole, and the unruly lock rolled over, reluctantly granted entrance to the sedate comfort of home.

A solemn stillness pervaded the dusky interior; the room smelled dank, stagnant. Chilled from the mountain drizzle, Clara gathered a handful of dry shavings from the wood box and laid a fire in the potbelly stove. She opened the damper and struck a match, its sulfurous smell lingered in the air. She held it below the splinters until they began to flare, then crisscrossed the glowing bits with larger pieces of kindling until they, too, erupted in flames. Only then did she allow herself to embrace the familiarity of her home.

She wandered from room to room, opening doors, peering into their slumbering silence as deepening twilight played surrealistic games with her senses. The fire crackled, snapped, ghostlike flickers danced on the walls. Light scratching at the door distracted her as she cracked it open, greeted GC's dog, Squim. He burst into the room wagging his tail like a victory flag. He rubbed against her legs and begged for attention, then welcomed her home with slobbering licks when she bent over to scratch his ears. She quenched the appetite of the fire with hunks of wood, then settled at the table and wrote a detailed letter to her kiddies telling them about her trip home, a letter enhanced with embroidered descriptions of fellow passengers.

She had never been separated from her children before. Bereft at abandoning them with Emma, she presented false smiles to the public and kept her sadness concealed. She tried to ensure their happiness as she wrote letters to each of them every day. She mailed copious batches of fudge and divinity along with boxes of nuts and oranges, apples, donuts, and bread several times a week. Once she mailed nine boxes in one day and imagined their delight when they ripped away the funny-paper wrappings and explored the contents.

Clara received frequent love-filled letters thanking her for the generous packages of goodies and telling about their adjustment to school. They begged her to hurry up and sell out; they wanted her back with them. Reading the words that they missed her renewed her energy to carry on alone. She reread their letters, she committed them to memory, then stashed them away in a box tucked up in the rafters where she intended to keep them forever.

Osakis, Minn.

Sept. 1929

Dear Mom,

How are you? everything is getting along fine here. How is the weather out there? I want to tell you some sad news. I passed in the sixth grade… [Note: The teacher didn't want to be burdened with another grade, so moved Melina into the sixth grade. Emma tutored her at home on the fifth grade curriculum.] Today Lou, Fred, and Charlie threshed. Emma took us over. Louis got his new car. He is going to take us all for a ride in it Sunday. We are going to town Saturday. Yesterday night we got stuck on the Bishop's hill. It was pitch dark. We had to go up to Bishops to telephone to Charley. And Charley come down and fixed the car.

Do you think you can sell out. I hope you can. If you don't sell out you got to come back here in a few days. And I don't mean maybe either. You got to come back here in two days. I pulled my tooth to night. Well, I can't think of any more to write about. So I will close.

From your toothless friend Melina Smiley

A few late summer stragglers, tourists without an agenda, wandered into the store for supplies, rented a room for a night or two before moving on. Display cases with fresh loaves of bread lured local customers back, but Clara sensed a feeling of abandonment. Nurturing children had never been one of her strengths; now she missed the responsibility of caring and cooking for them. She gathered some of their toys and displayed them on shelves around the store where they could be seen. She propped an orphaned doll on the piano where it could watch her work, follow her with its eyes. She didn't want to believe that she was really alone, that her little partners were a thousand miles away learning to cope without her. She watched the clock and waited for them to burst through the door after school, ravenous and sweaty after racing through the street with their friends. She sat at the piano and plinked out the first few notes of their favorite duet with dewy eyes. I'm acting so childish, she scolded as she gathered paper and pencil, and once again, wrote long, detailed letters to each of them.

Ed McManman, still lonely and cantankerous, continued to live in one of her log cabins even though he now paid rent. He shadowed her around the property as she did her chores, tottered behind offering unsolicited advice. Since he'd once tended the store, he felt an affinity for its success and made a nuisance of himself by becoming her self-proclaimed mentor. Clara tolerated his aggravation and turned a deaf ear as he expounded on how to operate a business, but she resented his presence when he arrived at supper time and hung around until the late hours of the night. She didn't mind sharing her food, but when Ed was there, others stayed away.

Strange thuds frequently erupted from his cabin; she stood in her open doorway and listened. She couldn't identify the thumping racket until the familiarity of its rhythm registered. That night when Ed arrived for a free meal, she confronted him at the door. "Ed," she said, "I don't want you splitting wood inside that log cabin. You'll ruin the floor, and I can't afford to put in a new floor."

He hoisted his baggy pants and snapped the suspenders. His stiff finger pointed at her in anger and denied her audacious accusation. "I don't split wood in the house," he retorted in a crackly voice. "I split it out back, then haul it inside."

"Well, I've heard you chopping wood in there, and I want it to stop before you damage my property," she said.

"I don't chop wood inside," he shouted into her face as though she was as deaf as he, then turned and scuttled away like a cockroach, but under the cover of darkness, Clara heard the thud of a hatchet echoing against the floorboards inside his cabin and shook her head in disgust.

Oct. 5, 1929
Osakis, Minn.

Dear sister:

Every evening since you left I have told myself to write you but did not do so. Today the children brought your letters from the mailbox on their way back from school. We were all glad that you made the trip okay and that nothing was missing, as I feared you might miss some of your chickens.

…The children really did surprise me. I looked for tears to be splashing about bedtime, but nothing doing along that line they were just as happy and contented as could be.

Interest in school is running high with them. Melina was put into the sixth grade, and they refused to miss school for threshing saying they would rather go after school…Hope you can sell and get your price. Don't give it away. Write again soon

Em

With the transparent hopefulness of a child, Clara walked

to the post office to mail her letters and packages every morning; she returned home dejected week after week when no letter from the buyer materialized. A query to the broker in Cut Bank clarified the situation when he assured her that business transactions take time, so Clara tried to maintain a positive attitude and continued to send bundles of funny papers, candy, and new overalls to the children.

Early snowfall frosted the mountains, the last fall flowers turned black, nipped by the season's killing frosts, rotted in clumps on the ground. Without Ed there to monopolize the conversation, friends returned to the store to sit around the fire and spin yarns about the old days when men were tough, and their women were tougher.

Black Tuesday, October 29, 1929. Wall Street collapsed. Newspaper headlines screamed doom across the nation. With a silent scream of her own, Clara, lonely for her children, followed the financial nightmare in the daily papers, fervently prayed for a miracle. Maybe the buyer keeps his cash around the house, maybe he doesn't need to go to the bank for money, she hoped. Gathering her courage after procrastinating for another week, she consoled herself with positive maybes, then trudged through the sleet-filled rain to the Log Cabin Inn and telephoned her broker.

"It's all over, Clara," the unctuous voice said at the other end of the line. "The buyer lost his money in the crash, and the deal is off."

Clara's mind searched for another way to entice him to buy her property. She couldn't give up. "He wanted my property real bad," she pleaded.

"Clara, he has no money. These are bad times. I'll do my best to find another buyer, but it won't be easy."

Dazed and discouraged, Clara replaced the receiver. With those few brief words her long-awaited hopes evaporated into thin air like early morning fog dissipating in the warmth of the sun, except that this time the swirling apparition was eradicated by wretched rain that pounded her elusive dreams into oblivion. How am I a-gonna tell the children, she worried as she sloshed home through the muddy street.

She prepared a pot of black tea and carried it to the table, savored its soothing warmth, pondered the plight of her circumstances. What will happen to my kiddies, she worried. They'll have to live without me for a few more months. Life away from the reservation is better for them, they've adjusted to school, and the family seems fond of them, so maybe they'll be all right for a few more months until I can sell this place. Oh, why does the Heavenly Father send me so many trials and tribulations, she sighed. Bearing the guilt for her inadequacies, she finished the last of her tea, pulled on a jacket and went out to close the chicken house door before the onset of darkness.

Then one night, unexpectedly, the Great Northern, the great deliverer of mankind, deposited John Smith at her doorstep. Like a guardian angel, the garrulous John swept her into his protective embrace. She hadn't seen him for months; it was incomprehensible that he should appear when she needed him most. Clara's eyes brimmed with tears as she grasped his hands in her own.

He was astounded. What had happened to the jovial woman he'd known? He solemnly listened with a sympathetic ear as her heart purged itself of woes and fears. He fathomed the depth of her disappointment and worried about her well-being. She seemed fragile, confused, totally bewildered about her dilemma. He'd always admired her kindness toward others, not to mention her good cooking, so he promised to stay in Glacier Park and help her with the business for as long as she needed him. John Smith's energy level never wavered; his boisterous spirits never ebbed.

Melina C. Smiley   Glacier Park
Osakis Minn   Nov 18th '29
My Dear Daughter,

I received your very sweet letter quite a few days ago —and
you can just imagine how happy I am to get your letters. So
glad you all are getting along so lovely and that you are well and
happy.

At last the winter is here in full blast snow and cold too. My
Dear Melina I would have written sooner, but I tell you we had
such nice warm days and I had Charlie Hickson saw up all of
my wood 18$\frac{1}{2}$ cords and John Smith began to neatly rick it up
in these 2 bedrooms. I thought it was to long a job for one person so I helped at all the spare time I could, and it seemed every
evening there was some company…so I never got at writing but
this evening the company went home early, so I thot before John
would come in I would write. He went up town. he as rule goes
up town evenings to see whats going on. he says its always very
quiet.

…I do miss you little pardners beyond words but I know the
best place is where you are. I have not sold yet I will for a good
price so far that hotle man didn't show up again that was going
to buy this place the way he talked.

Well every thing is as usual out here I surely am glad John
Smith stays at our place here—I tell you Melina the loneliness
in this empty cave was terrible. John you know is so nice and
always has jollie funnie things to tell of. I told him he was a God
send…he sure is a good worker at any thing—he was so delighted to hear what you Children *said* to tell him.

And *think of it* he has gained 5 pounds since he came here
about a month ago John seems to be perfectly contented and
happy as a lark right at home which I tell him he must make
himself. It is a pleasure to have any one around thats so good and
nice and pleasant all the time then like old Ed was last winter.

I talked to Ed today and nicely told him again about that

wood splitting in the house he told me he always done all his splitting out side but you see he dont he has the front room of that…house full of wood. and he never does go out side to split as I can hear the chopping Oh it surely makes an awful noise he thinks I can't hear, because he you know is quite deaf.

Last evening Mrs. Shannon was over too she is mad at Shortie because he dont put the water works in the house they live in. Shortie Hinse is just as usual —he talked to me yesterday: but Melina you ought to have seen his duds. I bet they hadn't seen water for a year, and talk of rich he is supposed to be the wealthiest man in town, and works every day like a real poor man.

Bill Buffalo Hide and Joe Buffalo Hide were in town Sat. they came in for supper they had been out hunting horses all day and they were about tired out after Supper they started for home, for a 14 mile trip by moon light.

Frank Shorts the Butter Flies and Bites were all in last week and got lots of groceries they are coming in next week again.

Violet wants to know why I dont make ice cream as I used to last year. I said well I done that to please my kiddies. Oh she said she was a kid she like ice cream above anything.

Well everything is at your school as usual…I am so glad you and GC are doing so nicely at school. and you are gaining to in weight you surely get your sleep there, isn't it great when you get to sleep like that its better then being up so late as we out here were always.

Well Dear Melina I now must close and write to GC too while the evening lasts as tomorrow I will be very busy baking.

With lots of love and many XXXXXXXXXXXXX I received your sweet tiny verses on that separate paper.

Your Ma   Write soon when time.

The winter of 1929 and 1930 after the crash didn't affect the residents of Glacier Park sequestered in their homes, tucked between snowdrifts that nearly covered the roofs as they waited for signs of spring.[1] Farmers, however, felt the brunt of the catastrophe. Unable to meet mortgage payments and pay their taxes, many lost their farms due to plummeting prices and shrinking markets for their commodities.[2] Three of Emma's neighbors committed suicide; the Lake Breeze Poultry Farm faced impending doom. She sold her poultry at a loss, sold a cow every few weeks. Too much responsibility drained her energy. Bedridden for weeks at a time, Pa was in declining health. Emma catheterized him, cared for his every need. That burden plus tutoring the children in their studies each night, the extra laundry and cooking, left her exhausted.

Melina and GC after moving to Lou's farm

She fervently longed for Clara's return, harbored secret dreams of her own to leave Minnesota behind, to join her longtime friend, Alma Larson, in Oakland, California, who was earning $80 a month. Emma yearned for an easier life. In addition, Clara's vivacious offspring irritated Pa, needed firmer guidance than she could provide alone, so in desperation, she leased her farm to a local family and on March 27, moved herself, Pa, and the children back to the old home place to live with Lou, a bachelor in dire need of a cook and housekeeper.

Clara bewailed the move where her children would be subjected to Lou's inflexible obsession with work. Worrisome memories of how he'd demanded more than she could give were rife in her mind. Up at 5 A.M. to milk the cows and do the barn chores before breakfast. Then the 8 A.M. meeting where Lou might say, "Okay, now, Fred, you take the milk to the creamery. Charley, you get the horses hitched up to the hayrack, and Clara, you get the water hauled to the house, then walk to the back forty and pump water for the young stock. Fill the tank, then come out to the hay field and help us until…" Wistfully she considered her kiddies. What will his exacting demands do to them, she wondered, but it was out of her hands. She couldn't afford to bring them back to Glacier Park nor could she abandon her property. It posed a conundrum to her as she discarded one unsuitable option after another.

John Smith readied the business for summer tourists. He mixed gallons of calcimine and whitewashed the inside walls

John Smith and Clara. The children begged her not to remarry.

of the cabins. He spaded the garden and readied it for planting. He felt that Clara needed a strong man around permanently, and after another exhilarating day of hard work, he proposed marriage, but his incantations of love fell on deaf ears. Widowed for nearly two years, she didn't resist his romantic endeavors, but she never seriously considered him as a likely candidate for a husband nor a suitable father for her children. When he departed for Rochester, New York, to visit his mother, he wrote her a passionate letter. She read it with amusement then passed it along to her children who giggled at his message, commented in their next letter that John sure was getting "lovey-dovey."

Effects of the depression finally descended upon Glacier Park. During the winter, local residents had little money to buy

Clara's baked goods, and the rent for her cabins arrived sporadically. The children needed money for clothes, and she sent what she could, but it was only a few dollars a month. She and her friends continued to gather and tell tales, but it was Clara who had a knack for spinning colorful yarns that kept the listeners on edge. Unable to afford the postage to send packages of candy and fruit, she sent money and wrote entertaining stories for the children to read. Sometimes she sent several stories at a time.

Dearest Mother,
...We received the $20 and was sure delighted to get it as money is such a scarce article around here. We also received the lovely bunch of stories and enjoyed reading them very much as they are so interesting. You sure must have a lot of time in order to write those stories...

Yours Lovingly,
Melina Smiley

As early as 1898, a federal geologist toured the area now known as Glacier County, with Tom Dawson, a pioneer resident.[3] They traveled by horse and buggy studying the rocks and terrain, after which the geologist speculated that oil seepage floating on ponds and stagnant pools east of the railroad tracks in Midvale left no doubt about the existence of great quantities of oil and gas in the area. In 1904 a wildcatter by the name of Fred Pike (Frank?) found evidence of oil near Lake Lubec. In 1907 drilling machinery was moved to Lubec, but the venture never materialized because of too much water and too little capital.[4]

After the discovery of oil and gas in other sections of Glacier County, a wildcatter by the name of R.C. Jeffries came into Glacier Park in 1931 and began drilling for oil near Clara's property. Ecstatic about the possibilities it presented, she checked on their daily progress. With the discovery of oil within close proximity of her land, she felt that her property might be more desirable to a buyer. In addition, she wanted to scrape together a few dollars of her own to confer on R.C. Jeffries, a man who encouraged local folk to invest in his speculative holes.[5]

The desire to invest with Jeffries tantalized her more than any venture she'd ever known. She sensed that he was close to black gold. If she invested with him and his well came in, she might become rich and could easily pay the back taxes and have additional money to send to the children. To convince her family of the wealth soon to gush skyward and shower investors with greenbacks, she collected an oil-saturated rock and sent it to Minnesota for them to examine.

Emma again offered timely advice.

Dear Sister,   April 30 – 31
    ...I had your letter the other day about the oil. It sounds pretty good. But I would not put too much confidence in what those people say. It may be that they are in earnest about buy-ing your place, on the other hand it may be just talk on their part so that you'll feel that your property is worth so much that you can afford to buy a good lot of their oil stock. They may have posted that night watchman to tell you about the finding of the oil, so it would seem more real. Sales people do all those things just to sell. Money is very hard to get these times around here with but-ter 29 cents a pound, eggs 11 cents a doz. oats 30 cents a bushel and barley 34, so if you get any money save it. I would like to see [the children] both go through high school. But money has to come in better than it does now on the farm before we can give them any help. I hope the oil will boost your pocket book so you can give them a lift. I always feel suspicious about that Smith. I think he'll fish hard to get your property. For a man to think of marrying some one older than he and a lively sort like the chil-dren say he is, I can't understand it. I guess it's because I consider

every body a crook untill they are proven honest and then you sometimes get fooled. You say love is the greatest power on earth, may be it is so as it seems to make people blind sometimes and that's why crooks stall it to put over deals they other wise could not...

Em

Compared to former years, few tourists appeared in Glacier Park during the summer of 1931, then a mid-July grease fire started in Olson's Pool Hall and burned all the main buildings in that block to the ground except the post office and the Glacier Park Trading Company.[6] Clara's property was not affected by the fire, but with the diminishing tourist trade, she faced a bleak future. She could no longer afford to pay board for the children's horses. In a quandary about what to do, she scraped a few dollars together and hired a local artist to paint the mountains of Glacier Park with Snip and Diamond in the foreground. She mailed it to the children and somberly explained her circumstances. After being gone for two years, they had little hope of returning home in the near future, so they suggested that she sell their horses and use the money herself.

Postage rose to three cents a letter and Emma had to limit the number of letters the children mailed. In addition, Clara's ponderous letters frequently arrived with postage due. The children did not attend high school that year; there was no money available to pay the cost of boarding in town nor to pay transportation fees back and forth to the farm on weekends. Christmas of 1932 was at hand. Emma wrote:

...We are cutting expense as much as possible, did not buy any presents as the children have all they need in wearing things. I am going to make some home made candy and popcorn balls.

Melina enclosed a letter of her own.

...Just think tomorrow is Christmas and I'm so hard up that I can't get any present for nobody. Oh well! I guess everybody is hard up this year.

Clara sent no Christmas gifts to the children; no money accompanied her letters. In desperation, she set aside her pride and petitioned the county attorney for a Mother's Pension as set forth by the Legislative Assembly of the State of Montana. The clerk of court appointed a local resident to thoroughly investigate the facts of the case and report to the county attorney, but Clara was unaware of the activity behind the scenes and continued to apply for the Mother's Pension month after month. No one told her that she could never qualify unless the dependent children lived under her roof, and they were a thousand miles away.[7]

The evening ritual of gathering at Clara's store to share adventurous tales provided free entertainment to the neighbors. Her romantic nature manifested itself in her stories where the good guys always won and the lovers lived happily ever after, ironical plots considering her own situation in life. With her charitable reputation, she was mercilessly exploited by the greed of those whom she trusted, and so best friends carried off a few pieces of wood with each visit while others stopped by the chicken house and gathered a few eggs or stole an old hen for soup. She was aware of their shortcomings, but it never occurred to her to confront them with their thievery, and they in turn could see nothing wrong with the arrangement.

On March 23, 1933, Emma wrote from the farm.

...How are you coming with the mother's pension. Have you had a reply? It will sure be a big help to you if you get it, you sure need it.

...Eggs are 9 cents a doz. for No. 1 and 7 cents for No. 2; Seems they are hardly worth picking up.

Clara struggled for survival in Glacier Park through the summer and winter of 1933-34 with her baking and her garden. Under the cover of darkness, hungry neighbors stole potatoes and vegetables nearly as fast as they grew, and Clara finally installed a padlock on the chicken house door to protect her diminishing flock. The local people had no cash, and tourism had come to a standstill, so when an honest neighbor offered to barter his battery radio for several heads of cabbage, she was more than happy to oblige.

John Smith made his yearly trek to New York in November as Clara continued to dismiss his aspirations of marriage. Her children repeatedly asked her not to remarry; they didn't want anyone to take the place of their father, so Clara spent the late winter nights alone with her radio to keep her company after the neighbors went home.

As she was confined to the store, weathered and battered by winter storms, empty shelves and vacant showcases became sordid reminders of a once-booming business. Through the late evening hours she reminisced about happier times on the Montana frontier; creativity blossomed as she wrote voluminous accounts detailed with vivid descriptions of her life at Lake Lubec. Radio dramas stimulated her lively imagination, while country music from the crackling radio awakened romantic inclinations; poetic endeavors flowed from her pen as she created lyrics of her own and submitted them to a music publisher.

Letters to the children included more samplings of plots from her latest stories; their letters complimented her on her whimsical tales, but it was her listening audience who praised her talent and compared it to the local author, Tom Fountaine, an early Lubec homesteader who wrote about Montana. Their suggestion that she, too, could publish her stories was appealing, so she submitted them to newspapers and magazines, but the editors rejected her creative attempts while her meager income continued to slip through her fingers.

For several months Clara entertained the idea of leaving Glacier Park for domestic employment, but afraid to abandon her business for fear that her property would be ransacked by those desperate enough to break the law, she tenaciously persevered. John Smith returned in April and found her still determined not to marry him, so he boarded the Great Northern and disappeared from her life. Her requests for a Mother's Pension went unanswered; publishers returned her creative endeavors with rejection slips. Dreaming dreams was her forte; making them come true was beyond her reach.

In late March of 1934, without capital to replenish her flock of chickens or purchase seeds for a garden, Clara counted her last few dollars, enough money for train fare to Great Falls where she might find a domestic position. Determined to survive the hard times, she prepared to leave Glacier Park.

She walked across her garden plot, still dormant under winter's icy coverlet. Dead stubble of Brussels sprouts protruded above dirty patches of snow, spasmed in the wind. Crystallized ice prisms reflected sunlight from glazed clumps of frozen soil, windowpanes of ice crunched beneath her feet.

She continued her trek to Ed's cabin and rapped on the door. He's been a good old guy, she admitted as she waited for him to respond to her knock. He opened the door a crack and looked surprised to see her; she seldom came visiting. "Ed," she said matter of factly, "you knew that I'd probably be leaving here for a few months, so today I'm catching the afternoon train for Great Falls. I'll be finding some kind of work down there, maybe cooking on a sheep ranch, who knows."

"What about your place and your garden?" he asked as he opened the door to better hear the distressing news.

"The store will be locked up, but maybe you can keep an

eye on things. I'll let you know where I'm at so you can send the rent money down. My kiddies really need that money. I've already spoken to the Tortensons about their rent." She wistfully glanced across at her spiritual oasis, the source of her summer pleasure. "When my flowers come up, maybe you'd be kind enough to keep them weeded so the neighborhood looks good?"

The lump in her throat choked her to silence as Ed watched her turn and hurry away.

Friends came to the house to wish her well as she secured the windows and stashed treasures out of sight. Too upset to speak, she nodded her thanks as they gave their regards and patted her on the shoulder, a simple gesture of encouragement. She packed faded dresses and well-worn shoes, gathered her aprons, underwear, and stockings and folded them into the battered leather suitcase. She secured its lock and buckled the two belts; with resignation, she placed it outside the door.

Checking the window locks one last time, she reluctantly removed the threadbare coat from the closet, slid her arms into the sleeves. She tucked back a strand of graying hair, adjusted her hat in the mirror and pinned it in place while studying the reflection of a plain, heavy-set woman in her early fifties.

She paused; her thoughts returned to the past. My children left this home years ago. Now it's my time to say goodbye, and I don't know whether there will be anything left to return to, she thought as she walked around the room caressing tender memories: the silent piano with the orphaned doll bidding a sad farewell, the showcases where mounds of donuts once beckoned, the children's toys still scattered across the shelves, her beloved talking machine, and the gleaming cash register, its once-reassuring voice now silenced by the depressed economy. She paused before the individual portraits of herself and Glenn mounted on the wall behind the counter. She contemplated their faraway gaze. "How hopeful we were then, Mr. Smiley," she said quietly.

Accepting her decision as irrevocable, she returned to the table and picked up her pocketbook. Without a backward glance she stepped into the brisk chill and pulled the door shut. She inserted the key and hesitated, remembered that five years ago she'd locked the door and returned to Minnesota with the intention of buying a farm, an intention that fell by the way-side. She now wondered what the next five years might bring.

The lock snapped shut. Dropping the key into the depths of her pocketbook, she turned and picked up her suitcase, walked stalwart and alone toward the depot where the Great Northern, once her great deliverer of dreams, would again surrender her to an unknown destiny.

And what about the family in Minnesota? After the death of Grandpa Charles Miller in 1931, life for Emma became somewhat easier, and Lou enjoyed Glenn's easy ways, his willingness to work. In turn, Glenn shared Lou's passion for the movies and frequently went fishing with Charley, who lived nearby.

Melina helped with the cooking, gardening, and canning every summer and finally attended high school in Long Prairie where she boarded in town during the week and returned to the farm on weekends. Uninterested in continuing school after eighth grade, Glenn worked full-time on the farm for his room and board. In addition, Lou gave him pigs to raise and a garden plot for growing early potatoes to put spending money in his pocket, but farming held no interest for him. The field work was too dirty, the drudgery without end. Like his father, he wanted to become a businessman.

Lou and Emma grew to love the youngsters as if they were their own. Lou took time out of his busy schedule to drive them on occasional sightseeing trips. Emma made sure that they attended local house parties, ice cream socials, and neighborhood picnics. In addition, she allowed them to drive her car, made sure they dressed in the latest styles, nursed Glenn through pneumonia and scarlet fever,[8] and had Melina's cavity-riddled teeth repaired, all paid for by the careful budgeting of money from Clara. With taxes to pay and the dry years with poor crops, Lou and Emma had no money of their own because the 240-acre farm also supported Fred and his family. Not a penny was wasted.

Clara arrived in Great Falls at 6:15 P.M. and walked one block to the Star Hotel, modest accommodations that would become her center of communication for the next few years as she moved from job to job. Rates were a dollar a day or three dollars a week. Each room had an outside exit, and streetcars rattled past her door to all corners of the city.[9] "I'll pay by the day," she said to the desk clerk. "I'll probably take the first job that comes my way."

In the *Great Falls Tribune* she read: Help Wanted Female, Woman Cook, Ranch. Montana Labor Office.[10] When she arrived at the labor office, she discovered that there were several jobs available. The next afternoon she interviewed for a domestic position as cook and housekeeper at a rooming house.

She reached 4th Avenue North and studied the two-story house from across the street. Styled after a French chateau, its stark simplicity with dormers on each side and tall, slender windows presented a style of architecture unfamiliar to her. A wrought iron balcony rail outlined the flat roof while gingerbread scrollwork decorated the expansive front porch. This looks like a nice place, she thought as she rapped at the door and waited.

Mrs. John Slattery, a stout, white-haired lady, opened the door and invited her inside. Clara entered the living room with its fine furniture and lace curtains; a clutter of knickknacks and collectibles adorned the tables.

Mrs. Slattery, a no-nonsense woman, loved to talk, and Clara found herself to be a captive audience as the woman described their conservative life, her husband's profession as a lawyer, and her expectations of domestic help. Overwhelmed by the woman's zeal for conversation, Clara listened and wondered when she might be able to ask a few questions, but Mrs. Slattery continued. "Now I'm looking for a strong woman who knows how to work. I will expect you to do all the cooking for Mr. Slattery, myself, and the grounds keeper who lives downstairs; you, of course, will take your meals with us.

"In addition, you will dust and clean the house every day and clean the rooms after people move out. I have two rooms in the basement and two cabins out back where the renters can cook. I rent a few other rooms just for sleeping purposes. I provide all linens and bedding that you will wash and iron every week along with the personal laundry for Mr. Slattery and myself. For your convenience, however, you'll do a few loads every day rather than wait for one specific washday. There are lots of clotheslines in the backyard. Oh, did I tell you that you have to get the laundry done early in the morning? You see, I have only one sink for rinsing the clothes, and the renters in the basement use that sink to wash their dishes. In addition, you'll have to share the washing machine with my renters on Saturday; Mr. Slattery and I won't allow any laundry to be done on Sunday."[11]

Clara listened with dismay as Mrs. Slattery's chatter continued about her lovely home, one of the oldest homes in Great Falls. She paused to straighten a doily on the back of the sofa then continued. "For your services we will pay you $20 a month plus room and board." Desperate for a job during those hard times when farm workers made less than $10 a month, Clara eagerly accepted the position.

During the winter at Glacier Park she'd done little except care for her own needs. Now she weighed nearly two hundred pounds and found herself exhausted before noon after rising at dawn, preparing breakfast, doing laundry, baking pastries and bread, and preparing the noon meal. She walked to the grocery store for fresh vegetables, returned to clean the house, gathered the laundry from the line, and ironed it all before starting a supper that always included three courses and seldom finished before 7 P.M., after which she again cleaned the kitchen, completed unfinished chores, and retired to her room.

The cooking and cleaning presented no problem, but the burden of laundry took its toll on her energy. Even though the Slatterys had electricity, they lived a frugal lifestyle, and Clara's laundry chores were done in a wooden washtub with an agitator that had to be worked by hand. She washed several loads each day by pushing and pulling the handle on the agitator until the clothes were clean. She fed each article into a wringer on top of the machine with her left hand while her other powerful arm turned a crank and forced the clothes through the wringer where they dropped into the lone, stationary tub of rinse water against the wall. She sloshed them up and down to clear the suds, then put them through the wringer again before hanging them on the clothesline to dry. Sometimes the white clothes had to be boiled beforehand to remove stains, sometimes they had to be submerged in a bluing solution to make them appear whiter. Whatever the routine of the day, laundry presented the biggest problem because the renters impatiently demanded to wash their dishes and monopolized the washing machine on Saturdays.

Clara used stoic restraint from complaining about the workload. She tried to follow Lou's motto: rise early, work hard, and sleep like a baby, but she wasn't sleeping well, and she resented not having time to write stories. She could hardly muster the energy to write letters to her children.

Mrs. Slattery, a kindly lady, frequently sat with her needlework and listened to details about Clara's children in Minnesota, but was oblivious to her exhaustion until the day Clara collapsed on the laundry room floor panting and wheezing for breath. Startled at seeing the large woman lying helpless, she summoned a doctor who revived Clara and examined her in the privacy of her room.

"Have you had these spells before?" he asked as he moved the stethoscope across her chest.

"Only when I'm overtired or worried," she answered. "I have this big house to keep up, but I need the job to support my children who live with my sister in Minnesota."

The doctor nodded in understanding but continued to give advice. "You've got to stop working so hard," he said. "I'll talk to Mrs. Slattery about this. Maybe she'll free you from some of your duties."

Pleased with Clara's cheery disposition and excellent cooking, Mrs. Slattery lightened her work load so she could rest and take care of personal business. Clara continued to correspond not only with her Minnesota family but also with friends in Glacier Park. She received this letter from old Ed written May 14, 1934.

I saw Bertha and the Davis and they told me that they would write to you. It is not very busy in the park yet not tell next month. There is a picture show in Mike's every Saturday evening. They are expecting a big crowd in the Park this summer, but I guess the world's fair will get most of the people. Floyd Lutz will have a nice building when it is finished. I suppose there is lots of people coming in to Great Falls every day. So I do not know of anymore to write. Hoping you will get better, Yours truly

Ed McManman

With more free time, Clara began to write again. She submitted fictional work to the *Great Falls Leader*, which published serialized stories in the daily paper, and she submitted autobiographical accounts of the homestead to the *Great Falls Tribune,* noted for its historical narratives about early settlers, but her manuscripts were rejected, so she sent them on to her children to read.

With a bit of extra money she bought a white shirt and tie for GC, now seventeen years old, but being unaware of the latest fashions for young women, she sent money to Melina, who was now fifteen. Touched by her devotion to the teenagers, Mrs. Slattery enclosed a necklace with a matching bracelet for Melina.

Clara bought a used typewriter and practiced with diligence; pen and ink could not keep pace with her creative ideas. Meanwhile, money from the renters seldom materialized, and property taxes were her nemesis. She continued to submit applications for the Mother's Pension and harbored aspirations of cooking on a sheep ranch, where she could earn a higher salary. Emma responded.

…Don't you think that work on a sheep ranch might be too hard for you, as long as you are not supposed to work so hard. If they pay $30 a month they have a lot of work, and nothing handy like it is where you now are. Of course you know what you can stand. With your ambition you are apt to do too much. …You should have had mother's pension, when you are not able to pay your taxes. If you did not ask Hines to come here to see the children, then he went for some one else. Any one especially wanting to see two children like that, would surely give them some little treat. He did not give them even a little piece of gum. Don't it look that way to you? I think he was asked to stop off by your town board so that they could say they sent someone out here to see how the children were getting along, in case you insisted on that pension. I think you could get back pay yet if you went after it. If I were you, I would talk to your employer about

it yet. That outfit in the park works against you all they can because they want to get your property cheap.

Emma

Clara's life was fraught with despair, filled with financial
woes. In desperation she wrote a letter to President Roosevelt
and asked him to intervene on her behalf for tax relief. Meanwhile, she poured her frustrations into the plots of her stories
and shared them with anyone who would take the time to read
them.

She explored the possibility of starting a writer's club. She
would advertise for stories in the local papers and charge ap-
plicants $2 for each submission, then offer luxurious prizes like
new typewriters and deluxe fountain pens for the winners. It
wouldn't cost her anything because the hundreds of applications and fees would pay for the prizes, and she'd have money
left over.

She intended to publish the winning entries in magazine
format, sell them at newsstands, and pocket the profits. In that
way, she wouldn't have to work as a cook, and could insert her
own stories in the publication. Clara wrote of the proposed
writer's club to her family. Glenn responded to her plan.

...It takes a lot of money to get any thing like that started and
where are you going to get it? That prize giving that you talk
might work and might *not*. If there isn't enough interested to
join at $2 each where would you get all the prize money that you
offered to pay out to the winners? Times are hard now and there
ins't many people interested in spending $2 like that they most
likely need it for something else. Maybe I am all wrong and don't
understand just how it works but thats what I think according to
my ideas.

In early October Mr. Slattery confronted Clara about her

spendthrift ways at the grocery store. His accusations accosted her delicate nature. Was he questioning her integrity? She felt humiliated. Even though Mrs. Slattery had been kind to her, she saw the scolding as an opportunity to seek work on a ranch where she might make more money. She contemplated the situation at hand, then answered with alacrity, "Gee whiz, I can't change my way of cooking after so many years, so I guess I'll have to move on. You'll just have to find yourself another cook." With deliberate intentions not to concede to his demands nor to Mrs. Slattery's pleadings to reconsider her hasty decision, she promptly cleaned out her room and returned to the Star Hotel carrying her suitcase and typewriter.

At the Montana Labor Office, she found several ranches advertising for a cook at $30 a month. With no applicants competing against her, she chose the best of the lot and decided that if the job was too demanding, there were plenty of other ranches needing cooks. During the next three months she moved three times, always returning to the Star Hotel between positions.

In mid-January of 1935, Clara accepted a position at the Lyman dairy farm nine miles from Great Falls, again salaried at $30 a month. The train rumbled past flat, fertile fields and deposited her at Gerber. Mrs. Lyman, a religious woman, welcomed her to the farm. Her graying hair framed a face with an unhealthy pallor. Her troubled eyes darted about the kitchen weighing the cost of every meal, every ingredient. Busy fingers tangled themselves in apron pockets as she informed Clara of her expected role on the modern dairy farm and described the conditions of employment.

"On this farm, Clara, we all work together. We milk fifty cows and have a lot of land, so we've hired six men to help us. Some of them get up very early for the morning chores, and you'll be expected to cook for all of them as well as prepare meals for the family. In addition, you will do the family laundry as well as that of the hired hands."

Clara looked around at the kitchen. Everything seemed handy; there were lots of supplies. "I see that you have an electric range," she said. "That should make it easier to cook for so many people."

"Because you'll also be cooking for the family, I'll help you in the kitchen at mealtime. We have an electric washing machine, too, so that will make your job easier," she said. "The hired men have been taught to wash before meals without creating a lot of unnecessary laundry. I've placed a couple of wash basins with soap and water outside the kitchen. Instead of having them dry on towels, I keep a supply of washcloths out there for them to use. It makes it much easier on laundry day, and they dry hands just as well as a heavy towel."

"Where are the meals served?" Clara asked.

"I'll serve the family in the dining room, of course, and you and the men will eat out here in the kitchen."

The idea of eating with the men appalled her. "But I've always taken my meals with the families on other ranches," Clara protested.

"No," Mrs. Lyman said, "our family prefers to eat alone. You'll eat out here."

Discouraged about having to eat with a bunch of men who probably smelled like cow manure, Clara complained to Emma who, surprisingly, offered no sympathy and sided with the Lyman family.

…I think you are getting real good pay. Men around here are only getting $15 a month and very few jobs at that. You mentioned about eating with the hired help. You can't blame people where they have a lot of help that way. Some eat so sloppy that it takes one's appetite. I remember one time they hired some one to shred corn here. He ate with his knife, gooped into the butter with it, even if there was a butter knife, and every once in a while, let out a hilarious horse laugh, over almost nothing and even spit on the floor.

Clara expected that she'd have to tolerate a great deal of male nonsense, but the men were an appreciative group who enjoyed her delectable meals and minded their manners. Mrs. Lyman, usually underfoot in the kitchen, watched Clara like a hawk.

"Clara, you're making too much food. No one needs to eat as much as you prepare."

"But these men are working hard. They should have more to eat than one helping," Clara protested, knowing from first-hand experience the amount of energy one expends on a farm.

Mrs. Lyman continued her lesson in frugality. "And don't use so many eggs in your baking. They aren't necessary; use half as many as you usually do." Clara couldn't understand such thriftiness, but she did her best to comply.

The convenience of an electric washing machine made her job easier than at other ranches where she'd worked. Mondays were reserved for sheets, towels, and the family clothing. She used the same wash water and rinse water with each load. First she washed the white sheets and linens. After she put them through the wringer into the rinse water, she set the next load of whites to agitate, then she put the sheets through the wringer, again into a second rinse water, and finally through the wringer a last time into a wicker basket. She carried it out to the wire clothesline where she doubled each sheet and secured it with clothespins until the length of the line looked like a regatta of spinnakers against the blue Montana sky. Then she returned to the house and continued with the next load, followed by the colored clothes, and finally the towels. The clothes dried quickly in the dry, Montana air.

When she washed clothes for the hired men, she used the

same procedure. She started with their underwear, followed with their blue work shirts, and finally their heavy denim overalls, stiff and crusted with muck. The men wore long underwear, short-sleeved cotton in summer and long-sleeved wool in winter; the "union suits" buttoned up the front and had a square trapdoor in the back that could be unbuttoned and dropped when necessary. She hung them up by the shoulders with the buttons unbuttoned and the trapdoors gaping open, and they danced on the clotheslines to the wailing harmony of prairie winds. She hung the shirts by the tails; she tossed the bibs of the overalls over the line and fastened them with clothespins, then turned the pockets inside out so they'd dry quickly as they flapped in the breeze.

With the convenience of electricity, Clara felt energetic again. In her spare time, her typewriter clattered away with letters to her children and new stories of adventure. Clara enjoyed her position at the Lyman farm and the camaraderie with the men at mealtimes, but the opportunity to become a publisher and make easy money tempted her, so once again she wrote to her family about the writer's club proposition, but Emma remained skeptical.

> …but it sounds to me too much like getting something for
> nothing, those schemes seldom work out good…You would have
> to publish a magazine for which you want these stories, and an
> outlay for that takes thousands of dollars…I think it would be
> a losing proposition. I think to manage anything like that one
> would have to have a high school education topped off with a
> college training along that special line.

Rumors of financial problems had been circulating for weeks amongst the hired help at the Lyman farm. On June 1, with Mrs. Lyman in poor health and the mortgaged farm expected to be dissolved, the family released Clara from her position and provided her with references. She returned once again to the Montana Labor Office.

"With this recommendation from the Lyman family, we have a job for you, Clara. Senator and Mrs. Blankenbaker own a ranch up at Virgelle. They own fifteen miles along the bank of the Missouri River and grazing land all the way north to Lonesome Lake. It's somewhere around 27,000 acres, and they raise mostly sheep with a few cattle thrown in. They're shearing the sheep now and shipping the wool to market, so they need a cook to feed the crew and work through the summer. It says here that you'll cook three meals a day, but Mrs. Blankenbaker will assign one of her house girls to assist you. There's no housework and no laundry. All you'll do is cook."

Clara enjoyed cooking in large quantities, and without the extra burden of housekeeping chores, it sounded like an interesting position. She had worked on large ranches, but none the size of the Blankenbakers', and she'd never worked for such a prestigious employer before.

"I think I'll like that," she said. "How do I get out there?"

"Catch the Great Northern to Virgelle. It's about an hour's ride north of here, and it's nothing but a whistle stop where the Blankenbakers built a mercantile store and operated a bank, but the bank's been out of business since 1927. The store is operated by her brother. They built the town and named it after themselves, Virgil and Ella, but nobody lives there. It's just the store, the old bank building, an elevator, and a warming hut for people waiting to catch the train, but the Blankenbakers have a real swell place right on the Missouri River. I think you'll like it," he assured her.

Working for a state senator required a more dignified appearance than that for her previous employers, so she purchased a few new cotton dresses, shoes, and stockings. There was no time to waste as she hurried to the Great Northern Depot, boarded the train, and settled down for a journey into unknown territory across relatively flat farmland until they reached the bustling town of Fort Benton on the Missouri River. There the flatlands turned into jumbled pillows of shortgrass prairie where the wind never slept. Deep coulees carved by waters from receding glaciers from the last ice age left ugly scars across the face of the earth. Outcroppings of wind-sculpted sedimentary rocks cluttered the ridges, while occasional grayish-green clumps of sagebrush sprinkled with wildflowers splashed color against the hillsides.

Virgelle, a hidden place, nestled in a valley with blemished, mutilated hills on one side and the Missouri River on the other, beyond which lay some of the bleakest badlands in Montana, windswept and bare, as dry as bleached bones.

The Virgelle Mercantile lay abandoned in the heat of the day except for the clerk who drove Clara down the narrow, dusty road to the Blankenbaker home site and deposited her without comment at the front door. The white, three-story Dutch colonial house was a grand affair with wide gambrel dormers and sweeping porches on two sides. Trellises covered three windows where sweetpeas and morning glories wrapped their tendrils around each other in unabashed, exuberant charm. Clusters of greening perennials along the foundation promised luminous blossoms while the warm, June wind ruffled the silvered leaves of the cottonwood grove, which provided a sense of seclusion from the outside world, a beautiful, isolated estate.[12]

The facilities and supplies were excellent, and her helper was eager to work. They set the table ahead of time with the plates, glasses, and cups upside down on the oilcloth to discourage flies; the knives, forks, and spoons lay in separate containers scattered down the center of the table within easy reach of the men. The women sliced loaves of bread into thick hunks, put out butter, jelly, and honey, and covered it all with a clean tablecloth until mealtime.

Trained by Mrs. Lyman to cook for a large crew, Clara set washbasins of water outside the door and rang the supper gong, but these men hadn't been trained by a woman with the genteel manners of Mrs. Lyman. These men were professionals who worked hard and moved from ranch to ranch without any inclination to savor the finer things of life. Time was money for a sheep shearer, and with over 25,000 animals to handle on this ranch alone, they exploded into the dining hall with churlish behavior and maledictions about the heat.

Clara observed them with horror as she removed the white cover from the table. Chair legs scarred the floor, grated her nerves as the hungry crew bellied up to the table, grabbed utensils, and emptied great pitchers of water into drinking glasses. Greedy hands wrenched steaming bowls of potatoes and vegetables to their plates, dumped mountains of grub, and assaulted it in ravenous haste while reaching for platters of meat. Each man slapped several slabs of mutton onto his plate as the next hungry soul grabbed the platter and mounded the mouthwatering delicacy before himself. They drowned their fare beneath quarts of gravy and ate with rapacious intensity to quell voracious appetites in their frenzy to get back to work, to make more money. The clatter of knives and forks bounced off the walls while the gulping and shoveling continued amidst hearty good cheer, grunts, belches, and derisive language, as the helper poured coffee and Clara served dessert. Within fifteen minutes the well-fed crew headed out the door leaving behind a table in disarray, a clutter of dirty dishes, tobacco stains and cigarette butts on the floor, but the worst offense was the fetid stench of sweat and sheep the two women tried to expel as they braced open the windows and doors and flapped dishtowels above their heads to start the foul air moving.[13]

Clara rose at 4 A.M. to set her yeast for bread, then slid several pies and cakes into the oven before the men showed up for breakfast, a repeat of her former routine at the Glacier Cash Grocery. After each meal, the women cleaned the kitchen and reset the table. Before long they had it down to a system that allowed them some free hours in the afternoon before supper. Mrs. Blankenbaker understood that there was enough work to keep the women busy all day, but she encouraged a rest break each afternoon. Clara used that time to walk a mile to fetch her mail from the mercantile store at Virgelle.

She could no longer cover great distances in the heat of the day like she'd done at Rudyard, so instead of walking on the dusty road, she cut across the untamed wilds of the shortgrass prairie, but it wasn't like the prairie at her soddy. This grass concealed sharp spines of prickly pear cactus that cut into her ankles. The knifelike blades of yucca brushed against her stockings, while cockleburs and thistles attached themselves for a ride. Her eyes were drawn to hillsides swathed in meandering gray masses that bleated and echoed across the valley as golden eagles floated silently on the air currents searching for a ground squirrel or rabbit, perhaps even a lamb. Once or twice she heard threatening rattles from hidden places, but she usually arrived at the post office without incident.

Emma wrote on July 19, 1935.

…If I were you I would let that publishing game rest a year or two.

The papers are full of rumors of war, if you have a paying bussiness your son would be one of the first called to go, but on the other hand if you are poor your son would be put off till the last, because you could say he helps to support you, another thing, suppose your adventure is a complete flop, how is Melina to finish her school? There is always a chance of any adventure to turn out a failure.

Your enterprise takes a lot of money to swing right from the start, so why not wait till Melina is thru school and then if you still feel the same, she with a good education might be of help to you, yes much help.

These are too poor times to start in any thing, many people without work, money is not moving. Grim determination will not carry one thru when the odds are too great against one.

That song you had published one time "My Blue Eyed Darling", did not bring you anything, at least I never heard you say that it did. Books and stories will not sell these times, I'm sure of that. Advice costs nothing for me to give nor for you to read. But you consider that a lot before you take the final step.

Clara was disappointed by the lack of correspondence from her teenage children and Emma's negative attitude toward publishing, but her enthusiasm for writing never waned. She wrote stories as the summer moon rose above the eastern banks of the Missouri River turning the prairie sagebrush into silvered filigree. Yucca pods waffled in the wind while nighthawks rose and circled, dived and flitted in their search for nocturnal insects, while the staccato outbursts of Clara's typewriter thrust romantic fantasies into the night air. Dense clouds of mosquitoes bred in the stagnant backwaters of the muddy Missouri descended with bloodthirsty zeal, but Clara kept a mixture of bicarbonate of soda and water in her room to sponge over infected bites and soothe the itching as she pounded out her sagas.

During the month of August, in addition to their cooking duties, the women canned hundreds of jars of garden produce, sometimes not retiring until after midnight. Preserving the earth's bounty in jars reflecting the radiant abandon of ripe tomatoes and garden vegetables offered satisfaction as she carried them to Mrs. Blankenbaker's cellar and proudly displayed them on white-papered shelves.

In late September with the wool shipped and canning completed, Clara returned to the Great Falls area where she passed the next six months working at six different ranches. She saved nothing for property taxes, spent sparingly for her own needs, and sent the balance of her wages to the children.

In February of 1936, she accepted a cooking position on the Carmichael Ranch eighteen miles south of Augusta, an expansive spread that covered nearly fifty square miles and was hidden away in the valley of Flat Creek where the amethyst splendor of the Rockies hovered on the western horizon.[14] Clara was enthralled with the lovely automobile ride across the top of snow-covered hills. She observed rock cairns stacked on distant hilltops, where bored sheepherders competed against each other to create the highest pinnacle.

The terrain of the land changed abruptly. Unaccustomed to riding in a car, Clara's stomach knotted and lurched as the driver negotiated hairpin curves down through the coulees, then accelerated around steep corners and climbed up the dizzying gradient until, once again, the tortuous track dropped away and dissolved into a creek bottom where they repeated the roller coaster adventure. She grasped the door handle. "How far do we have to go?" she moaned. "Can I get out and walk?"

"Oh, no, we're almost there," the driver said as he braked for the turn. They traveled the level road up through the valley where Flat Creek meandered through ice-shrouded willows and snow frosted the tops of towering hay stacks like mounds of whipped cream, along the driveway up to the ranch where the house and barns sought shelter in a protected pocket between the hills.

Because of the enormity of the ranch, Clara had hoped for a house as beautiful as the Blankenbakers', but it lacked the luxurious amenities of the senator's estate along the Missouri River. In addition, it was located miles from Augusta. Mail service was a haphazard affair, so after a few months, she called it quits.

She returned to Great Falls and accepted a number of other unsatisfactory domestic positions in town; one family kept cats in the house. She detested cats. "Momma always said that every hair on a cat's body was pure poison and sometimes the dirty things would hop on a baby's chest while it was sleeping and suck the air out of its lungs trying to get at the child's milky breath," she wrote to her children. One wealthy family had two unruly siblings who frequently flipped up her skirt and peeked at her voluminous bloomers,[15] while one female employer demanded an hour massage each night before retiring.

Ranch life paid better with less hassle, so in April she accepted a cooking position a few miles out of Shelby, but in addition to cooking, she was expected to tend several hundred chickens, plant and nurture the garden, and do the canning. Too tired to continue any longer, she pocketed her wages on June 15 and climbed aboard the Great Northern bound for Glacier Park and her own garden.

But the woman who returned was not the woman who'd left. There was little gentility at the ranches where she'd been cooking for the last two years. Depraved conversation assaulted her modesty with improper suggestions, and randy cowboys swatted her fanny like profligate Romeos when they wanted another piece of pie. Witless palaver interspersed with curses and oaths whooped across the table as they wolfed down their food with open mouths and splattered their work mates in good-natured camaraderie.

She'd smelled the best of them when men slathered themselves with cologne before visiting the ladies of leisure. She'd smelled the worst of them retching and vomiting rotgut whiskey. Dry sweat mingled with manure as fetid breath from neglected teeth frequently complimented her on a tasty meal. Drunken cowboys with stuporous eyes sometimes regarded her as the Aphrodite of the prairie; they groveled like petulant children and begged for sexual favors as she swore at them from behind a locked door and shook her head in disgust. Profanity was what they understood.

The Whiteville Methodist Church was built by the rural community sometime between 1880 and 1885. The Todd County Museum in Long Prairie has a quilt made by the ladies of the church with the names of all church members embroidered on it. By 1950, when the author was a child, the church was no longer used. In 1995, only rubble remained. Photo courtesy of Todd County Museum.

Although she tired from the hard work, she had reveled in the mealtime banter with untamed ranch hands who, unknowingly, provided raw material for literary endeavors that spewed out of her typewriter. She'd worked too hard and seen too much to return to the docile, polite society of the Whiteville Methodist Church and the pastoral peacefulness of the Long Prairie River Valley, but she was unaware of that fact as expletives and colorful language augmented her letters to the family, and caused Emma to throw up her hands in exasperation at Clara's explicit descriptions of life at the ranch.

Glenn and his mother Clara after his return to Glacier Park to live.

PART VII

Going Home

When you live so close to the bare bones of reality, there is little room for sentiment.

Nannie Alderson[1]

At fifty-three years of age, Clara boarded the Great Northern and lowered her stout figure into a window seat. She gazed south across the prairie as the train liberated her from another summer of arduous labor; she looked forward to a slower pace of life in spite of the hardships that awaited her back at Glacier Park. Old Ed had passed away, and recent letters from the winter caretaker of the Log Cabin Inn described how Clara's latest renters had abandoned the cabins in a filthy state and stolen most of the contents. *I wonder if anything is left to clean up after that low thievish bunch moved out,* she thought as she watched the flatlands of Shelby and Cut Bank merge onto the foothills of Browning as the Great Northern began its ascent toward Glacier Park.

As the train approached the depot, she leaned forward in her seat and searched the streets for a familiar face, but only deterioration and hopelessness welcomed her back. The Depression had left its mark with dilapidated buildings and streets scarred with potholes. Hurrying toward the comfort of home with her suitcase and typewriter, she approached the derelict property with speechless astonishment. Buried in weeds as high as the windows, the dark, foreboding cabins sprawled before her. The greening spears of hollyhocks, the lobed leaves of columbine feebly struggled to rise above the choke hold of tall grass and pig weeds that thrived in the garden. The chicken house door complained on rusty hinges, the open doorway yawned its welcome before slamming shut in the breeze. She couldn't see the log house rental, but felt that it was probably as sorry-looking as the rest. "How will I ever get this mess cleaned up," she mumbled as she set her suitcase aside.

The dismal store and its surroundings presented another disappointment. Flower beds, once so beautifully manicured with rows of yellow and purple iris nestling against the foundation, now bulged with clumps of quackgrass and dandelions. Spiked leaves and pale magenta flowers of Canadian thistles bobbled in the breeze. Shingles, ripped from the roof by the tempests of winter, lay scattered amidst debris of rusty cans, shredded inner tubes, a chair with two missing legs, a broken cup, a leather boot chewed into strips by local dogs, abandoned possessions by those who'd moved on in search of a better life. A heavy padlock prevented entry into the store. She turned away in frustration. "I can't even get into my own place," she fumed. "I guess those lousy thieves got in here, too."

A female voice welcomed her home. "Oh, Mrs. Smiley," she said. "I'm so glad you're back to take care of your property. Your renters nearly wrecked the place with their boozing and parties. When they left, they bragged about how they'd stayed here for nothing, then took all your furniture with them."

Clara turned. Peggy Shannon, a short woman in her early thirties, stood at the corner. With marcelled hair cut just below her ears and secured with a tangle of bobby pins, her pretty eyes and round face showed the worried lines of hardship.

Clara snorted in disgust. "That lousy booze stuff sure causes lots of trouble. All booze joints should be ordered shut up." She rattled the padlock. "What's this all about?"

"That wild bunch jimmied your door open and stole a lot of your personal stuff and made a mess in there."

What a rotten homecoming, Clara thought to herself. "Those dirty, thievish liars in the log house told me they'd send the rent money to my kiddies, and they never sent one dime. He had a good job, and she took in washing, so they could afford it. I'm as mad as a hornet!"

Mrs. Shannon gnawed at a hangnail, removed a bobby pin from her hair, pried it open with her teeth, jammed it into the tangle behind her ear. "My husband and I were desperate for a place to live. Your letter said that you wouldn't care if we used your place since you had no renters anyway, so we moved into the back part of the store and cleaned it all up for you. After the people moved out of the log house, we calcimined the walls and moved our stuff in there, then padlocked this door shut so your place would be safe," she said.

Unwavering in her disgust, Clara trampled through weeds, high-stepped over a pile of debris to the paned window for a look inside.

Peggy Shannon recalled Clara's former generous nature, her jolly disposition. This angry woman frightened her. "Oh, please don't make us move out, Mrs. Smiley. We need a place to live, and there aren't any other houses in town. We'll gladly pay $10 a month rent and help you repair the rest of the place. When we get the cabins fixed up, we'll move into one of those, and I have another renter lined up for the big house."

Clara compressed her lips and nodded vacantly, waited for more information. The young woman searched her pocket for the key, then removed the padlock and swung the door open. She returned to the street to retrieve the battered suitcase while Clara stepped across the threshold and paused until her eyes adjusted to the dimness. The interior of her store was neat and clean, but few of her possessions remained. Thieves had plundered every closet, every drawer. The kitchen had been robbed of her best pots and pans. Empty shelves gaped where the children's toys once perched. Even the orphaned doll had been kidnapped. In the bedrooms bare mattresses lay open and stained. The neatly ironed sheets and pillowcases she'd so carefully wrapped in newspaper had been selectively pilfered from the dresser drawers. The best hand-made quilts she'd crafted over the years were also gone; only tattered blankets remained. The children's sleds and saddles, skis and pedal cars were all gone. Even the counter was missing. With a quick glance into the living area she took inventory of the rest of the furniture. "Rats!" she exclaimed in disappointment. "They stole my talking machine!"

"The renters in the big house took it with them. Their kids bragged around town about how they hadn't paid any rent, and they even had your phonograph. When they told me that they said, 'Swell, ain't it!'" She chewed her lip, reached down and pulled up a frayed sock that had worked its way beneath her heel; she watched Clara's reaction before continuing. "They moved out to a ranch somewheres, but we don't know where, and I talked to the ones who stole your counter, and they said you could have it back if you come and got it."

Not one to hold a grudge against her neighbors and knowing the desperation of the families migrating back and forth across the country during the Depression, Clara gratefully accepted the woman's help and soon had the cabins disinfected and rented to more responsible people. She battled the weeds and coaxed the flower beds back to life. Energized by warm summer days, she stirred the garden soil with her hoe from earliest light, and planted rows of vegetables that grew to maturity since the light-fingered neighbors had moved away. The lovely smell of warm bakery goods floated through the streets once more and plump, sugared donuts tumbled out of the showcase. She opened a small soup and sandwich shop in her store using her garden vegetables and bakery items, but her generous nature compelled her to serve too much food for too little money, so the soup and sandwich enterprise fell by the wayside. That was a lousy investment and a quick way to lose money, she berated herself as she resurrected former dreams of becoming a publisher.

Glenn, a handsome young man now twenty years old, detested the hard, dirty work of farming and wanted to move back to Glacier Park to manage the business for his mother. He wrote:

> ...As long as we have got any property out in the Park...there is sure something that I can do out there it seems to me...I don't say its a nice place to go but everything we got is tied up there, and thats where anyone should be instead of out working some other place. There surely is something one can do somehow.
>
> Maybe that idea of yours about publishing is good, but it takes lots of money to get any thing like that started, and where are you going to get the money?

Meanwhile, Clara continued to discourage Glenn from coming. "You can't go back to the old days," her letters kept telling him throughout the year, but nothing could quell his determination. The desire to rebuild the remnants of his father's estate was stronger than the signs of the times, and Melina, soon to be a high school graduate, anticipated rekindling childhood friendships and dancing at the new Mike's

Place. Clara repeatedly warned her that she wouldn't like it; she wouldn't last two days in the crumbling community after the easy years in Minnesota, but Melina laughed it off and asked to be her own judge.

After nearly eight years of laughter, hard work, and good times with Clara's children, Lou and Emma couldn't bear to think about life without them. The children's hopes of returning to Glacier Park, where the future promised nothing, worried the aging aunt and uncle as they tried to discourage them. Emma wrote to Clara:

> Glen still thinks he'll go to Montana. He thinks the times are now like they were when he left, things have changed since then. To convince him on that Lou wrote to Shorty Hynes and he wrote back that things are very bad there. Said that if it was not for the W.P.A. work many would go hungry, no work to be had, said his house was empty as he could get no renter that could pay the rent, and the people living in your house were not paying anything he thot.
>
> He has a little money saved up about $100, his car is paid for. You know how long $100 will last when you pay for your board and buy gas for a car...I hope Glen decides not to go as I'm afraid all his savings will go for expense. When one has no income his car will have to set, can't even have it in shelter, as it takes quite a little to keep a car going, gas, oil, tires, and a repair bill now and then.

Emma's Victorian ways had influenced the children with polished manners and a gentle demeanor, but they did not embrace her innate distrust of others; they anticipated a future of adventure without mishap. They refused to foresee hazards on the western horizon, but Emma feared the realities of life that awaited them in Glacier Park. Mostly, she dreaded their reunion with Clara's raw, frontier ways and rough manners.

In a letter of April 15, 1937, Emma cautioned her sister about inappropriate language.

> …Glen and Melina seldom use any swear words or slang. Glen is always kind of peeved when you use any in your letters especially some of the descriptive words for some of the people that visit at your place. He's always saying "suppose some one saw this letter." Some times a mail carrier may leave it in the wrong box, some people will steam a letter open. So he said that he was going to tell you to be a little careful and not make them too strong. Melina and I insisted that he not mention it but we could not change him any. I especially did not want him to say any thing as I thot you would think I told him to, which I absolutely did not…

Although Emma's farm had been forfeited to the bank, she sacrificed her meager savings to accompany the young people back to Glacier Park. She felt that her comforting presence might temper the shock that awaited them at the other end. Perhaps her close scrutiny of strangers would discourage any rogue from taking advantage of two trusting young people. Maybe the youngsters wouldn't like it there and would return home with her to live for a few more years.

The dream of driving to Glacier Park had been uppermost in Glenn's mind when he shopped for a car of his own.

Glenn and Melina with the Chevrolet.

He finally selected a 1928 Chevrolet coach that could withstand the perils of washboard country roads as well as the abuse of a journey across Montana. Emma hated to drive; it made her nervous, so she gave him her car as a trade-in. The dealer allowed him $35, took a $50 down payment, and monthly payments of $10. The total cost was $110.

Now with Melina's graduation at hand, Glenn prepared for the trip west. He checked the water level in the battery and radiator. He got the car greased and the oil changed. He washed and polished the exterior until the green paint matched the sprouted wheat fields in the bright Minnesota sunshine. He dusted the interior and wiped down the seats. Lastly, he checked the tire pressure all around and bought a new patch kit in case of a blowout in the Montana wastelands. He studied the road maps for the easiest route and worked out a timetable for each day's travel. The success of the trip rested on his shoulders; he did not want to put Emma at risk.

Melina rushed through days of final exams with her mind on her packing. What should she take, what should she leave? She packed and sorted as Emma watched in dismay seeing her own happiness disappear into the depths of the luggage. "You'd better leave some of your clothes here so you'll have something to come back for," she said hopefully, but Melina packed with the determined finality of going home forever. With high school behind her, there was nothing to hold her interest in Minnesota. She'd applied for a scholarship to Staples Normal School, a teacher-training institute, but so had eight other girls from Long Prairie High School, and she had little hope of being selected. No, she was returning to her mother, her home, and her dear friends.

Emma worked hardest of all in preparation for the trip. Glenn wanted her to stay with them for a month in Glacier Park, but two weeks was all she could be away from her garden and Lou's housekeeping needs. She hoed the weeds, watered the tomatoes, cleaned and dusted, baked extra loaves of bread, finished the washing and ironing, and suggested menus for Lou to follow in her absence.

Monday, June 7, dawned dark and drizzly, but even bad weather couldn't dampen the children's intoxicated state of mind. They were going home after eight years, going home to the freedom and beauty of Glacier Park, going home to ride Joe McGregor's horses to the homestead to visit Charlie, to cascade down the shale banks of the Two Medicine River, going home to dance at Mike's Place, and going home to enjoy their mother's huge loaves of homemade bread and famous donuts.

Nonplussed by his own emotions at the thought of losing the two young people who'd brought so much vitality to the farm, a sorrowful Lou offered a gruff goodbye at breakfast and headed to the fields for the day. He couldn't bear to watch them drive away.

Glenn loaded the luggage into his Chevrolet. Emma and Melina packed sheets, quilts, and pillows for their stays at tourist cabins along the way. They rearranged the pots and pans, the boxes of food, Melina's graduation gifts, and Glenn's guitar. Melina sat in the back seat with possessions stacked beside her and jars of soup arranged around her feet. Emma, who now weighed 260 pounds, settled herself into the passenger seat as Glenn once more checked the tire pressure. Satisfied that all was well, he eased the green machine out of the driveway toward home.

Devastation from the drought surrounded them as miles of loose, dry soil lay vulnerable to the winds across North Dakota and Montana. Farms lay abandoned and decayed where green fields of winter wheat once riffled in the breeze. With the topsoil blown away, what remained was too parched to produce hope.

In Glacier Park, Clara lived in poverty. Since returning home a year ago, she'd had no source of income except for a few eggs, a bit of produce from her garden, plus rent that dribbled in from time to time. She continued to dream of publishing her stories, but survival became her main goal, and now the children were coming home to stay.

She had tried to discourage them from coming. She repeatedly assured them that they wouldn't like it, that things had changed, but what could she do? They were her children, and they wanted to come home. The park offered no employment for young people; she had no income. How will I feed them? she wondered. Growing children require a lot of food.

Weathered, unpainted boards lay warped along the sides of the ramshackle store where they rattled in the wind, struggled for freedom. The shingled roof, a jigsaw puzzle with gaping spaces, offered little protection. Clara scrubbed the wood floorboards, washed down the walls. Wet, heavy snow moved into the park. She set buckets around the room to collect drips that seeped through the ceiling. "I hope this lousy snow falling lets up," she murmured. "This lousy old Montana weather can't be trusted, and here it's almost the middle of June."

Humiliated at her lack of money, she tossed and turned through sleepless nights as she sought a solution to her problem. They are accustomed to getting duded up to go to dances. What will they think of me, she worried. I want to look good. She filled the days before their arrival by washing and ironing her dresses, now faded and worn. I'd like to see my kiddies, she admitted, but it would be better if they remembered me as I was.

On the afternoon of their expected arrival, she baked bread and made several pies. She stoked the potbelly stove to provide a cozy atmosphere and hoped that the heat would dry the floor and ceiling if it ever stopped snowing. She had plenty of fuel. One of the renters supplied her with wood instead of paying monthly rent. She prepared a bed for Glenn in the back room and used the last of her bedding on two double beds in the living area, then set the table. She washed her baby-fine hair. As usual, a few untidy tendrils framed her face. "I never can get my hair to do what I want," she complained to her reflection, then slipped her best dress over her head, fastened the buttons down the front, and adjusted the belt.

Anxious about seeing her children again after eight years, and not sure whether she wanted them home at all, she nervously bustled about the place emptying drip cans and wandered to the window to search the street for their car. She wondered how in the world she and her friends could continue their evening story sessions around the stove with those two young people underfoot. She reset the table a different way, hauled in a few more armloads of wood and stacked it behind the stove to dry. Water droplets slithered down the steamy windows, dripped off the edges of cracked windowsills that hadn't seen a coat of paint for fifteen years, splashed onto the floor creating puddles. She stoked the stove again; beads of perspiration formed on her upper lip. She sat down to await their arrival.

The farther west they traveled, the worse the weather and roads became. Emma relived her fear of the mountains when they began to descend Looking Glass Pass in the evening storm. She clutched the door handle in terror; she felt faint as the car slid dangerously toward the precipice before Glenn guided it back on course. Tips of snow-covered fir trees jutting up from the bottomless chasm reflected the car lights and invited her to enjoy their beauty, but she saw no beauty in the mountains, only imminent death if they plunged over the edge. The car shimmied and pulled to one side as Glenn maintained his death grip on the steering wheel, guided the car back to the center of the road. His hands ached from the steady grip, the cold temperature both inside and outside the car, stress of the unknown, as they entered the outskirts of Glacier Park; it was nearly 11 P.M.

They passed the familiar sights of John Clarke's art studio, the train depot, and Glacier Park Hotel. They crossed through the underpass to the east side of the tracks and saw the decay of abandoned businesses and a few fortunate others that managed to survive, but the boom times of the town of Glacier Park that they remembered no longer existed. Beyond the incessant clatter of the windshield wipers, the headlights exposed broken windows and boarded-up doors; the relentless siege of the Depression lay before them as they observed the wreckage in silence. Despair confronted them at every turn. They each wondered what daylight might reveal.

Clara sat with her mending and watched for headlights to break free of the storm, listened as syncopated drips from the ceiling composed a Depression sonata into tin cans on the floor. The wood shifted in the potbelly stove and thumped against the side, the lantern flickered and hissed overhead as she contemplated her children's arrival.

Headlights of a car swept across the wall as it turned the corner and parked. Her heart lurched. Will my little pardners remember me? she fretted. She sat and waited for the slamming of car doors, then set her sewing aside and walked to the door where she waited, waited for their knock as she smoothed her skirt, patted her hair. Waited.

Their sharp rapping echoed through the old store. Clara opened the door. Three large adults confronted her. Who are these people? she wondered for an instant. Although Emma had gained over forty pounds, she recognized her, but the two young people were strangers. She studied their faces without comment. Yes, that must be Glenn, she decided. He resembles Charley and Fred; he has the build of my brothers, but his hair is so curly. He never had curly hair. And that must be Melina. I'd forgotten that she had to have glasses. She looks like me, but she's tall and slender like her daddy.

Eight years had gone by, hundreds of letters had passed back and forth, yet no warm hugs broke the chill of the night as the travelers stood in the doorway and waited for an invitation to enter. "Well, here we are!" someone blurted. Still stunned by the maturity of her children, who both towered above her, Clara stepped aside and motioned them into their once-familiar home, but she felt uncomfortable with these strangers. They'd sent school photos as well as snapshots taken with the Brownie camera, but in her mind, she'd continued to picture them as the kiddies she'd taken back to Minnesota.

They crossed the threshold into a wall of heat. Melina's glasses steamed over, she removed them, waited while Emma slipped her a clean handkerchief. They took off their coats and draped them across the counter that Clara had retrieved. Emma removed her hat and laid it on top of the piano. Clara watched silently, studied her children as they glanced around in muted shock.

The store had diminished in size from the way they remembered it. Shelves that had once loomed overhead were now eye level. Glenn reached above his head, touched the dilapidated ceiling that pressed downward; he felt claustrophobic. Did our family of four really live in this cramped space, he wondered. He stroked the empty shelves that once sagged with canned goods, tried to regain a feeling of familiarity. Melina slid the cover of the piano open. Her nimble fingers wrenched a reluctant scale from the untuned instrument. She grimaced, dropped the lid, concealed the leering grin of the ivories, turned away. Except for the portraits of their parents that hung on the wall behind the counter, the potbelly stove, and the cash register, nothing was as they remembered.

Except their mother. She looked about the same. She was stout; the veins stood out in her strong hands, muscular arms. Strands of gray streaked her reddish-blond hair; her face was smooth, she looked well. A distinct feeling of unease swept through them; everything was backward. It was as if they were visiting some distant aunt with their mother instead of the other way around. And the smell. They could never forget the cinnamon-nutmeg aromas that once wafted from the kitchen, but now there was the odor of wet wood, rotting timbers, musty and mildewed, in spite of Clara's freshly baked goods.

Most comfortable while cooking, Clara bustled into the kitchen, set out platters of bread. She cut two pies into oversize wedges; she poured tea and brought out a fruit cake for the weary travelers. They sat around the table and teased each other about Emma's death grip on the door handle and Glenn's two-handed grasp on the steering wheel as the car meandered from side to side down the pass.

Accustomed to participating in lively discussions with friends, Clara wanted to contribute adventures of her own, but she couldn't relate to this conversation. She listened with amusement to Emma's detailed account of their night at Wilbert's where she and Melina shared a three-quarter size bed and Glenn slept on a daybed with his long legs dangling over the end. Only then did she participate in the chit-chat of her guests, relating Wilbert's winter visit when he became snow-bound in Glacier Park for a period of time.

She helped carry suitcases and boxes from the car. They followed a path through the living area with its two double beds and strategically placed tin cans, made sure that they unpacked their luggage in a dry place. Exhausted after the perilous drive from Rudyard in the spring snowstorm, Glenn quickly retired into the back bedroom leaving the women to settle their own sleeping arrangements. Emma silently questioned why Clara would have two double beds in the cramped quarters since she no longer rented out rooms, but kept her thoughts to herself as she and Melina prepared to share one of the beds. Melina glanced up at the stained, fiberboard ceiling that sagged above her mother's bed, but put it out of her mind as Clara extinguished the lantern.

Several inches of wet snow accumulated during the night.

The heat from the stove drifted upward and melted it drip by drip. It seeped through the battered shingles. It fell from the ceiling, plinked into the containers, splashed onto the floor. It collected into the ballooning swell over Clara's bed until the weight of the water gushed through.

Her angry shouts at the lousy roof and rotten Montana weather brought the women to their feet. Clara lit the lantern; she was thoroughly drenched. Emma and Melina brought in a dry mattress from a back bedroom and prepared a fresh bed from the bedding they'd brought along from Minnesota, but the delicate dawn promised a beautiful day of blue skies, so while the rest of them went back to sleep, Clara got dressed and prepared a batch of fresh donuts.

After breakfast, Glenn and Melina walked around town to call on old friends, Bud Lutz, Leo Hickson, Johnny and Alene Parrent, but everything had changed. Melina's friends had married or moved away; few of Glenn's friends remained in the area. The siblings returned to the store. "Ma," Glenn asked. "Where does Bobby Shannon live? He hasn't written to me for years."

"Oh, he died of complications from the scarlet fever epi-

Mike's Place

demic that swept through here in '32," she said. "He's buried out at the cemetery."

"Why didn't you tell me?" he asked incredulously.

"Oh, it would have just made you feel bad. That's all."

After years of hard work, Emma enjoyed her vacation away from Lou and the farm. Although they'd never been close as sisters, she and Clara shared a strained relationship, but eventually warmed to each other. Now that Melina was back in home territory where she'd once roamed at will, she announced with authority, "Glenn and I are going to the Saturday night dance at Mike's Place. It might provide a chance to see some old friends from Browning or Cut Bank."

After years of diligently chaperoning the two young people, Emma was not about to shirk from her duties. Concerned about their safety in this unruly frontier town, she declared, "Well, I think I'll just go along with you and see who these friends are! Clara, you should come, too."

"Oh, no," Clara said. "I don't have a nice dress to wear. You go along without me." She didn't want to chaperone the children. She felt uneasy in their presence. She couldn't talk to these modern young people with their newfangled ideas; she had nothing in common with them.

"Well, you can wear one of mine," Emma decided as she walked to her suitcase. "This one is a bit tight on me." She and Melina stood Clara on a chair while they altered the waist and shortened the hem, and on Saturday night the four of them strolled two blocks up the street to Mike's Place.

The sisters sat on a bench along the side wall and jokingly gave names to Melina's dance partners such as Baggy Pants and Big Chin. Reveling in the popularity of the children, Clara boisterously visited with those around her and returned the following Saturday night as well. Emma realized that the only way she could get the young people to return to Minnesota was if the business in Glacier Park no longer existed. For two weeks she harangued Clara to sell out and come back to the family home in Minnesota where they could enjoy the children together, where life was more civilized.

Disillusioned about Glacier Park in spite of the warnings they'd received, Clara's children considered returning to Minnesota with Emma, but Glenn found a job building fences at a remote site where he could make money of his own while Melina fried hamburgers at the soda fountain and did housecleaning in the afternoons, so they decided to remain with their mother.

While waiting on the station platform for the Great Northern to take her back to the farm, Emma turned to Melina and said with determination, "Now you are going to come back."

"Well, I surely am if I get to go to school in Staples, but if I can stay here and work…"

"But what would you do in the winter?" The question hung on the air without response.

Unaccustomed to being responsible for anyone but herself, Clara reluctantly accepted the children's presence in her home. Eight years ago, knowing that she could neither educate nor discipline them alone, she'd taken them to Minnesota to be raised by her family. She'd had good intentions of buying that farm next to the home place, but once her potential buyer failed to materialize, she decided that maybe the children were better off without her. Glenn needed to grow up with non-drinkers, virtuous men like her brothers; Emma could guide Melina toward becoming a lady, while she would provide the money for their needs.

The children's letters had begged her to come for a visit from time to time, but she had felt that her money for their support was more important than her presence, and the best thing to do was to leave them undisturbed. Besides that, they might have wanted to return to Montana, and she had nothing to offer. And they would have interfered with her attempts to become a published author.

Ambivalent in her own mind but succumbing to Emma's desires that she sell out, get rid of the dilapidated buildings, take the money and seek a better life, Clara escaped to Great Falls and left the children to fend for themselves. For two weeks she advertised her property in the daily papers and waited for a response. Meanwhile, Glenn used his first paycheck to patch his mother's roof and collected overdue payments from negligent renters.

Emma missed the children more than she'd ever imagined possible. Even though a thousand miles separated them, she continued to instruct Melina in good manners. She wrote to Melina on June 29.

> …Robert [Fred's son] asked me about the swell guy you hooked. I asked him how he knew anything, and he said you had written to one of your friends to that effect. I hope you did not write *hooked* as that sounds very slangy, and unladylike.
>
> You'll wonder why I rushed off the way I did, but I had to snap along, or the sobs would have got me before I got out of the yard. The sob bug bit me a plenty after the train pulled away.

On July 2, Clara mailed a post card to Glenn and Melina from Great Falls. It's message was brief but inspiring.

> Dear Children,
> Will be home soon. Expect Sat. have our Deeds and Abstracts. Let's hope to sell out Sunday or Monday. Hope you are fine. Same here.   Lovingly, Your Ma

Clara arrived home accompanied by her potential buyer. With the flat terrain and a view of the mountains, he assured her that the property encompassed the perfect site for a motel. For three days the interested party methodically researched the abstract and the property lines before offering $10,000, half of her asking price for an entire block of property. Totally disgusted, she refused his miserly offer; he'd wasted her time, insulted her intelligence. No further negotiations materialized, no other buyers came forward.

For the rest of the summer the Smiley family survived on eggs and mulligan stew. Glenn collected her rents and contributed a bit of his hard-earned money to repair the ceiling, but he and Melina sensed that it was time to move on.

Clara didn't especially care to have them around. She didn't know them any more; they weren't the children she remembered. They were adults with interests of their own. And she missed the late night chatter with gossipy friends, the flirtatious escapades with male admirers who now stayed away.

In July, Melina received the scholarship to attend Staples Normal as a representative from Long Prairie High School. She returned to Minnesota in late August to pursue her life-long dream of becoming a teacher.

Tourists and summer folk scattered with the early leaves of autumn; by mid-September the hotels lay dormant. Mother Nature tucked the inhabitants of Glacier Park beneath an icy blanket of down, and the drowsy inhabitants drifted off into hibernation for the duration of winter. "What will we do here all winter, Ma?" Glenn asked.

"By golly, I get quite a kick out of writing stories. Even if I have no editor take a mess I write, I soon can write new stuff. You see, we all have hobbies here." She added, "And I never know when company may blow in to tell a story or two."

No longer employed, confined to the mean interior of the store with its drafty floor and creaking walls, Glenn abhorred the desolate isolation of Glacier Park. In late October, discouraged and disillusioned, he departed for Minnesota in his green Chevrolet.

Relieved to be alone again without responsibility, enjoying the solitude, Clara brewed a strong cup of tea and sat down to review her life. She tried to be fair to everyone concerned, but facts were facts. She and Emma had shared a pleasant two weeks together talking about Minnesota, reminiscing about the old days, talking about their friends the Hubbards, the Christiansens, the Kienbergers and the Hickeys, "but those people are Emma's friends, not mine," she admitted to herself.

Maybe they never had been her friends. She'd never felt any real kinship for the Whiteville Methodist Church nor the local communities of Clotho and Gutches Grove. Actually, she'd never been close to her family. Her childhood had been crushed under Pa's devotion to hard work, Momma's watchful eye for perfection. And Lou had always demanded his pound of flesh for every favor he'd granted; Fred seldom offered encouragement. Now Charley had a wife and son to think about.

And the Depression? She'd listened to Emma's detailed descriptions of hardships the family had suffered during the Depression from eggs at seven cents a dozen to overdue taxes. Well, she thought to herself, the Depression was hard on everybody and still is. Families all over the country were torn apart. Didn't I sacrifice my home and my children to work on the ranches? Didn't I send them all my money so they could have a good life, go to school, attend ice cream socials, and go to parties? Now Glenn has his own car and Melina is going to become a teacher. They have their own lives, so why should I move back to Minnesota? she reasoned.

She roused herself from the chair and poured another cup of tea. Attempted to translate her emotions into thoughts. I've lived in Montana for twenty-five years, suffered here, married here. My true friends are here, Mrs. Thompson, Mrs. Young, Mrs. Edkins, Charlie Tobin who bought the old homestead. I'm fifty-five years old and this is the first time that I've had the freedom to keep my money for myself, to buy some clothes, to have nice things, she thought.

But the rentals were vacant, her cupboards were bare. She had no money to spend on herself; her small reserve had been wasted on the folly of selling out. Once again the sordid specter of winter bared its teeth, threatened to devour her last bit of self-esteem with impoverishment, but Clara was a survivor, determined to be free, to break loose. She didn't owe anything to anybody; the children were adults.

She rose from the chair and set the teacup aside, retrieved her battered suitcase from the back room, began folding aprons and faded dresses, packed them within its dark recesses.

Once again she examined her reflection in the mirror, but this time she liked what she saw, a liberated woman unencumbered by feelings of failure, family commitments, obligations to submit to the will of others. The portraits that hovered behind the counter on the back wall no longer condemned her for leaving. They looked toward the door encouraging the rebirth of her carefree spirit, her love for adventure.

Clara pulled the tattered coat from the closet. "This will be your last winter in this lousy Montana weather. You're a-gonna be replaced," she promised as she collected her purse, the last of her money. Setting the suitcase outside, gathering the typewriter under her arm, she padlocked the door and walked toward the depot.

Clara returned to the nomadic life. The family received new forwarding addresses every few weeks from Great Falls, Big Sandy, Wolf Creek, Augusta, and Choteau, but money and gifts no longer arrived. Back in her element again, she wrote letters infrequently as she kneaded great loaves of bread, bantered with cowboys, sent fanciful stories to reluctant publishers, and drifted from ranch to ranch across western Montana for several more years.

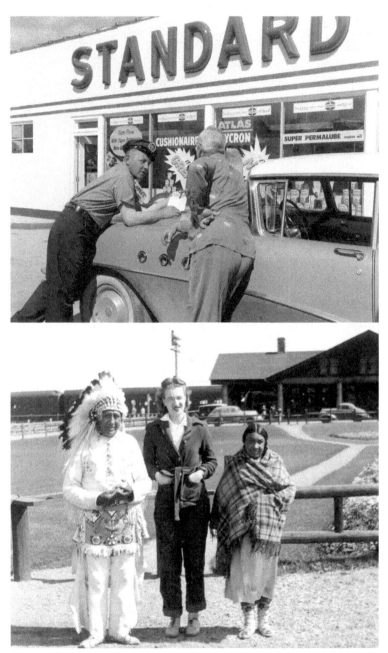

Above: Melina frequently returned to East Glacier Park. This photo from 1934 shows her with her friend Jim Blood and his wife in front of the train depot. *Top*: Glenn Smiley (GC) leased the Standard Station in his name in 1951. He was an astute businessman like his father and easily made friends.

PART VIII

Closure

What one loves in childhood stays in the heart forever.

Mary Jo Putney

In 1942, as she neared her sixtieth birthday, Clara abandoned the nomadic life and returned to Glacier Park where she continued to live for another twenty years. Glenn and Melina paid the taxes so that in the twilight years of her life, Clara found peace. She continued to write stories that her friends enjoyed, but nobody published. She converted the log rentals into chicken houses and spent uninterrupted days in her garden with the power of the soil beneath her feet and the comforting feel of the hoe in her hands. And the earth gave forth bountiful harvests.

Glenn bought the Standard Gas Station in the town Glacier Park. He lived near enough to help her market her garden produce and eggs, while Melina, now a teacher at Whiteville School, contributed money for her mother's welfare. Glenn installed electricity and running water in her aging abode, but fastidious about cleanliness, Clara refused a bathroom. "Toilets don't belong in the house," she said.

In 1962 at the age of eighty, Clara pleasured herself with work-filled days, but cataracts began to film her eyes. Caring for the chickens and weeding the garden became impossible tasks, yet she refused to have surgery. Worried about her diminishing vision, Glenn demolished the original log house behind the store and replaced it with a new house where she wouldn't have to haul firewood or go outside to the toilet, but the closer it came to completion, the more distressed she became.

Without her garden and chickens to tend, her mind slipped back to the past. On late summer afternoons while the sun slipped below the horizon, she sat in the doorway of the old store with Glenn's wife Shirley and reminisced about the years at Lake Lubec with her two babies, her good life with Glenn Cecil, and her hard times on the ranches. She wept for those she had loved and those who had died. On moving day, she declined Glenn's offer of the new house and asked to be placed in a rest home to be near old friends.

With undiminished ambition, Clara volunteered in the kitchen and served meals to the residents, but she hated the "lousy T.V. racket." She wrote letters for those unable to see until thickening cataracts obscured her own vision, and friends had to read to her.[1] She continued to write stories by feel, keeping one hand on the left edge of the paper while the other hand scribbled at steep angles in a large, childish scrawl across the page. Sometimes she strayed off the edge, but she wrote with a passion; she knew that her days were numbered, and she had so many stories to tell.

At the age of eighty-one, Clara became a published author.

On Sunday, April 19, 1964, the *Great Falls Tribune* included one of her historical accounts; the paper paid her eight dollars.

Homestead Community of Lubec
Once Again Quiet Wilderness
By Clara Smiley

In 1916, Lubec was an area of about 10 square miles located six miles west of the east entrance of Glacier National Park. The area had a seven-acre lake where the wild ducks nested all spring and summer.

Tall, green rushes grew thickly along the west side of Lubec Lake, making it a splendid place for the ducks to nest, hatch and feed safely. After nesting time was over, hundreds of ducklings were on the lake swimming about with the older ducks. The lake was a waterfowl paradise.

Wild flowers grew everywhere in this newly settled area. Log cabins were built on the homesteads of 160 acres each. Many of the settlers had small gardens, chickens and a few milk cows.

Mr. and Mrs. Frank Pike took care of the post office. At times that post office was a busy place. Every homesteader took pleasure in going to get his mail, because there he could visit with his neighbors and exchange a few stories. The post office part of the Pike house was a large room with a big heater and plenty of benches and chairs for patrons' use.

Many of the homesteaders ordered their clothing and other goods from mail order houses; many packages came into the post office.

Lubec had a small log school. It also served as a meeting house and center for social affairs. Enrollment was small, but they usually succeeded in hiring a good teacher for the fall, winter and spring months. Some of the homesteaders had hopes for a high school.

One homesteader had a logging outfit. He sold building logs, corral poles, fence posts and firewood blocks all over the nearby prairie country. He kept about 40 head of strong work horses for this operation. Many of the homesteaders worked for him during the winters. Others trapped and sold furs for a good price; some worked on nearby cattle ranches at times.

Sometimes as a homesteader came home from brush cutting or stump grubbing, he would find a neighbor had left him a large pail of huckleberries, or fresh fish, or a platter of sliced elk steak ready to fry. Or there might be a loaf or two of fresh bread or a container of cookies, or a few pounds of fresh butter.

The homesteaders were thoughtful of their neighbors; they were always helping one another. I thought of them as the best people on earth.

All the original homesteaders are gone now. A lonely log cabin here and there is all that remains to testify to the hopes and dreams of the early settlers. The log school and post office were closed years ago, and the buildings have been taken down.

The country is once again in its wilderness state. Wild flowers bloom where radishes once grew, and the elk roam undisturbed where horses once grazed.

Her room became the gathering place for women who wanted to talk about the old days of Glacier Park, Mrs. Oscar Peterson and Marge Fox among others. She referred to her room as the Glacier Park Convention Hall where friends gathered in wheel chairs and sat on the beds listening to her stories. She enjoyed the attention, but felt that precious time slipped away when her writing was interrupted.

March 65

My Dear Darling Children,

...I began a story, the tital is How I Completely Got Lost in the Forest Wilderness Then How I Got Out Again...gosh at times just as I am writing a story 3 or 4 women come in to help pass the lonely hours away, and I can't tell them that I am to buisy

writing. I must keep at it to finish my story. gosh if I do that
I will hurt their feelings so I begin…to talk of story plots, but
when anyone is just deeply interested to get a story completed
then to quit and let it go, often the story turns out a wreck.
Women are at times hog wild to hear the complete ending of a
story in a few minutes. gosh that can't be done but they are not
experienced in the story writing field.

She worried about becoming incapacitated and senile like
so many of the residents in the nursing home. She frequently
wrote to her children that she didn't want to linger on to an old
age and become a bag of bones.

Aug 23 65
…I love to be in the Park but the bygone happiness floats as in a
vision, and I shed tears about all the time when we get so overwhelmed in the past happy places. I felt I better stay away for
awhile. Emma used to…say Clara never long to get very old as its
terrible to be old and helpless…so when we go to heaven earlier
before we get into a shape like that, gosh no fooling its a blessing
to be in our heavenly home where everyone is healthy and happy.

As her life drew to a close, Clara shared childhood memories with her children.

…I feel fine only I get to crying and thinking over our child
hood happy hours and what a mess that is, but time ends all
stuff.
     gosh I so often live in the happy years when Emma Louis
and I used to go to school, of the grand times we kids had
walking to school about $^3/_4$ mile or more. All wer the German
children. no one ever thought of talking English the first school
years because every one talked German.[3] gone are the days when
our hearts were all young and gay, but gollie so its all over. Youth

can't stay forever. The small nut grows up into a big tree but God knows we love all our Darlings in heaven and someday we will all meet again.

The power of the earth continued to beckon as she described the local crops in her letters, but never again would she inhale its richness nor embrace the land with her hoe. Gone were the days when the soil caressed her hands as she crumbled clods of earth between her fingers and entrusted tiny seedlings to its nurturing care.

The vibrant woman whose imagination and dreams soared beyond her everyday world, the woman who believed in the goodness of mankind and gave away so much to so many, the woman who worked with tireless energy for the welfare of her children, wasted away before her loved ones. She suffered no illness nor discomfort; she simply lost her will to live; it was time for her final passage. Clara slipped away on December 28, 1965.

She rests in a small cemetery on the Montana prairie outside of Cut Bank where her spirit soars with the strength of an eagle and the gentleness of a butterfly just as it did in life. It watches the sun set behind the majestic peaks of Glacier Park then swoops and ripples the waters of Lake Lubec in remembrance of good times. It dances through the pine boughs of East Glacier Park, creates summer dust devils in the streets, and whispers secrets about the wonders of the earth before swirling and twirling across the prairie flatlands to visit those who passed away before her. Her adventurous spirit lives on.

Afterword

Clara Miller Smiley was a gifted storyteller whose vivid memory brought the past to life. Her years on the high plains of Montana as a homesteader, a spinster who craved independence and her own piece of land, are based on stories she told to her children. The details cannot be verified, but the hardships she endured cannot be doubted. Attempts to locate the site of her soddy have been unsuccessful. The fate of her organ is unknown; she either abandoned it or gave it away.

She enjoyed many romantic liaisons after her husband's death, but the author found no proof of remarriage. The only love letter in the vast collection of letters she left behind was the one from The Land Man. The Christmas letter written after the birth of GC was found tucked away in the attic of the Minnesota house when the children lived with Lou and Emma. The detailed accounts of life at Lake Lubec are retellings of stories she wrote to her children in later years. The letters have been lost, but the stories survived, stories that include Clara's words and phrases as Melina retold them to me.

The descriptions of people who touched her life are based on interviews and historical records. In addition, Clara saved hundreds of letters that I studied to round out the story line. In one of her letters, Emma referred to a song Clara published, "My Blue-Eyed Darling." Was the song about her husband, about John Smith, about The Land Man, or another of her many suitors? We'll never know.

During a recent move, Glenn's widow Shirley discovered a cache of letters Clara had written during her two years in the rest home, long rambling letters about her daily life and reminiscences about the past. Some of the letters, twelve to fifteen pages in length, outlined her latest stories. At the time of her death, she was working on a novel, *What Sadie Saw and Heard Through the Keyhole*. No one remembers finding the manuscript.

And what about the real Sadie Dowen? She remarried after Claud's death and moved to California, but returned to her homestead suffering from dropsy and heart disease. She was alone and nearly destitute. She said that her husband had cheated her out of her money. She bought a cow that she milked by hand. She rolled the milk can down the steep driveway to Highway 2, and the Trailways Bus picked it up every day and delivered it to the creamery in Kalispell.

During her last summer, as a favor to a friend, Sadie watched over two small children, ages four and seven. She provided little supervision. Her nearest neighbor saw smoke coming from his barn and saw the children running away. His barn burned to the ground. Shortly thereafter, Sadie's home caught on fire, and she barely escaped with her life. The sheriff took her back to Glacier Park, and within the month, she passed away.

Many of Clara's neighbors moved away during the Depression, while others persevered in Glacier Park. In 1930 Charlie Tobin bought the Lubec homestead from Clara for $1000. In 1936 he married a newly arrived nurse from New Jersey. They dismantled the homestead cabin and barn and moved the logs across U.S. Highway 2 where Charlie constructed a large house. At that site, the Tobins operated a rest home for several years before moving to Columbia Falls.

Shorty Hynes died of a heart attack while splitting wood at Two Medicine Lake. He died intestate with no known relatives. Several of Clara's friends who stayed in East Glacier Park now rest in solitude in the unmarked cemetery east of town sheltered in a copse on a quiet hillside where range cattle trample the wildflowers and elk graze their way to lower pastures in the fall.

After leaving her children with Emma, Clara never returned to Minnesota. Of the five Miller children, she experienced the hardest life, but she outlived them all. Lou died of peritonitis from a ruptured appendix in 1947. Neighbors found Emma upright in a chair where she'd passed away in her sleep during an afternoon respite from gardening in 1954. Charley died in 1962, and Fred died in 1964. They are buried in the cemetery in Long Prairie near their parents.

Melina, the little girl who used to perch at the end of the bench at Mike's Place and watch the pianist's fingers glide over the keys, became a teacher and taught at Whiteville School and District 77 before she moved to Buhl, Idaho, where she married the local postmaster and worked as a clerk for the Draft Board for 22 years. After her husband retired, the couple invested in real estate and bought a cottage in Stanley, Idaho, where their neighbor, Bill Harrah of Harrah's Casino in Reno, soon made them an offer they couldn't refuse. They sold out, and became caretakers of his Stanley estate for two years.

They continued to invest in real estate but moved to East

Glenn and Melina return to Glacier Park and old friends.

Glacier Park where they lived for twelve years before a final move to Choteau, house and all. In poor health, her husband died in 1993 after which she sold her home and moved into a nearby retirement facility.

She spent her widowed years among friends where she enjoyed music and the seasonal kaleidoscope of beauty on the distant slopes of the Bob Marshall Wilderness. On August 19, 2005, she passed away in her sleep. She had no children. Her ashes were scattered in a secret field of wildflowers where her spirit revels in the tranquil beauty of Glacier National Park, and the memory of hoofbeats of her beloved pony reverberates across the meadow.

In 1941, Glenn returned to Glacier Park and lived in the store building while Clara continued to work on sheep ranches. He worked for Glacier Park, Inc. until WW II. When the park closed for the duration of the war, he was unable to enlist because of an enlarged pulmonary artery, the result of his bout with scarlet fever. He worked at a dairy farm in Washington until the war ended, then he and the tourists returned to Glacier Park where he worked as a gas station attendant. Always eager to be a businessman like his father, he leased the Standard Station in his own name in 1951.

Clara never received any money from the property that she had so diligently protected in Glacier Park. At her death, it was inherited equally by Glenn and Melina, but Melina signed over her share to her brother because he'd been the caretaker of their mother. Tragically, Glenn passed away due to his heart condition in 1967, two years after Clara's death. He is buried in the cemetery in East Glacier Park.

His widow Shirley remained in East Glacier Park and raised her five-year-old daughter alone. To support herself and pay the taxes, she developed Clara's property into a trailer park in 1970. The Glacier Cash Grocery building was ravaged by time, and it was used for storage.

In 1973, a potter inquired about renting the derelict building to use as a showroom for his wares. Shirley updated the electricity, installed water and sewer, and rented it to the couple for $30 a month. In 1983, they purchased the property.

The Glacier Cash Grocery, now known as The Brown House, on the corner of Dawson and Washington Streets, has changed only its name. The owners have kept the spirit of the Smiley family alive as they rent rooms to tourists and specialize in pottery and local works of art. There, in the interior of the old store, the portraits of Glenn and Clara hang on the wall behind the counter with its glass case where Glenn so proudly displayed his wife's baked goods. Upon entering, the visitor can almost smell the sweet aroma of cinnamon and sugar. The nickel-plated cash register reflects light from the window while the potbelly stove with its Grecian urn continues to exude warmth. The children's piano, the beloved instrument they rescued from

The bunkhouse is the only remaining building on the Smiley homestead at Lake Lubec.

an abandoned cabin, maintains a quiet dignity against the wall as if waiting for their return.

Six miles west of town on U.S. Highway 2, one can catch a fleeting glimpse of the log bunkhouse at the edge of a small mountain lake, a lonely sentinel, an isolated reminder of the homestead family that once carved a niche out of the wilderness on the shores of Lake Lubec.

B. L. Wettstein

Acknowledgments

Dream Chasers of the West would not have been possible without the following people who helped with the research of public documents:

Loretta Barron, Deputy Clerk of Records, Glacier County, Shelby, Montana

John Barsness, Executive Director, Montana Arts, Bozeman, Montana

Vicki Cwiok, Archives, Public Affairs Department, Sears, Roebuck and Company

Jan DeLaney, Co-curator of Rudyard Museum, Rudyard, Montana

Judy Ellinghausen, Archives Administrator, Cascade County Historical Society, Great Falls, Montana

Wilma Finseth, Assistant Director, Todd County Historical Society, Long Prairie, Minnesota

June Liebelt, Records Clerk, Hill County, Havre, Montana

Julianne Ruby, Archive Administrator, Cascade County Historical Society, Great Falls, Montana

Barbara Van De Pete, Genealogy Volunteer, Havre–Hill County Library, Havre, Montana

A hearty thank you to Warren and Lorraine Augdahl, who explained how to harness a team of horses and patiently instructed me in the finer points of farming. Thank you to Shirley Smiley, who provided letters, photographs, and her memories of Clara's last years; thank you to Donald Miller and Norma

Morrison for sharing their photographs of Clara's siblings; and thank you to Sandra Bareither, great-granddaughter of Ernestina Ruck, who provided the photographs of the Ruck family. Finally, I am forever grateful to Melina Hlavaty, whose hundreds of letters, photographs, and brilliant memory of the daily routine at the Glacier Cash Grocery made this story possible.

In addition, I would like to remember those who read the manuscript in part or in whole and made valuable suggestions, and my husband David who not only helped me with the research and provided technical assistance, but listened to my ramblings and revisions for several years without complaint.

NOTES

Introduction

1. Michael P. Malone and Richard B. Roeder, *Montana: A History of Two Centuries* (Seattle: University of Washington Press, 1977), 182.

2. K. Ross Toole, *Montana: An Uncommon Land* (Norman: University of Oklahoma Press, 1959), 233-34.

3. Malone and Roeder, 183.

4. Joseph Kinsey Howard, *Montana: High, Wide, and Handsome* (New Haven, CT: Yale University Press, 1943), 178-9.

5. Michael P. Malone, *James J. Hill, Empire Builder of the Northwest* (Norman: University of Oklahoma Press, 1996), 257-61.

6. Malone and Roeder, 183.

7. [Big Sandy, Montana] *Bear Paw Mountaineer,* February 15, 1912.

Part I: A Woman Homesteader

1. Howard, *Montana: High, Wide, and Handsome,* 181.

2. Malone and Roeder, *Montana: A History of Two Centuries,* 184.

3. August Ruck and Charles Miller were immigrants from Germany who settled in Fond du Lac, Wisconsin. Charles Miller married Clara Fischer in 1880. August Ruck married Marie Fischer, her sister, when she came from Germany in 1883 with her mother and another sister, Ernestina. August and Marie had four children: Wilbert, Elmer, Freda and her twin who died at birth with the mother. Ernestina came to care for the children and eventually married August. They had three children: Elwood, Walter, and Bessie.

Charles and Clara Miller had five children: Emma Henrietta, Clara Augusta, Louis August, Frederick August, and Charles August, names that suggest the close relationship between the two families.

4. Howard, 182-3.

5. Daniel N. Vichorek, *Montana's Homestead Era,* Montana Geographic Series, #15 (Helena: Montana Magazine, 1987), 109.

6. Horn, Huston, and Editors, *The Old West: The Pioneers* (New York: Time-Life Books, 1974), 189 ff.

7. *History of Glacier County, Montana* (Cut Bank, MT: Glacier County Historical Society, 1984), 32.

8. *Great Falls* [Montana} *Leader,* Saturday, March 8, 1913.

9. Lydia Langel, interview with author, Rudyard, Montana, October 12, 1995.

10. *History of Glacier County, Montana,* 39.

Part II: Entering Grizzly Country
1. Stan Cohen and Don Miller, *The Big Burn: The Northwest's Forest Fire of 1910* (Missoula, MT: Pictorial Histories Publishing Company, 1978).
2. *Water Resources Survey, Liberty and Toole Counties, Montana* (Helena: Montana Resources Board, 1969), 11.
3. Beth M. Volbrecht, "Homesteader's Wife," in *Toole County Backgrounds* (Montana Institute of the Arts, Compiled by Shelby History Group, 1958), 40.

Part III: Homesteader's Bride
1. Dennis J. Lutz, M.D. and Montana Chapter No. 1, National Association of Postmasters of the U.S., in *Montana Post Offices and Postmasters* (Rochester, MN: Johnson Printing Co., 1986), 39.
2. Andrea Merrill and Judy Jacobson, *Montana Almanac* (Helena, MT: Falcon Publishing Company, 1997), 45.
3. *History of Glacier County, Montana,* 206.
4. Ibid., 32.
5. Ibid., 206.

Part IV: Vignettes of Glacier Park
1. *History of Glacier County, Montana,* 37.
2. Ibid., 40.
3. F. Mike Shannon, "Erection of New Mike's Place Recalls Olden Days of Park Resort; 'Emporium' Too Rough for Eastern Dudes," *Cut Bank* [Montana] *Pioneer Press,* Friday, April 15, 1932.
4. "J. J. Smith, the Outlaw of Glacier Park, Is Hero of Many Wild West Yarns," *Cut Bank* [Montana] *Pioneer Press,* January 15, 1932.
5. "Paroled Prisoner Killed By Officers In Desperate Duel," *Browning* [Montana] *Review,* June 30, 1922.
6. *History of Glacier County, Montana,* 41.

Part V: Voices of the Children
1. Melina had a lisp; she pronounced her name "Melina Thmiley." Snipacasnooze was the name Glenn chose for her pony. She could have it only when she learned to pronounce Snipacasnooze without a lisp. She worked with determination. She sat on Glenn's lap and had him show her repeatedly how to place her tongue; she wanted that pony more than anything. After two months she could pronounce the "s" sound perfectly, and she was rewarded with Snipacasnooze at the age of six. Thereafter, she called him "Snip."
2. *History of Glacier County, Montana,* 41.
3. Ibid., 42.
4. Ibid., 40.

Part VI: The Depression
1. *History of Glacier County, Montana,* 38.

2. Malone and Roeder, *Montana: A History of Two Centuries,* 226.

3. "Tom Dawson Tells How Oil Rumor Started," *Cut Bank* [Montana] *Pioneer Press*, October 21, 1927.

4. *History of Glacier County, Montana,* 29.

5. Ibid., 24.

6. Ibid., 38.

7. Twentieth Legislative Assembly of the State of Montana, 1927, Chapter 12, 15-18.

8. In the spring of 1931, Glenn contracted scarlet fever, a severe disease that often left physical defects of one type or another. When Glenn became delirious with a high fever, Emma sat up with him all night and sponged his body with cool water while Melina helped restrain him. After the fever subsided, his skin peeled off in big sheets; the disease damaged his heart, narrowing the pulmonary artery. Because the disease was highly contagious, the family was quarantined for three weeks; Lou couldn't sell the milk or go out in public. He was disgusted. He said to Melina, "Are you going to catch it after he gets all done so we have to be quarantined for another three weeks?" Although she'd stayed at her brother's bedside, she escaped the disease while it swept through the entire community.

9. *Great Falls City Directory, 1929-30,* 44.

10. *Great Falls* [Montana] *Tribune*, April 1, 1934.

11. Betty Ehman, interview with author, Great Falls, Montana, May 29, 1996.

12. Jim and Terry Rettig, *A Gathering of Memories: A History of the Big Sandy Community* (Big Sandy, MT: Mountaineer Printing, Compiled by the Big Sandy Historical Society, 1990), 287-89.

13. Malone and Roeder, 119.

14. Lois Handy and Lucile Orcutt, "J. H. Carmichael," in *In the Shadows of the Rockies: A History of the Augusta Area* (Fairfield, MT: The Fairfield Times, 1978), 130-33.

15. Connie McNamara, telephone interview with author, Big Sandy, Montana, May 28, 1996.

Part VII: Going Home
1. Malone and Roeder, *Montana: A History of Two Centuries,* 128.

Part VIII: Closure
1. Tom Fountaine, a published author and fellow homesteader from the Lubec area, lived at the rest home in Cut Bank when Clara arrived. When she could no longer read family letters, he read them aloud for her. He encouraged her writing, but confided that the rest home was too noisy for him to concentrate and moved to a small apartment. He published *Buffalo Prairies and Buffalo Men* in 1967.

2. Clara Smiley, "Homestead Community of Lubec Once Again Quiet Wilderness," *Great Falls* [Montana] *Tribune*, April 19, 1964.

3. Clara and her siblings were born in Oshkosh, Wisconsin, where the

family rented a small farm near Eldorado Mills. A few years later they moved to another farm near Austin, Minnesota. There the entire family was struck down with scarlet fever, and Edward, two years old, succumbed to the disease. His parents buried him at night somewhere on that little farm. Because of being quarantined for an extended time, the family was destitute. Once again they placed all of their possessions in a horse-drawn wagon and made the long trek north to Todd County to live near the Ruck relatives. Mrs. Miller and Mrs. Ruck were sisters.

INDEX
Italics indicate photographs.

About the Author

B. L. Wettstein was born during a blizzard in rural Minnesota, where she attended the same one-room country school as her father and grandfather. She became a teacher and taught in public schools in Michigan, Oregon, Washington and California. She and her husband later taught in the international schools of Istanbul, Cairo, London, Jakarta, and Aruba.

After retiring, she contacted Melina in Choteau, Montana, a woman she hadn't seen since childhood, to learn about her mother Clara, an adventurous woman she'd never met, and the story of the homestead in Glacier Park unfolded in Clara's own words as she described frontier life in letters to her children that frequently contained her unpublished stories.

This is the author's first book.